STARTUP ARABIA

STORIES AND ADVICE FROM TOP TECH ENTREPRENEURS IN THE ARAB WORLD

AMIR HEGAZI

Ordering information: Special discounts are available on quantity purchases by governments, NGOs, schools, companies, associations, and others. For details, contact the publisher at StartupArabiaBook.com.

Printed in the United States of America.

Hegazi, Amir. Startup Arabia: Stories and Advice from Top Tech Entrepreneurs in the Arab World

Print ISBN: 978-1-7325421-0-5
Ebook ISBN: 978-1-7325421-1-2

1. Business & Money, International, 2. Business & Money, Entrepreneurship, 3. Business & Money, Management

First Edition

Cover design by Fathurohman

TRANSFORMENA PUBLISHING
1223 Wilshire Blvd., No. 738
Santa Monica, CA 90403

www.StartupArabiaBook.com

CONTENTS

Dedicated to anyone
who dreamed of changing the world
and decided to do something about it.

1

INTRODUCTION

ALL HUMANS ARE BORN ENTREPRENEURS.

— MUHAMMAD YUNUS, NOBEL PEACE PRIZE WINNER AND FOUNDER OF GRAMEEN BANK

The year: 2005. The place: Dubai. I had just landed in Dubai International Airport for the first time. This had to be the biggest airport I'd ever been to. I didn't recall ever seeing immigration lines this long. Where were all these people coming from, and where were they going? Dubai sure seemed to be a travel hub connecting east and west.

I came to realize later that Dubai was also a sort of international oasis, drawing folks from everywhere set on finding something they didn't have back home. For some, Dubai represented a chance; for others, an opportunity. For both, it offered hope. This sure was starting to feel all too reminiscent of "the American dream" and the story of New York at the turn of the 20th century. Could Dubai possibly be the new

New York at the turn of the 21st century, or was it all just hype? I was about to find out.

As I stepped outside the airport, I was greeted by the sprinkling water fans at the sidewalk attempting to cool off the steamy air. Even past midnight, you could feel the warm, moist air. It made me wonder, "How hot does it really get here?" This was late spring 2005; Dubai was certainly warm and about to heat up, literally and figuratively.

As I rode in the cab through Sheikh Zayed Road, the lifeblood highway that cuts across the city, my eyes were fixated on the tall skyscrapers surrounding us. "Amazing, right, sir?" I heard my southeast Asian taxi driver ask. "None of this existed just two or three years ago," he proceeded to tell me in a semi-British accent. He was right. It certainly was amazing. Equally impressive were the cranes in the background that spread through the desert and seemed to stretch forever. I recalled hearing that 50 percent of the world's cranes were in Dubai at the time, all in just one, small emirate with no more than 1.5 million residents.

This wasn't like anything I had expected. Sure, I'd lived in the Middle East before, in Egypt, where I grew up. I'd also heard all about Dubai and how fast it was growing, but for all I knew, this part of the Middle East was new to me. In spite of priding myself on staying connected to my Arabic culture during the dozen years I had lived in the United States during my adulthood, I might as well have been a foreigner. Riding around the city, I tried to take it all in. Little did I know or could have imagined the transformation that was going to take place here just a few short years later. Dubai had certainly set the tone for many things to come in the region.

This trip was the first leg of an extensive business development roadshow I had planned with my CEO at the time, covering a dozen countries in the region. I was working at a multinational startup back then, overseeing the region, a region I soon realized I didn't know much about after all. Our company was a pioneer in the online video space, well before YouTube, Netflix, Amazon Video, and Hulu. We were going to be traveling throughout the region, meeting television broadcasters to pitch them on joining our online live streaming platform. We eventually signed every top television broadcaster and media company in the region on an exclusive basis for all their digital rights. It was my first encounter doing business in the region, and it was an adventure in every sense of the word.

I remember my boss asking at the time, upon seeing the itinerary I had planned for the trip, with Dubai and Doha as our first two stops, "Why are we starting with the small countries?" Little did he, or I for that matter, know what those gems in the desert held in terms of potential yet to be mined, not in terms of oil or so-called "black gold," but rather in terms of human imagination and the relentless spirit to catch up to and even surpass the rest of the world.

I practically lived on a plane for a good part of the three years that followed, hopping from country to country across this vast region, from Qatar and Egypt, to Lebanon and Morocco, to Sudan and Palestine, literally on a daily basis. I was everywhere, always on the move. The pace was insane, but I couldn't have asked for a better crash course into the culture, the political-economics scene, and the business landscape.

It never failed to amaze me, traveling in this part of the world, how similar and different each country is: similar in the instant connection and rapport you feel with someone, as a fellow Arab, given the shared language, history, and culture everywhere you went, but diametrically different in every other way.

You get on a short flight of just forty-five minutes to the next country over, and suddenly everything seems to change; the mood in the air itself is different, the scenery, the extent of openness, the level of formality, the pace of business, you name it. Every place had its own flavor and seemed to resemble its own unique era, like you were in a time machine of some sort, from the futuristic science-fiction landscape of DIFC (Dubai International Financial Center), to the Bedouin villages at the outskirts of Amman, to the nightlife scene in Beirut, to the ancient ruins in Cairo. It was all too surreal and yet captivating at the same time.

Another striking element was, no matter where you went, the language and spirit of business was always the same, being focused on fixing existing problems and creating new opportunities. Remarkably, there was an undertone of admiration for successful American businesses and businessmen whenever the topic came up among local business leaders, though combined with an air of national and patriotic pride and resolve to build something great of their own locally.

Through all this travel and the countless number of projects I got involved with, I saw it all. I was fortunate to experience firsthand business conducted at different levels and from different corners of the region, and from different roles and perspectives, where in some cases I was a mere fly on the wall, and in others I ran the show. More recently, I oversaw Souq.com marketplace, the largest e-commerce platform in the Arab world, where I was quite involved in the inner workings of this thriving startup as we strived to "make history" per our internal mantra. I also got to engage and work with hundreds of SMEs (small and medium-size enterprises) across multiple markets and witness both their success and growing pains. I'm proud of our accomplishments at Souq.com, which are a great testament to its leadership and the commitment of its staff.

Looking back, I wouldn't trade any of this experience for the world. It was quite an eye-opener and transformative on a personal level. In a way, I got to sit in the driver's seat, watching globalization in action. Change was happening right before my eyes, not just in terms of the ever-changing skyline and infrastructure, but less ostensibly in terms of the mindset and attitudes around business, especially among the new generation.

Things have evolved quite a bit from the days where I had to polish my shoes before and after every meeting, walking up the unpaved sandy roads and under construction sites at Dubai Internet City; when I had meetings with small, unheard-of young companies with funny logos in small squeezed-up offices and nearby hookah cafes and hearing their ambition to become the next Yahoo!, PayPal, or eBay of the region; when fortunes were made and lost in the real estate market in the background. It was definitely the wild, wild east, as anyone who was there at the time will attest.

Fast-forward to today's environment with a more thriving startup ecosystem, which was unheard of just ten years ago. Mature and sophisticated companies are on the rise. There are even a few exceptional ones that managed to lure global investment and acquisitions from world-class companies.

Certainly, things have changed significantly in the region since 2005, when I first set foot in Dubai, and are changing as we speak. Though perhaps international perception influenced by international mainstream media has yet to catch up to this new reality. Granted, there are serious and unresolved issues that continue to haunt and pose a serious risk to the stability of some parts of the region. Nevertheless, that's not the full story, and there are many untold positive stories that get brushed by the wayside.

This book is meant to shed light on a few of those insightful and inspiring stories being created by remarkable tech entrepreneurs in the Middle East who refused to accept the status quo, managed to transcend cultural beliefs and limitations, and are now rewriting the region's destiny. It attempts to capture their own personal stories, the companies they built, their advice to fellow entrepreneurs, and their perspectives in general.

Whenever possible, I tried to present diverse types of entrepreneurs, with diverse nationalities and locations, with diverse backgrounds, in diverse fields, at diverse stages of company development, and with diverse experiences and perspectives, though all are founders of very successful or very promising tech companies, or both.

Many business books try to box success into a neat set of qualities, when the reality is that successful entrepreneurs are as different as they come. Entrepreneurship is perhaps the only profession, if you consider it as such, where success isn't tied to any given set of qualities or skills. It offers you the opportunity to fully utilize your strengths and all the while work around your weaknesses, by finding the right co-founder, eliciting the help of mentors and advisers, hiring personnel with specific skills you lack, etc. In a way, it's the most malleable profession of all, whereas in every other profession, your success is directly tied to your given domain expertise.

My "shot for the moon" aim for this book is to help awaken dreamers and encourage them not to abandon their aspirations by accepting their current realities in the name of "being realistic." Quite the contrary: I hope they will think, act, and live up to their dreams. There is hidden power in such pursuit. Whenever you set out pursuing a dream (or for many, searching for a dream), you're already a success. Failure stems only from inaction. I encourage you to go after your personal dream and follow an entrepreneurial path. You owe it yourself to tap the best from within you and never hold back.

I would very much enjoy hearing from you. I hope you find value in the following pages and commit to apply whatever lessons you may learn.

Amir Hegazi
amir@StartupArabiaBook.com
www.StartupArabiaBook.com

2

SAMIH TOUKAN

Catalyzing the tech revolution in the Arab world

Founder and Chairman of Jabbar Internet Group
Co-Founder of Souq.com
Co-Founder and CEO of Maktoob.com

WWW.JABBAR.COM

WWW.SOUQ.COM

WWW.MAKTOOB.COM

SAMIH TOUKAN is the founder and chairman of Jabbar Internet Group. In 2000, Samih founded and became the CEO of Maktoob.com, the world's first Arabic email service and largest Arab online community, with more than 16 million users. Maktoob.com was acquired by Yahoo! in 2009 for $164 million. He is the co-founder of Souq.com, the largest e-commerce platform in the Arab world, which was recently acquired by Amazon.com for about $600 million. He is also the founder of several other startups in the tech space. Previously, Samih had several years of experience with Andersen Consulting in technology consulting, systems development, and internet services. Prior, he co-founded Business Optimization Consultants in 1994.

On September 9, 2009, Samih received the Al Hussein Medal for Distinguished Performance of the First Order from His Majesty King Abdullah II in recognition of his contribution to the IT and telecommunications sector in Jordan and the region. From 2003 to 2005, he was appointed by the Jordanian government as a member of the board of the Social Security Investment Fund (a fund of several billion dollars). He is also an active angel investor, investing in several startups in the region. He also acts as a mentor to several entrepreneurs. He holds a bachelor's degree in electrical engineering from the University of London and a master's in management and international business from HEC University in France.

How did you initially become interested in technology?

My passion for technology and engineering started very early on, as long as I remember, and that was a few ages ago (laughs). In 1985, I graduated from Bishop School in Jordan. I then went to England to study for A level. While studying in England, my dream was to create something that makes an impact on the Arab world. Everyone is capable of contributing something meaningful. I had that belief and ambition from a very young age.

Growing up, I loved computer programming. Outside of my studies, I spent a lot of time programming. Back then, computer language was very basic. I also went beyond programming and learned machine language assembly. I remember I had a ZX Sinclair personal computer. It was a British-made, powerful, small personal computer. At that time, "powerful" meant less powerful than any smart phone you are holding in your hand right now! It was even pre-floppy disk. We used to have to load programs through a tape recorder, and every program would take half an hour to load. If there was an error, you had to repeat the whole process all over again, until you loaded that program into the computer.

EVERYONE IS CAPABLE OF CONTRIBUTING SOMETHING MEANINGFUL.

My passion for computers and giving back to the Arab world was the basis for my obsession with Arabic, more specifically creating an Arabic interface for the computer or what is referred to as "Arabizing." So my passion for Arabizing was there very early on and intertwined all throughout my path.

At that time, one of the most popular pieces of software was a game called "Football Manager," which I Arabized when I was just 16 years old. I actually contacted the owners of the company in Bournemouth, England, and went to see them. I showed them the Arabic version of the game and said, "I want to distribute this in Jordan." So we signed the contract. That was the first business contract I had ever done in my life. I went back to Jordan for the summer holiday and tried to sell the Arabized version I had developed to bookstores. I didn't have any experience in distribution, marketing, or sales, or any business experience in general. I was just a kid, and I went around and showed them this program I created and tried to convince them to buy.

The computer at that time wasn't anything like today. A very limited number of people had access to computers, mainly through libraries or universities. Having a personal computer was such a luxury and not common at all. Without really any planning or studying, I tried to distribute the program. I naturally failed miserably. I sold just two or three copies. So, that was the first failure in my life. I like telling that story and the fact that I started my career on top of a failure and I have no shame of that. Of course, it was a personal success in the sense of following my passion and actually creating the program, but it was a failure in a business sense. I could not execute, distribute, market, or sell the program because I didn't have any understanding or skills to do so.

After I graduated from engineering, I decided to go to France and study business management and business administration. I finished in two years. I then moved back to Jordan. At that point, I had developed both technical and soft skills. Though everything I'd learned so far was theoretical since I had only done internships. I didn't have any real-world business experience.

My first job in Jordan was with Andersen Consulting, which is now Accenture. I worked in management consulting. I developed software and technology for companies in the region. I did that for three years. That's when I connected with my longtime friend Hussam Khoury, who ironically also worked for Andersen Consulting in Canada. He and I talked about him coming back to Jordan and transferring from the Andersen Consulting office in Canada to its office in Jordan. His family wanted him to come back home as well. I told him, "Why don't you come back to the region? The region is quite stable now, and things seem to be on an upward trend." He ended up returning to Jordan in 1992, and we worked together for a year or two at Andersen Consulting. Then we decided to start our own business.

We left Andersen Consulting in 1994 to start our own consulting company in Amman. We called it BOC (Business Optimization Consultants). At the time, management consulting was a new concept in Jordan and the region. Not many companies understood it. The market was not that big, but we decided to give it a shot nevertheless. We managed to raise $30,000 seed capital and signed our first client, Aramex, the top local logistics company in the region. We developed their website, which was the first Arabic website in the region.

We developed a website for a company, I remember, called Zara Natural Dead Sea products. They were selling their products all over the world. So they accepted our idea because they thought putting a website online would get them sales. It actually worked. This was way before there was any e-commerce in the region.

We developed a rental car booking website for Thrifty Rent-A-Car. We developed websites for King Hussein of Jordan, companies, banks, and other websites all across the Arab world, in Syria, Egypt, and Saudi Arabia. We were quite good in creating websites. This is also how we picked up the skills to eventually create Maktoob.

Looking back, BOC was modestly successful, though I wouldn't say it was an easy journey. We managed to get a few clients but faced a lot of challenges. It was somewhat like a roller-coaster; sometimes we did great, and other times we struggled. This is something the youth need to understand. In a startup, things take time, and you will face many challenges. Early on, we faced lack of funding and a small consulting market in Jordan to work with. Nevertheless, we persevered and survived. We acquired different projects. Some succeeded, and some failed.

How did the idea of Maktoob come about?

After three years, Hussam and I decided that it was time to move beyond management consulting and launch our own product, instead of continuing to develop websites or solutions for other companies. Besides many of the challenges we faced with BOC, consulting had its inherit limitations. You're managing other companies' projects. So it's never really your vision, nor are you in full control. Those projects are also never scalable enough. They weren't going to create the real impact I was after or deliver products that could reach a bigger scale in the Arab world.

So, in 1999, after different ideas and trials, we came up with an experimental project under BOC, which we called Maktoob. The idea was based on creating the first Arabic email on the internet. At the time, Hotmail was the first webmail product brand, and it was the email that everybody used. So, we thought, "Why don't we create Hotmail in Arabic and make it available to the Arab world?" Back then, the number of internet users in the region was relatively small. It was really in the thousands. I'm talking 1999 here. Our vision was that if the internet was going to spread to millions in the Arab world, then the Arabic language will become a key factor. So we decided to focus on the Arabic language when we created the webmail product. After all, email at the time was the most important internet service out there.

In a way, the riskiest thing in business is not taking any risks.

I remember early on, we participated in a big technology exhibition in Jordan and another one in Egypt. We got 5,000 users right off the bat and realized there was a gold mine there. We got very excited about the potential. We realized right then and there that this was the future and this was the product that we should focus on. It was scalable and had the potential to reach all of the Arab world, much better than any consulting project we undertook with BOC. So we decided to stop our consulting work and focus on this Arabic webmail product. That was really the birth of this new dream, Maktoob.

Sure, it was a risky move. We already had a successful consulting business. We had paying clients. We had a good name, and we were good at what we did. Nevertheless, we saw the future in Maktoob, and we just went for it. It was definitely a calculated risk. This is a lesson for entrepreneurs: Sometimes you need to just go for things and take that risk. Sometimes you make the wrong decision, but if you don't take that risk of changing, you may not survive. We all have seen big, world-class companies disappear because they didn't take risks and change. You barely hear of Nokia these days or Blackberry. There are many examples. Companies need to keep changing and adapting. In business, you need to re-evaluate yourself every few years and see where the trends are going and adapt to these trends and make the necessary changes, even if it means taking on new risks. So, in a way, the riskiest thing in business is not taking any risks.

Our next goal was to go from 5,000 users to 100,000 users. I remember our first marketing campaign we called "Sajjil, Ana Arabi," meaning "Register, I'm an Arab," based on a poem by Mahmoud Darwish, a very famous Palestinian poet. We played on that theme, with the idea that we needed to be proud Arabs and create our own personal Arabic email and start using the Arabic language for communication online. The campaign was a success.

We started to see that this was starting to spread virally and became very excited about the potential. At the time, Hotmail used a clever thing, which was a simple tagline at the end of every email, "This email is sent by Hotmail." We used the same, "This email is sent by Maktoob. Register for free." So, with every email sent, you had an embedded call to action. When you email people, they get to see that. It was automatic viral marketing. That worked quite well.

So, in 2000, we officially registered Maktoob as a company. We were no longer an experimental project. We were now a real business. We then went to our first investor meeting with EFG Hermes in Egypt. I remember we presented them with our business plan. It was simply based on increasing the number of users to reach millions of users in the Arab world. It also had different revenue streams, mainly advertising. Other revenue streams would come into the picture later, including revenues from e-commerce, online payments, and other online services.

We continued to focus on Arabic email. That was now our forte. We would not do anything else yet. We had a business plan to start adding other services later, but not until we got email right. We also focused on growing our user base. We relied on what's referred to as "guerrilla marketing" and "viral marketing" tactics, as well as exhibitions that reach directly to our target users. We used to get a hundred users per day, then a thousand users per day, then two thousand users per day. It just continued to grow and grow. It was fascinating!

Did you ever encounter skepticism about the idea of Maktoob early on?

Definitely, at the beginning when we started Maktoob, many people were skeptical. Even our families, they were saying, "What are you doing? Why would you drop your current established business and do Arabic email? There is Hotmail already. People already use email in English. Why would they switch to Arabic email? People will keep using the internet in English. Why are you wasting your time on this?"

At the time, the small minority who used the internet, the thousands who had access to the internet, were the privileged. They were either educated outside or they already spoke English. They were not the masses. We thought if the internet is going to spread, and it will eventually, Arabic will be a key factor. So we didn't listen to the naysayers. We stuck to our vision and continued to focus on language and email because it was the fastest thing that we could spread.

What were some of the challenges you faced during this period?

We faced many challenges in those early years, mainly related to our exponential growth. For one, we struggled a bit with the technology and making sure we had uninterrupted service. Sometimes, our servers went down and we had to fix them or add more capacity quickly. So, we were always asking ourselves, "How could we make our email more reliable? How could we decrease downtime?" With email, your uptime rate should be at least 99.999 percent of the time. Meanwhile, in the beginning, our uptime rate was probably at only 80 or 90 percent.

It was a very challenging phase. This was a new industry, and the technology was very new. Nobody in the region really knew this technology or had scaled their user base to the level we did. So this was certainly uncharted territory. We had to learn a lot and develop those skills in-house. We called ourselves a "university" with our own internal workshops and training center.

Once we fixed our uptime rate and some basic metrics, we started experimenting by adding new features and services to the email. We added the first Arabic chat, for example, which was a very important feature. It helped further attract and engage users and accelerate our growth. At the time, Java programming had just come out, so we decided to create a Java virtual keyboard. That was a huge hit back then. Millions of Arabs in the U.S. and Europe wanted to use Arabic email or Arabic chat to communicate but did not have an Arabic keyboard. They were now able to click our virtual keyboard that pops up on their computer screen. We even used to send Arabic stickers that users ordered, so they could stick Arabic letters on their keyboard. Then suddenly people in the U.S. and Europe had an Arabic keyboard and could communicate virtually in Arabic for the first time!

These were innovations at the time. By today's technology standards, they are nothing, but at the time, they were amazing innovations. They really helped us grow around the world, not just in the Arab world, but in the U.S. and Europe as well.

We eventually started generating revenue and eventually profit. By then, we were ready for the next step, which was to start creating other services and to become a portal rather than just an email. We added news, games and sports. Eventually, we got in everything as we continued to do Arabic email. Our positioning was still "The first and the largest Arabic email," except now we were becoming the largest Arabic portal as well.

All the while, we kept trying different things. We succeeded in many things. We also tried projects that didn't work out. For example, we had a project called Maktoob TV at the later stages of Maktoob, where we tried to display UGC (user-generated content) on real TV. We had a TV station on air. The concept allowed you to submit material from your laptop or computer straight to live TV. Unfortunately, that wasn't a very successful project, and we had to shut down and move on. On the other hand, Souq and CashU were obviously two very successful projects that we started.

We initially started Maktoob Shopping, which didn't work out great. Then, we turned it into Mazad Maktoob, which eventually became Souq. So we founded Souq in 2005 with Ronaldo Mouchawar, who remains its CEO till today. Ronaldo is a world-class leader, and his accomplishments over the years speak for themselves. Though Souq strategy shifted multiple times and the company had to pivot a number of times, it eventually settled into being an online marketplace model. It sold products it owned as well as enabled third parties to sell on its platform, including brands, merchants, and individual sellers.

Amazon had invented the model in the U.S., but Souq had to adapt the model to local needs. I really believe Souq wouldn't have survived if it didn't continue to listen to its local customers and solve for local problems. Of course, Souq went on to become the first and largest e-commerce platform in the region. It enjoyed tremendous success. It was ultimately acquired for about $600 million to Amazon in 2017. This was, of course, a huge milestone for Souq, the group, and the region as a whole.

CashU was another project we undertook in those early days. It was created to provide an online payment method and a digital alternative to credit cards. CashU was successful, even profitable. It was a very innovative product. You could open your CashU wallet (or electronic funds) and you could buy scratch cards from different distributors and use them as a form of online payment. We had agreements with different offline distributors and retail outlets, in which you could just walk, say, in a neighborhood store, give them cash, then fill your account online. Then you could use your wallet to pay online merchants on our network. Our network, of course, was growing. Had it not been for the heavy financial sector regulations, CashU could've really grown way beyond what it did. Unfortunately, there were too many hurdles to overcome to really scale regionally. This was another great product ahead of its time. CashU was eventually sold to a regional investor.

EVENTUALLY, MAKTOOB REACHED SIXTEEN MILLION USERS WHEN WE SOLD TO YAHOO! IN 2009. IT WAS A GREAT ACHIEVEMENT AND OUTCOME FOR THE TEAM AND MYSELF, AS WELL AS INVESTORS AND EVERYONE WHO WAS INVOLVED IN BUILDING THE COMPANY THOSE TEN YEARS.

Out of CashU, PAYFORT was born. PAYFORT is a digital internet credit card processor that remains under Souq.com Group, which owned 100 percent of it and is now owned by Amazon. It's a great company that has grown very fast and is now one of the largest internet credit card processing companies in the region.

All in all, Maktoob evolved from email to portal, hosting multiple services, and then to what we called the Maktoob Group, an umbrella of various companies. I'm talking here maybe three years in each stage that made up the entire nine or ten years' journey.

Eventually, Maktoob reached sixteen million users when we sold to Yahoo! in 2009. It was a great achievement and outcome for the team and myself, as well as investors and everyone who was involved in building the company those ten years. We were proud of what we had accomplished and how far we'd come.

When we sold to Yahoo! in 2009, they decided to take the Maktoob portal and ran with its team, all 250 people, and the management team including its exceptional general manager, Ahmed Nassef, who was now to oversee Yahoo!'s business in the region. They all became Yahoo! employees. Yahoo! left all the other Maktoob group companies, which we had to spin off into another entity, which remained under Jabbar Internet Group, including Souq and CashU.

Both Souq and CashU were now incubated by Jabbar, operating under our offices, and were part of our daily management. They used our financing. A lot of internal services were shared including legal, accounting, HR, etc.

How different was Souq's journey pre- and post-Yahoo! acquisition?

I think Souq before Yahoo! was different from Souq after Yahoo! The reason is that while Souq before Jabbar was growing, we were still experimenting and learning. Also, on the financing side, we didn't have the full financial bandwidth Souq needed. We had some financing that was being distributed to different projects. After the Yahoo!-Maktoob deal, there was more financing available for Souq. As a result of that deal, we were able to inject more money as investors into Souq, so that gave Souq a big push.

I would say after 2010, this was the beginning of the real growth of Souq. We had more money, more focus, and we started to gradually develop Souq into a company on its own and detach it slowly from Jabbar. We knew Jabbar was a platform that supports startups and would incubate them. At some point, these companies will have the potential to grow and have the right financing to continue to grow on their own.

So we spun off Souq fully with its own team. We even transferred

Jabbar CFO to Souq, and I helped Ronaldo hire a top management team. We continued to be involved with Souq, not so much on a daily basis, but maybe on a weekly or monthly basis as active members of its board. We also started raising funds for Souq over several rounds, with Tiger Global Management in New York and with Naspers from South Africa, and then with the last round, two years ago, from a diverse range of investors.

Again, I always trace back all this to Maktoob. For me, Maktoob was like a tree; for every branch, there was something. You had Maktoob.-com, you had Souq.com, you had CashU, and from CashU came PAYFORT and so on. Even though not under our group, many employees that were at Maktoob and left decided to start their own companies utilizing a lot of the learning they had at Maktoob. So out of that Maktoob tree branched out twenty, twenty-five, or thirty companies and maybe more, now. Now, Souq itself is branching out into several companies.

For our industry in the region, this was the beginning, and from it, a lot of things came out. This is the direct effect. Now, if we talk about indirect effects—like how much did Souq help in employment, how many people; small merchants and individuals at home could sell, buy, trade and so on—this has indirectly affected hundreds of thousands of people.

You also have the indirect effect of the whole Maktoob-Yahoo! deal. You now have increased investment in the region, more interest from global players, more interest from local and regional big investors, who did not want to invest in online business initially. They then saw an example success story when Maktoob was sold to Yahoo! and now Souq to Amazon. I think this significantly accelerated the pace of investment in the ecosystem. Not to mention, it inspired and continued to inspire entrepreneurs to follow suit and build their own success stories. It pushes them; it motivates them to create new ideas and products and think big.

> REGARDLESS OF HOW MUCH MONEY YOU HAVE, YOU NEED TO MANAGE YOUR CASH FLOW VERY CAREFULLY. IN BUSINESS, YOU HAVE UPS AND DOWNS, AND THERE ARE CYCLES. YOU NEED TO PLAN VERY WELL. YOU DON'T NEED TO START SPENDING MONEY YOU JUST RAISED. JUST LIKE YOU CANNOT RUN BEFORE YOU WALK.

To what do you attribute Maktoob's success?

Looking back, one thing we learned early on and did very well was that we were extremely prudent in using our funds. We did not spend left, right, and center, and we were very strategic and measured in where we allocated our money. Our competition at that time was a company called Arabia Online. It was funded $22 million by Prince Waleed Bin Talal, the famous Saudi billionaire businessman. Meanwhile, we had just raised $2 million. So we naturally had to cut down on our expenses. We managed cash flow very carefully.

I always give this advice to the startups we invest in and the ones I mentor: "Regardless of how much money you have, you need to manage your cash flow very carefully. In business, you have ups and downs, and there are cycles. You need to plan very well. You don't need to start spending money you just raised. Just like you cannot run before you walk."

Arabia Online at the time was hiring very expensive expats and very expensive management. They were spending millions of dollars on TV marketing. I think that was a waste. The market was still small. It was growing, sure, but you cannot go on TV and create TV ads when internet penetration was only 5 percent. Maybe TV ads today make more sense because internet penetration is more like 50-60 percent, but at that time, 95 percent of your money spent on TV advertising was wasted.

Meanwhile, we were more of a bootstrapped kind of company. We hired people slowly and accounted for every dollar spent. We also insisted on focusing on Arabic email for the first few years, to keep our operating cost down and not to spread our resources too thin or on too many projects. Meanwhile, Arabia Online focused on doing everything from the outset—news, games—and ended up spending the money very quickly. Eventually, they went out of business. Believe it or not, $22 million vanished in just a few years!

What lessons did you learn from this journey you can share with entrepreneurs?

The first lesson I would say is related to passion or "shaghaf" in Arabic. It's very important for a person to love and be passionate about something and to be convinced about every job they do. If you work in something you are not passionate or convinced about, you are not going to produce good results. This is probably one of the many issues we have in the Arab world. People do not follow their passion, or they are not able to for some reason.

Success in the world and the Arab world is not limited to technology, engineering, or medicine as previously thought. People can be passionate about anything, whether it is physics, music, history, or whatever. For example, we are now investors in a weather company, ArabiaWeather, which was founded by Mohammed Al-Shaker, a Jordanian entrepreneur. When I first met with Mohammed, I felt his passion. He was telling me that when he was a kid, he was always looking at the weather and the clouds. So he was able to translate his lifelong passion in weather into a thriving company now. It started as a Jordanian company, and then we supported him and helped him transform it from a Jordanian company into a pan-Arab company. Often people who do not have access to funding or certain privilege or education are able to succeed if they have the passion and the ability to execute and persevere.

The second lesson is related to having a vision or "ruaya" in Arabic. When I was a young student, I always thought, "How can I help contribute to the Arab world entering the era of technology? How can I build a product that makes an impact, that is able to reach a large number of Arab users?" I didn't have an idea of what that product was at the time; nevertheless, the intention sets the direction you will be moving into. So you learn and build the skills you will need down the road. So always look three, five, or even ten years ahead. What is the vision that you want to reach? This vision is much bigger than financial gain. Many entrepreneurs might be thinking, "Oh, I want to make money, and I want to become a millionaire." That's not a vision.

> IF YOU WORK IN SOMETHING YOU ARE NOT PASSIONATE OR CONVINCED ABOUT, YOU ARE NOT GOING TO PRODUCE GOOD RESULTS.

I believe, in the end—with success—profit and financial gain will come for everybody who is serious and hardworking. Ultimately, you will get the financial gain and the profit, but that should not be your purpose. Your purpose should always be on making a difference.

The ones that create companies and say, "OK, I'm going to sell it in two or three years and make millions," these I don't think are the successful ones. The successful ones are the ones who persevere. It took us ten years for Maktoob to exit; it took us twelve years for Souq to exit. It requires a lot of vision. It involves a lot of hard work, a lot of challenges to overcome, a lot of patience. It just takes time. It's not something that you can flip in a few years.

The third lesson was how to deal with failure, more specifically to not get discouraged by failure, rather use it to be more determined to succeed. Failure is a great teacher. Use failure to identify and learn new skills you're missing and that you need to succeed. You can always try in different ways, with different skills, and on different projects, but with the same vision.

The lesson for the youth is not to be scared of failure; rather, embrace it. Whenever you fail, you should get up and be determined to learn the reasons you failed. How can you try again? Eventually, you will succeed. Many, many successful people failed several times before they succeeded. It's a continuous thing. Even today, we work on projects and with companies that fail. We learn and we continue. If you give up, you will never make it.

What's your advice to entrepreneurs regarding creating a team?

It's also very important to work as a team and think about creating a team. Make your team feel that they are part of the company and that they own the company.

Maktoob was the first tech company in the Arab world to offer stock options to our employees. At that time, we did not know what stock options were. We had to research that and bring it in. We thought it was a great tool to motivate our employees.

Our employees didn't understand it initially, but we explained it. At the beginning, employees favored getting a slightly higher salary than stock options because it was a new concept for them. There weren't success stories before us to prove anything. When we sold Maktoob to Yahoo!, things changed, and everyone made money. They were part of the success.

Now most startups if not all offer stock options from the very beginning to their employees. I think that is very important. It is also important for an entrepreneur to not keep the whole cake to themselves. Share it with your co-founders, with your employees, with your stakeholders, and so on. At the end, the more you share and the more you collaborate, the more successful you will be.

In your experience, what makes an effective co-founders partnership?

Hussam and I are different. I am more on the risk-taking side, and Hussam is more on the wiser, calmer side. We complement each other nicely. If you think about it that way, in terms of the relationship being complementary, I think you will succeed in your partnership. So, when I disagree with Hussam, we would always work things out at the end of the day. When I think about it, I ask myself, "Could I have done it without Hussam?" and the answer is always "No," because when I was down, he would motivate me, and vice versa. We've always supported each other. Sometimes, when I am making a decision, he might just give me an angle, a thought, or something that I didn't think of or I didn't see. I might be too excited and want to do the idea tomorrow, and then he comes and says, "Calm down, look at this, there is a risk here and there is a risk there," and I realize he's right and I shouldn't jump too quickly.

It's the same from his side. If he takes it too slowly, I push him to move faster. So, when you think of a partnership, it's OK to disagree and fight, but you always need to look at the bigger picture to make this work as a partnership. Rarely do you find companies with one person; no one person can do it all. I always encourage companies to at least have two founders who complement each other but share the same passion and commitment and vision.

As an entrepreneur, when do you know if you should stick to an idea or when you should give up?

This flows from the last question. I tend to stick very much to the idea, to a strategy, to anything, until the last minute. Meanwhile, Hussam tends to give up quicker than me. We learned with time that there has to be a balance. It's somewhere in the middle. I can't give you the exact stage where you give up on a product or you stick to it. I often stuck to things too long and Hussam often gave up too early.

So it's a balancing act. Sometimes it's wrong to give up too early, because sometimes things need more time. If you've launched an online product, for example, where internet penetration was not there, your timing was off. So you need to stick to it until the market catches up and things start to happen. With Maktoob, we passed through difficult times. We could have given up easily, but we didn't; we stuck to our plans. So it's important to stick to it when you have a vision.

At the same time, if you see that something is not working and is consuming a lot of money and has little or no upside, you must decide if that is something that you need to put your ego aside, close it down, and say, "I failed in this." Then move on to the next one. At one point you will need to do that; we've done it with many projects. On the other hand, you cannot give up too early on projects because they need time, they need financing, they need to run their course. You also cannot stick around too long with failed projects or the wrong people.

The lesson for the youth is not to be scared of failure; rather, embrace it. Whenever you fail, you should get up and be determined to learn the reasons you failed. How can you try again? Eventually, you will succeed.

Do you believe there's such a thing as work-life balance in early startup days?

Well, I don't know if there is such a thing in the early days of any startup. Initially, we used to work day and night, to be honest. I would say I am a big believer in a balance between everything in life. Try to balance your work, life, family, health, and so on. I say that in theory because in my early stages, I was working 24-7. I had passion and went after it with everything I had. I liked what I did, and I wanted to do it.

When you have a startup, you need to work hard. You need to put in a lot of effort and time. It's not a nine to five job, for sure. It's your life, and you're going to spend many years doing this, and there's a lot at stake. It's pretty much all you're going to think about day and night. You're going to dream about it. So, it's definitely an all-consuming effort, but try as much as possible to find some balance.

What's the single biggest missing thing needed to empower the next generation of entrepreneurs in the Arab world?

There are many missing things, and obviously there is no one solution fits all. The one thing that comes to mind, though, is a company in Jordan called Hello World Kids that we just invested in. They created a coding curriculum for schools starting at the age of ten and have already signed fifty schools, both private and public schools. So kids that are ten years old will learn programming. This is very important. In my own journey, I learned to code and developed passion for technology at an early age, and that really shaped me. So imagine if this becomes a language like English or Arabic that our kids learn from an early age.

Do you believe that business leaders have responsibility to give back to the startup community?

An entrepreneur by definition implies creating value and contributing. When you create a company, hire people and become successful, you are giving back. That means you employ people, solve problems, find solutions that can help your society, country or the Arab world in general. You are, by definition, giving back, even if not officially. Take Souq, for example. When you hire 3,000 or 4,000 people and you are enabling thousands of merchants on your platform, you are really giving back.

As an investor, you're also giving back. After the Yahoo! acquisition, I started thinking, "OK, now how do I give back even more?" So I decided to invest more in startups. There are a lot of young people with ideas that need angel investing, and they need venture capital. So I'm now also looking into creating a social fund that is geared to making an impact. I want to encourage startups that can solve massive local problems or offer scalable solutions for their society, whether in transportation, healthcare, or whatever. Thus, further helping develop the overall ecosystem. That's one area I'm looking at now.

If Souq and Maktoob didn't create the impact they are creating regarding solving local problems, motivating the young, pushing the ecosystem, generating more investment in the region, and more companies and ideas, I wouldn't consider them as successful no matter how much money they generated.

Of course, There are many ways of giving back. You can also give back by being a mentor and mentoring startups and young entrepreneurs. We've done a lot of that for no return and continue to do so. We sit on advisory boards and just give a few hours with companies every month to teach them things that we've learned over time. We don't want them to repeat the same mistakes we made, and we don't want them to fail. We can do this just by giving them advice.

I think if Souq and Maktoob didn't create the impact they are creating regarding solving local problems, motivating the young, pushing the ecosystem, generating more investment in the region, and more companies and ideas, I wouldn't consider them as successful no matter how much money they generated.

3

MONA ATAYA

Creating the go-to online shopping destination for mothers

Founder and CEO of Mumzworld

WWW.MUMZWORLD.COM

Mona Ataya is the founder and CEO of Mumzworld, which she founded in 2011 and is currently one of the leading e-commerce brands in the Middle East. Mona is also co-founder of Bayt.com, one of the pioneering recruitment platforms in the region. She graduated with a dual honors degree in marketing and finance. Mona has also worked for such companies as Procter & Gamble and Johnson & Johnson.

Tell us a bit about your life growing up.

I am the second of five children. There are two boys and three girls in our family. We come from a family of entrepreneurs. My father and his father were entrepreneurs. They moved to Lebanon from Palestine in the late 1940s, when they left their home in Zeeb on the Sea of Palestine and moved to Beirut. My grandfather set up from nothing. My father was the eldest of thirteen children, and so we grew up and thrived in a large family and extended-family environment.

We were brought up in Kuwait, where we attended British schools. We were taught early on that hard work was the reaper of all benefits and not to feel entitled to anything. Education, sports and community involvement were the cornerstones of our upbringing. We were encouraged and rewarded as we excelled in our academics and sports and were taught to always look at improving ourselves and our surroundings.

Our younger years were very fun and happy. Our parents were not strict at all; they gave us a lot of autonomy. They were fun, loving and trusted us a lot. I think it's that environment of trust, happiness and comfort that allowed us to be confident in our abilities. This combined with high expectations allowed us to feel that hard work was what it was all about. We learned that every effort you put in eventually comes back to you—in your work, in your successes, perhaps even in your children. Nothing goes to waste. These were the values I grew up with.

In 1990, I graduated from college and planned to move back to our home in Kuwait. I shipped all my belongings home while my family and I were vacationing in Europe. I was excited because I was planning on getting a job, working for a couple of years in Kuwait, and then going back to do my MBA. It was all planned out. About two weeks before we were all supposed to return home, Kuwait was invaded. So returning home was no longer an option. We were uprooted and had to start from scratch and build a new home. Our lives took an unexpected turn in a heartbeat.

As a family, we decided that we would mobilize and move to the United States. We moved to Washington, D.C. I was at this intersection point. I needed to decide whether I wanted to go back and do my master's or look for work. So I decided to explore both options and looked at the possibility of doing an MBA and finding work.

I had met the head of human resources of P&G (Procter & Gamble) during a career conference. I sent them my resume even though they were only looking at hiring MBAs. I had worked throughout my college years and had many internships. I knew that I had the profile that a company like P&G would want. They were looking for leaders; they were looking for problem-solvers; they were looking for people with initiative who were smart and had good grades. I believed I checked off all of those boxes and had those qualities.

The only thing I didn't have was an MBA, so I had nothing to lose by applying. I went to the library and spent the next few hours writing my first official resume. I knew that I didn't have an MBA, but what I did have was a caliber of skills that others didn't have, skills that were uniquely me. I articulated that in my cover letter and mailed it. Two weeks later, they invited me to an assessment. A couple of weeks later, I got a call to attend the second assessment. Following that, I was invited to fly to Cincinnati for my first round of interviews. I was just 20. I was very excited. This was the first time that a company had sent me a plane ticket. I flew to Cincinnati and stayed in a wonderful hotel. It felt surreal; I felt grown-up. This was the real world.

I stayed up all night researching Procter & Gamble and everything that P&G stood for. Who were they as an organization? What did they look for? What made them successful? Why would I be the right fit for them? What were my experiences? What about my character made me the right person for this organization? I spent the entire night formulating my answers in my mind. It was important for me to be convinced, too. They were a global brand that was looking for exceptionally smart people who would create impact. That is what I was about. I was formulating my thoughts so that I could articulate what I knew I had.

I had a few rounds of interviews. Those interviews were rigorous, but I enjoyed every minute. Eventually, the HR team invited me to lunch, and afterward, they offered me the job right then and there. I was over the moon.

It's OK to be different because leaders are not the same. Leaders are not the herd; they are the ones who dare to be different, who are authentic in their values and steadfast in their beliefs.

They then invited me to the local bar to celebrate. I don't drink. They all took out champagne glasses. They gave me one and said, "Let's celebrate your offer." I turned down the champagne glass and asked for a glass of water instead.

I remember later on, one of the managers told me that I should have taken the glass and sipped a little rather than decline. That was my first experience with pressure to conform to "make the crowd happy."

No, I don't drink. So why should I pretend to be something that I'm not? I always aim to be authentic and true to who I am, even if it is different or out of the norm. My integrity has served me well, and it's what I teach my children. It's OK to be different because leaders are not the same. Leaders are not the herd; they are the ones who dare to be different, who are authentic in their values and steadfast in their beliefs.

That was how I got started in my career. I learned so much during those formative years about how to develop, validate, and execute a business concept, relying on my insights and understanding of certain key dynamics and trends, as well as being diligent about understanding the data. As an entrepreneur, you really need both: intuition and data.

How did Dubai and Bayt come into the picture?

My brother called me one afternoon in 2000. He said he had an idea: He wanted to revolutionize the recruitment ecosystem in the Arab world, and he wanted to connect job seekers and employers in a faster, easier and more effective way. Back then, internet penetration was less than 2 percent. Putting a resume online was inconceivable. His vision was very admirable, but I initially thought the idea was a challenging one to bring to life. We were living in a region where confidentiality was ingrained in the culture and where the majority of employees and job seekers weren't even online.

After a lot of thinking and soul-searching, I made my decision to resign from Johnson & Johnson, where I was working at the time, and joined his new startup. I fundamentally believed in the social impact story of Bayt. At the end of the day, my motivation was always to create social impact. I was driven by the constant urge to do something relevant for the region I loved and was proud of.

We set up offices in November 2000 on Sheikh Zayed Road in Dubai, and the years that followed were very exciting. We were on an adrenaline rush from day one. We didn't have a lot of money. Our offices were small and basic. We had a black sofa that we took turns napping on because we hardly slept. We were working 24-7. I think that's what made Bayt successful early on: The team gelled together very well; we had a great idea and solid execution; and our timing was just right.

As a marketer, it was the first time I was exposed to this startup reality—build a business and ecosystem that's underdeveloped with money that you don't have. I had to figure out how to be creative in all my decisions. I recall how I managed to get a $100,000 media campaign and not pay anything for it by bartering. I challenged myself to improvise and to create win-win solutions to add value to partners and suppliers, with very limited resources.

We grew and became a leader in the jobs market in the region and became a highly admired and respected brand very quickly. I felt very proud to be part of Bayt and continue to feel very proud to be part of that evolution.

While I was at Bayt, I became a mother. My first children were twin boys. My third child was a boy. I have two teen boys now and a 10-year-old.

How did the idea of Mumzworld come about?

As an entrepreneur, you're problem-solving day in and day out. For the first time in a very long time, I was unable to find solutions to what I needed as a mother-consumer. I was pregnant with twin boys, and I was overwhelmed. I had no guidance, no playbook that told me what to do. Sure, there was a lot of advice and content on international sites, but my needs were different. I'm a mother from the Middle East, and I was exposed to different challenges. Who could help me with certain questions that I had? There were no resources for me to tap into.

This lack of information didn't allow me to make informed decisions. For example, I needed to buy a stroller for my twin boys. I had no information to guide me. Do I buy a double stroller that's face-to-face? Do I buy a double stroller that's back-to-back? There is dust there in the U.S. and Europe; meanwhile there is sand here in Dubai. I can't buy a stroller with certain types of wheels; instead I need a stroller that will move on the sand, move through narrow doors. How do I find that?

I also didn't know how to tap into a community that would guide me. Who could guide me with information about twins? I knew I was not alone in these frustrations. I was very deeply entrenched in many mother communities, and all of them were as frustrated as I was. Accurate, comprehensive, regional, reliable information about baby and mother problems simply did not exist.

The second problem I had as a consumer was choice. Quality choices in the region are limited. Retail stores typically carried what buyers "historically" bought without a clear understanding of global trends, bestsellers and consumer pain points in the market.

The third problem was price. Regional prices for baby and child products were significantly higher than anywhere else in the world. The region's retail landscape was dominated by distributors who traditionally held exclusive contracts with global brands that gave them freedom to inflate prices. Consumers, however, were becoming more discerning, and with the transparent world of the internet, it was becoming increasingly clear that the region's prices were no longer competitive.

The fourth challenge was lack of community. Mothers gravitate to one another for guidance, support and empowerment. While there were a few pockets of mother groups here and there, there was no go-to community that I could tap into to guide and support me and answer endless questions for a new parent.

When the boys were born, I took two years off work. I was a fully committed, passionate mother with only one objective: to do the best for my children and give them the best opportunity to do well. I needed to be empowered, informed and inspired and have the right books and information to support me. I was not, so I turned to international sites for information and products.

When the boys went back to nursery at two years, I went back to Bayt. In 2011, when the twins were eight, I wrote a business plan, driven by the frustrations that I felt as a parent. I didn't initially have any intention to launch the business. I was already overextended as a parent and entrepreneur of a fast-growing organization. I wrote the business plan out of a passion for solving pain points for mother-consumers like me.

While I was writing the business plan, it became very evident that the better way to solve these problems was through e-commerce, the biggest trend of the coming decade. The value of global retail e-commerce reached almost $2 trillion in 2016, representing 9 percent of total retail sales and 3 percent of global GDP. By 2020, retail e-commerce is expected to top $4 trillion, representing a 21 percent annual growth over a five-year period.

In the MENA (Middle East and North Africa) region, B2C (business to consumer) e-commerce represents just 1.5 percent of total retail sales and .7 percent of the region's collective GDP, so there is a long runway of growth ahead of us. There are 82 million e-commerce shoppers in MENA, representing more than half of the connected population, and each spends $313 per year on average on e-commerce purchases. Due to their higher internet penetration, more developed payments infrastructure, and higher spending power, the GCC (Gulf Cooperation Council) markets are particularly attractive e-commerce markets.

On top of the e-commerce wave, our region enjoys strong demographic tailwinds that very much support the Mumzworld thesis. There are almost 350 million people living in the MENA region, of which 90 million are between the ages of zero and 12, which is the target market for Mumzworld. Every year, 8 million newborns are added to this pool. At that rate of compounding, Mumzworld's target market is poised for tremendous growth.

What were some of the challenges you faced in the early days?

We were pioneers in the vertical e-commerce space for all things mother, baby and child in the Middle East. We faced a lot of challenges in the early days around building an e-commerce ecosystem and e-commerce brand. There are many touchpoints in the ecosystem that support or hinder success in e-commerce. Given that the ecosystem was still very much in its infancy, many of these touchpoints did not exist or were very basic. For example, payment gateways were unreliable, and consumers had little confidence in them. Last-mile delivery providers were slow and still not used to the volumes and speed that e-commerce mandated. Technology talent was, and continues to be, rather scarce. In addition, the process of setting up a business was expensive and complicated. In a nutshell, the barriers to entry were many.

The infrastructure at the time wasn't as developed as it is today. We had to build our own infrastructure. We had to build partnerships that allowed us to scale fast and cost-effectively. We learned the art of being creative, resourceful, and doing more with less. We were then able to establish momentum very quickly.

We launched the business, and on day one, we had 25,000 products or "SKUs." We locked in the key brands, who were skeptical about e-commerce. We had to knock on their doors and sell them our vision and create the same passion in them that we had in the potential of this brand. It was a leap of faith that a lot of these brands took with us but was critical for allowing us to start a business with a very strong catalog right from the outset.

Very quickly, we were able to establish ourselves as the largest catalog for the mother, baby, and child segments. We had to be the deepest catalog in the region for these categories, combined with speedy delivery and everyday low prices. Today, we are the largest community of mothers in the region, building a brand that has already become a household name and an indispensable online extension of mothers' lives.

How does Mumzworld build its community and empower mothers today?

Mumzworld today is home to a community of almost 2 million mothers in the region, but with 15 million mothers out there, we are still at the beginning of the road. Our community today is the result of many years of hard work building grassroots relationships across the region. Whether through our strategic partners (of which there are 100+ in the region) or our network of influencers, every mother that joins the "Mumz" community raises the value of the community to all of its members—the true definition of a network effect. Since the start, we've sought to be a mother's trusted partner and advisor in her challenging but rewarding journey of motherhood. By positioning ourselves in this role, we gained the trust and loyalty of an initial core group of mothers. That core group then became the beachhead from which the community grew by word-of-mouth at an accelerated pace.

MUMZWORLD TODAY IS HOME TO A COMMUNITY OF ALMOST 2 MILLION MOTHERS IN THE REGION, BUT WITH 15 MILLION MOTHERS OUT THERE, WE ARE STILL AT THE BEGINNING OF THE ROAD.

There is still a lot to do in building out this community. Empowering mothers is multi-dimensional, and while e-commerce is the starting point, where we empower a mother to make the most informed purchase decisions for her child, it is only one component in our vision of building the largest mother, baby and child company in the Arab world.

Another area we focus on is corporate social responsibility (CSR), especially as it relates to mother and child education. Supporting underprivileged mothers is something that we discovered that our consumers are very keen to do. Today, women are 60 percent of our staff. We've found that women who understand this business and understand our products do very well. We also hire women who want to come back to work but prefer to work from home because of their children or simply because of geographic distance. We have hired a lot of freelancers out of markets like Lebanon, Jordan, and Palestine who work remotely and are now empowered to work, contribute and earn a living for themselves and their families. This is a first ever in the region, and we have started to create a network effect and partnerships with other companies who are adopting such a model.

Three years ago, we also opened an investment round only for women, inviting women who wanted to come back and contribute to the region to invest in Mumzworld and become part of this growth story. We received tremendous interest in that opportunity. There were eight women investors who came on board as silent partners, though they add substantial strategic value to the business and have become very important ambassadors of the brand. These are women who are educated movers and shakers in the region. Some of them work; some of them don't work. This is another initiative that demonstrates the kind of impact story that we are creating with this brand.

What's your advice to entrepreneurs?

Be passionate about your vision, have a clearly thought-out plan and execute—*fast*. We give members of our team full ownership to run with their ideas. I tell them to "just do it. If you're going to fail, make sure to fail fast, learn, and fix it. Don't execute and fail and then sit and whimper." That's how you get breakthroughs. Innovation comes from continuous iterations of great ideas and unique, exceptional execution. Another advice is to surround yourself with people smarter than yourself, who have skills that compensate for your weaknesses.

At Mumzworld, we tried many things that did not get off the ground. But those that did, the results people see, did very well. We had no idea what we were doing in the beginning. We were shooting in the dark. I had no e-commerce background at all. We had to give ourselves a crash course very early on. We were always in trial-and-error mode. We were failing fast, and if I did something last year and I failed in it, I was not repeating that mistake. On the contrary, I was going to become an expert really quickly.

In that sense, this kind of failure was essential to our success. On the other hand, I think real failure is not trying. It's being apathetic and sitting back and watching. Real failure is knowing that I can, but I choose not to, or I'm too afraid to try. It is also about not living according to your values and doing things for the wrong reasons.

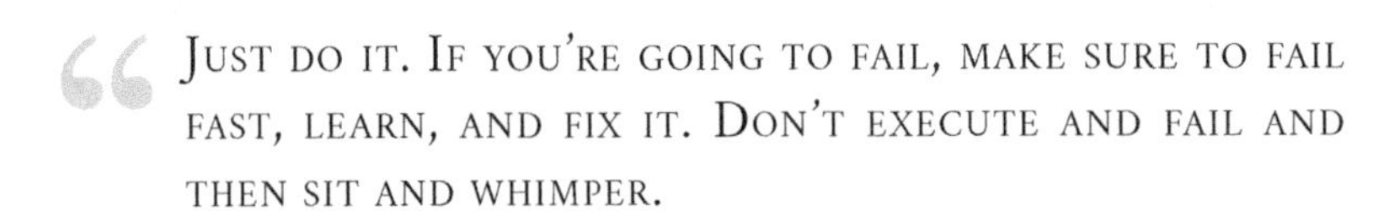

> "JUST DO IT. IF YOU'RE GOING TO FAIL, MAKE SURE TO FAIL FAST, LEARN, AND FIX IT. DON'T EXECUTE AND FAIL AND THEN SIT AND WHIMPER.

Any advice regarding recruiting and building corporate culture?

Working at a startup requires you to work harder than you've ever worked. You work longer hours than a normal company would ask you to. You get paid less because a startup typically can't pay you as much as the market, and you are often surrounded by uncertainty and change. You're constantly inventing and reinventing yourself. You're constantly editing, especially in the first year. Recruiting people into that environment of constant change, long hours, less pay and high stress is very difficult. It requires a certain type of person who will accept that level of chaos. It's challenging, and you're going to get a lot of turnover at the beginning.

What typically keeps employees in an organization is not the money. That is only part of it. The other part is the corporate culture and vision. You need to aim so far that you can attract people who are sold on your vision and energized by your purpose. You need to keep reminding them of that vision and the impact you are creating.

We have always strived to only hire entrepreneurs into the organization regardless of the role. These are people who are energized by challenging the status quo, seek to be different and are problem solvers and not complainers. We hire people who believe that opportunity is created and not handed to them on a silver platter. We hire people who are driven by social impact and want to make a meaningful mark in their community.

We hire people who believe they are "lucky." I found that people who feel lucky and positive can always figure a way around the maze. In contrast, people who feel that life treats them badly are the complainers, the problem creators as opposed to the solvers, the people we don't want around us. Finally, we hire people who believe in the impossible and are resourceful and creative. As such, we have built a corporate culture that rewards positive energy, innovation and excellence.

What's your philosophy on bootstrapping and fundraising for a startup?

We work on efficiently building our business and being innovative, with the philosophy of doing more with less. This is the way we have scaled from the beginning. It is quite a ride because every time you raise money, you feel that the people around you become almost complacent. They say, "OK, I have $100 here; I'm going to spend $100." The reality is, if you have $100, you now need to be 100 times smarter in how you spend it because you need to multiply your business faster. The more money we raised, the more we challenged ourselves to be better and to make less mistakes. We are building a business that is here for the long term— a business with strong unit economics, unique fundamentals and offers intrinsic consumer value. We operate with a bootstrap mentality although we are a well-funded company. We operate with very lean metrics and with the DNA of being efficient in everything we do.

It's so important to find the right investors because they are your partners. They are going to ask lots of questions, which is natural. As long as they are aligned with you strategically and executionally from the outset and clear on your vision, and you deliver what you promise, the relationship is a win-win. We as founders are always balancing the focus we give to our three most important stakeholders—the customer, our team and our shareholders—and strive always to give adequate attention to each. Our customers, because they are the reason we do what we do. Our team, because great people build great businesses, and without their tireless effort, we cannot build a great brand. Our investors, because they provide us with the financial and support resources to fulfill our customer promise and employ great people. As founders, our success is the impact story we create for the customer, the employment opportunity we create for our team and the impressive returns we give to the shareholders for their trust in us.

CUSTOMER SERVICE IS YOUR FRONT LINE. THEY ARE YOUR SOLDIERS. CUSTOMER SERVICE IS YOUR ANCHOR. IT'S WHERE YOU HAVE TO FOCUS YOUR TRAINING, AND IT'S WHERE YOU HAVE TO FOCUS YOUR TIME. IT'S WHERE YOU HAVE TO FOCUS YOUR BUDGET.

What's the role of customer service in a startup?

Customer service is your front line. They are your soldiers. Customer service is your anchor. It's where you have to focus your training, and it's where you have to focus your time. It's where you have to focus your budget. They are the guys representing you on the phone, on chat, and on email. They are your eyes and ears to the customer, and they have to be the most customer-obsessed department in the organization.

We were always customer-centric and customer-obsessed, but you must have the right metrics, quality metrics, support metrics, and constant checks and balances. We didn't have those metrics at first because we didn't have the resources or thought we didn't need them. When we moved warehouses last year and had a lot of hiccups in the move, that's when we recognized that our customer service department needed to climb to the next level in training, development, and customer communication. If you have a dollar to invest, that's where you should invest it.

How important is it for leaders and organizations to give back?

I think everybody has a responsibility to give back, whether it's a leader of an organization, an employee within an organization or the government. We all have a responsibility to give back. Here at Mumzworld, although we are an e-commerce player, we give back to employment. We employ mothers at home and outside. We give back to our customers by being customer-obsessed. We give back to our employees by providing them with a great learning experience that sets them up for successful careers. We are homegrown and built for the region but operate with the vision of being a viable global brand as well. Accountability is on every one of us.

What are your views on the Middle East's prospects?

I think the Middle East region is on the right path. There is a lot of potential here. There is a huge population. It's a young population. We are at the tipping point of some exciting times. Sure, it's going to take time, but I'm very optimistic and excited about what will unfold in the coming years. What needs to happen is that entrepreneurship must become more affordable. As an entrepreneur operating today with limited budgets, it's very difficult to succeed. You need to make resources accessible. You need to make entrepreneurship viable. Today it's not. I hope that will change over time.

What's your vision for Mumzworld?

We are building the largest mother, baby, and child company in the Arab world, and our vision is to be the indispensable online extension of a mother's life. Ultimately, "where there's a mother, there will be a Mumzworld mum." We are building a 360-degree solution for mothers in the region. It's a customer-obsessed organization empowering mothers to make the most informed decisions for their children by giving them access to the widest choice of products throughout their journey of motherhood in the context of a "community" that they can relate to and trust and turn to. We give them curated, comprehensive and localized content to make informed decisions, a superior customer experience and unique laser-focus services that address the many important milestones throughout their parenting journey. We are building a focused vertical business that will answer to all mothers' needs and empowering her with tools, information and resources to be the best she can be.

To me, Mumzworld is a business of passion. If it weren't, I would feel every hour I spend on Mumzworld is an hour away from my three children and my family. It's creating a social impact, empowering mothers, and doing something important for this ecosystem, even though it's not an easy ride. I believe it's an important ride, and the end path, the road, and the journey we are on is a very exciting one. We've achieved a lot already to date, and we continue to pave the way to being that indispensable online extension of a mother's life.

MUDASSIR SHEIKHA

Reinventing the local ride experience

Co-Founder and CEO of Careem

WWW.CAREEM.COM

Mudassir Sheikha co-founded Careem Networks in 2012 and serves as its CEO. Prior, Mudassir served as the Vice President of Solutions at Keynote DeviceAnywhere. He was responsible for the Solutions organization, managing all aspects of delivery of products to customers. Before that, he spent two years in Karachi, Pakistan, where he established and headed Mobile Complete's offshore development center. He also founded Solerent and served as its director. Previously, he was part of the Venture Finance group at Garage Technology Ventures, where he worked with seed-stage companies in the software and consumer internet industry. Before Garage, he held various technical positions at Brience and Trilogy Software. He started his career as a consultant at Ernst & Young. Mudassir holds a master's in computer science from Stanford University and a bachelor's in computer science and economics from the University of Southern California.

Tell us a little about your background.

I was born in Karachi, Pakistan. I'm the eldest of three siblings. I have two younger sisters. I come from a relatively middle-class family. My parents did not have the opportunity to go to college, so they had a deep desire to give us an education. They sent me and my sisters to English-medium school so that we could acquire the education that they were not able to get.

My dad came from a business-oriented family. He had worked in the rice trading family business from the time he was a teenager, and that became his life. He still works there today and has managed to raise us and give us an education.

My mom was a very good student in school. She was one of the very top students in high school. In Pakistan, they had these annual rankings. She was number three in the entire city of Karachi the year she graduated. She was also quite ambitious, but like what happens with most women in Pakistan, she got married quite early, started having kids and was not able to pursue a career and realize her potential. So, from the very beginning, my mom's untapped ambition and her unrealized potential became a part of our lives. We had to be at the top of our class, and nothing less was good enough. She would work extremely hard with us to make sure that we were doing our homework and that we were working hard on a daily basis. We were always getting 200 percent of her attention and focus.

My dad, on the other hand, was not able to get much education, but he was a hard-working individual who would focus on something and do it really well. If anything had to be done, you called my dad, and he would take care of it. The entire family would call him for fixing their houses, fixing relationships, fixing whatever. He was the youngest of seven siblings and was known to be the guy that would go out and fix things for everyone.

I grew up in a joint family household, so my uncles were living in the same household with us. It was a very interesting upbringing. It was very much influenced by the ambition of my mom and the humbleness of my dad. Growing up in this environment, I always had lots of people around me, so I thrive on and get energy from having people around me.

I did my schooling in Pakistan and ended up getting the highest GPA in all of Pakistan when I graduated from high school. I wanted to go to college in the U.S. and hoped to get a scholarship because my family did not have money to pay for it. I applied to a bunch of schools. My grades were awesome, so I naturally expected I would get into a good school and get a full ride. As it turned out, for some reason, I got lots of rejections. I eventually got into a big college in Los Angeles, USC (University of Southern California), with a full scholarship.

I initially started studying economics at USC in '95-'96 when dot-coms were about to happen. Technology was a big topic in California then. I always enjoyed physics and math, so I found myself gravitating toward computer science. Since I loved both majors, I decided to pursue both and graduated in three and a half years from USC.

What was your first business experience like?

In 1999, California was at the height of the dot-coms. I graduated, and I didn't want to do anything but a startup. I really wanted to be in the San Francisco Bay area, where this whole, exciting technology thing was happening. Since I had a computer science degree, it was relatively easy to get a job straight out of college. After a few months, I found myself at another company working at a very early stage startup in San Francisco, called Brience. Brience was an exciting and foundational experience for me, because up until now I was the nerd. I was the one that was working hard and getting the best grades in school, and that was the only thing that mattered in my life. Then, all of a sudden, here I am in Silicon Valley, working at a startup that has raised a ton of money. They had raised more than $200 million in the first round of funding. Even by Silicon Valley standards, that was by far the best ever investment round, in fact, best ever series of investment rounds for any startup. The objective was to bring this thing up quickly and go public in nine months.

When I joined Brience in March 2000, the objective was to go public in December 2000 in nine months, hopefully make a ton of money, and not have to work for the rest of our lives. That's how the pitch was sold to us. There's a lot of things I ended up learning not to do as a result of that experience. This was a very artificial build-to-flip mindset where, let's build something extremely quickly, that we don't care if the foundation is solid enough or not, but we just need to build it quickly. We need to go public. We need to make a lot of money and then we'll go and do the next thing if that day comes.

That was the mindset, and a lot of things were done that were not right, we were getting short-term gains at the cost of long-term liability. In spite of the shortcomings, what I did get out of that experience was the ability to dream big. In a way, we were trying to achieve the impossible. The founders of the business said we would do it. They actually showed us by doing whatever it took to make it a reality. Ambition within the company was through the roof.

I also learned how to work extremely fast, because this company wanted not only to build the business, but also to go public in nine months. So literally in three months, we had hired three or four hundred people in Silicon Valley. That was incredible, because at that time, it was literally impossible to hire people with so much competition from other startups. We acquired a company in Florida and Armenia. We also had already acquired a whole bunch of customers. This is all just from the start of the business to the six months mark.

Then, of course, there was a small correction of the markets. We had already filed our S-1 to go public. We felt this was just a correction, that the markets would come back. They came back and then they went down again, and then down again, and then we realized that this was the new reality and eventually accepted that this IPO wouldn't happen after all and that was the end of that.

I did that for about three years, which is around the time that I got my green card as well, and over time I became a U.S. citizen. I went to Stanford and did my master's in computer science. I came out with the aspiration to return to Pakistan. I felt I had spent enough time in California and in the U.S., and it was time to head back home. I'm the only son, so I felt it would be good to be close to my parents. So I moved back to Pakistan in 2003 to be with my parents.

Once I was in Pakistan, I started a small IT business there and met up with some friends from the last startup I was at. They were starting a business called DeviceAnywhere. It was a startup that I eventually joined as a third co-founder. I was responsible for the operations in Pakistan initially and then, as fate had it, had to move again to the U.S., where I looked after professional services out of the U.S.

I did that until 2008 and then felt that I had to move back once again to Pakistan because my parents were all by themselves. At the time, things were quite unstable in Pakistan. I decided to move to Dubai to be near my parents and basically park myself there until things got better in Pakistan and then move back there. I joined McKinsey's management consulting Dubai office and did that for four years. All the while, the aspiration has always been to either go back to Pakistan or do something entrepreneurial.

How did your experience at McKinsey prep you to become an entrepreneur?

McKinsey was the best way for me to get a business education, because I was an engineer all along, and I hadn't really done business. In the startups that I worked at, I felt a void of business education. I would do things and would not have the confidence that these were the right things to do because I was not trained in them. McKinsey was amazing in building that confidence. I learned to look at business problems and solve them. I also learned how to communicate to top executives. I would present to them, and it really built confidence in my ability to solve problems the right way and articulate my message the right way.

When did Careem enter the picture?

In 2012, the startup that I left in 2008, which I had shares in, was acquired. I made some money and felt that now was the time to move and do something on my own. Around the same time, I was starting to feel that I should do something else, and as part of that thinking, I joined a group of Pakistanis in the McKinsey office in Dubai. They were working on opening an office in Pakistan.

Since I was thinking of leaving anyway or going to Pakistan, I felt this was the perfect opportunity to be a part of that initiative. I joined that team and did the due diligence to make the Pakistan office happen. I had to make a list of all the companies that McKinsey could serve in Pakistan.

We started making a list of the largest companies in Pakistan. We ranked them in order of size, and the results of that exercise were quite shocking to me. Guess how many billion-dollar businesses were in Pakistan at that time, in 2011? There was only one business that was a billion dollars plus. This does not include the oil and gas industry; that tends to be a bit larger. Pakistan was a nation of 200 million people, and we, unfortunately, had produced only one billion-dollar business. I didn't care about the billion-dollar number so much, but the fact that we, as such a large nation, had only built one large corporate institution, I felt, was really embarrassing.

I would often joke around with Magnus, who later became my co-founder at Careem, that Sweden, where Magnus comes from, is a nation of nine million people, and they have produced an IKEA, Volvo, Erikson, Skype, Spotify—there's so much that has come out of that country. Even in the times that I spent in the Silicon Valley, every 300 meters there were large corporate institutions, and for some reason in Pakistan we had hardly built one that was big enough.

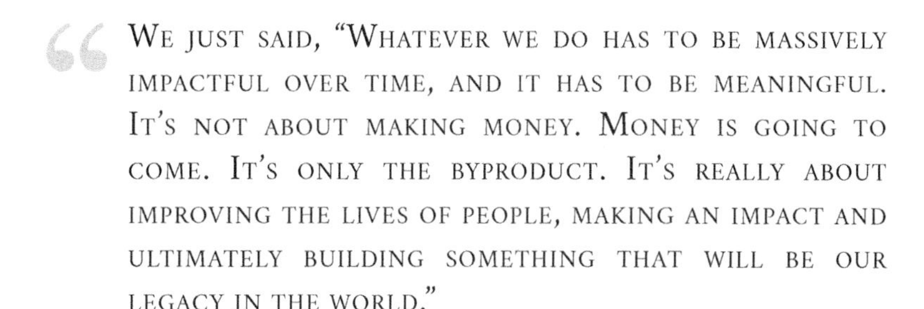

> We just said, "Whatever we do has to be massively impactful over time, and it has to be meaningful. It's not about making money. Money is going to come. It's only the byproduct. It's really about improving the lives of people, making an impact and ultimately building something that will be our legacy in the world."

The story is not different from other parts of the Middle East. That is why I associate myself with the region, with the Muslim world. I felt that it was more than just a Pakistan issue, that this is a region-wide problem. This is where I was coming from as I was thinking of leaving, and there was a deep desire to build something big in the region for the region. So that was my thinking then, which really planted the seed for Careem.

How did you and Magnus start working together on Careem?

I first met Magnus at McKinsey. We were the only two people at McKinsey in the Middle East who were working in technology. He similarly had a background in computer science. He also had been at some startups before, hence both of us were assigned to anything that was closely tied to technology in some shape or form at McKinsey.

I ran into Magnus again in 2012. He had just had a life-changing event where he was diagnosed with bleeding in the brain and was told that he may not survive. He had to go through a brain surgery and resolved to himself that if he survived, he would pursue becoming what he called "Magnus 2.0." Fortunately, the surgery was successful and he was healthy again. Through this experience, however, he realized that his true calling in life was to build something big and meaningful. That would be his legacy in the world. We were both coming from a place of yearning to build something big and really make an impact.

Magnus is married to a Palestinian. So he was also connected to the region as I was. We decided to partner up and said, "Let's figure out what to do." At that time, we didn't have any ideas. We just said, "Whatever we do has to be massively impactful over time, and it has to be meaningful. It's not about making money. Money is going to come. It's only the byproduct. It's really about improving the lives of people, making an impact and ultimately building something that will be our legacy in the world."

How did you become interested in transportation?

We looked at opportunities that could be impactful in the region. We started looking at impactful sectors like education and healthcare, looking for something that could become massive. We knew of the opportunity in transportation from our days as consultants, because every time we would travel the region, we would struggle to find reliable and convenient transportation.

As consultants, we would often spend most of the days on the road. It was always trouble finding someone to pick you up from the airport in Riyadh, then take you to your business meetings. They would not always know the directions of the place that you needed to go to, and you had to pay them in cash, which you would not always have. You had to go to the ATM. It was a quite cumbersome process, and what we ended up doing, for the most part, was for every city that we would have to go to, we kept phone numbers of one or two drivers that we would typically call when we would land in the cities, so that worked. The problem was that the minute those drivers were not available, then we would be without reliable options, and it would be quite a pain to get around.

We knew there was this opportunity. We weren't sure how big it could be or if this was meaningful enough. What's meaningful about providing a taxi service for people? This is essentially what we would be doing. When we started digging deeper, we realized that ground transportation is quite broken and in many of our cities is nonexistent, so it was a huge opportunity to come and fill this gap.

When we spoke to some of the drivers that were servicing us, we realized that their lives were quite challenging. They were working long hours. Most of them in Dubai or Pakistan were working sixteen-hour days. They would save 90 percent of the money they would make to send back home to their families to educate their kids and to keep up their families. They were living in very challenging conditions. Literally, in one room there would be four beds, and in four beds these people would sleep in shifts. We really saw this opportunity as a way to improve their lives, and we found that if we could build this thing, we could end up creating a lot of jobs, and this would then make it especially meaningful.

So that's why we took this opportunity a bit more seriously. Our first stop was McKinsey, the consulting company that we had worked with. We asked them if they would come on board as a client. I think there was a small pilot period after which they joined, and that's really how we got started. It was just our own pain as consultants traveling the region and finding this as a potentially big opportunity and one which would allow us to create a lot of jobs and improve the lives of drivers, or "captains," as we call them now.

What did you initially imagine Careem to be?

We started in 2012, and I remember on the first day, I took a bus from Dubai to Abu Dhabi, where Magnus lived. We met in his home office, and the first thing that we did was we put in order the five values to which we would guide Careem. We had selected the name "Careem" already. Careem means generous in Arabic, and we felt this was a strong value from the region, generosity. We said we wanted to be generous on three dimensions.

We wanted to be generous to our customers, meaning that we would provide exceptionally outstanding customer service, something that you don't see much of in the region. We said we wanted to be generous to our captains. This means that we would look after them, not just by giving them work, but look after them holistically. We would be looking after their health, looking after their families and everything else they would need help with.

Finally, we would also be generous to our colleagues, the people at Careem. We would make sure that they became partners of success and that we looked after their professional development. We would pay, for example, to have stock options in Careem. They have been very well rewarded since then as a result of Careem's growth.

We found the name Careem and the value that it represented as a way for us to be generous to customers, captains, and colleagues. That became a central value at Careem, and this is something that we decided very early on in the life of this business.

Initially, we were building a B2B (business to business) service for large companies. We didn't have a consumer app. We didn't have an on-demand service. We basically had a web-based service that we would target to large companies. We understood their pain points firsthand.

When you're servicing large companies, you are as good as your "last screwup," so to speak. You have to be very particular about the call to your service. You may have delivered a thousand trips really well, but if one trip goes wrong with the wrong person, it would completely destroy that relationship for you. So we had to build a service that was very reliable. We wanted to offer very high levels of customer service, so if things went wrong, which they often and inevitably do in this business, we would respond very professionally through customer service. We would do things even before people would complain, just wow them with our customer service. We built very strong capabilities in delivering a reliable service and exceptional, high-quality customer service.

How did you deal with outside competition entering the market?

In 2013, nine months after we had started, someone sent me a job description from Uber looking for a general manager of Dubai. We didn't know much about Uber at that time because we were delivering a corporate service and we weren't doing app-based on-demand service. We saw our future on the consumer front to be an app, to be on-demand. When we heard that they were coming to the region, we naturally felt quite concerned; maybe there was a risk that we would remain corporate-focused and they would take the big consumer market opportunity right from underneath us. Uber had already raised a lot of money by then. They had an app, and it was undeniably very slick. We had no app. We had no on-demand service. We didn't even have our first round of funding closed.

It was frankly a very high-stress time for us, but there's nothing like competition to get you running really, really fast. Instead of sleeping six hours a day, we started sleeping three hours a day. We said, we have to launch an app, and we have to have it up and running before they come to the market. And we did just that. We were live on the app store in a matter of weeks before Uber came to town. It was very much a basic app, but we were up and running. Uber hit Dubai with their much more advanced app and serious financial backing that affords them to do whatever it takes to land-grab. Not only did this offer them more marketing opportunities; they used their buying power to try and get our captains to exclusively work for them with huge incentive schemes. What happened next was interesting. Since the Middle East tends to be somewhat challenging from an infrastructure standpoint, the maps in the region were not accurate, and a lot of these captains are not as educated as drivers that Uber may have worked with in the U.S. It resulted in a lot of behaviors that were unexpected for them.

> It was frankly a very high-stress time for us, but there's nothing like competition to get you running really, really fast. Instead of sleeping six hours a day, we started sleeping three hours a day. We said, we have to launch an app, and we have to have it up and running before they come to the market. And we did just that. We were live on the app store in a matter of weeks before Uber came to town.

When Uber first came to Dubai and launched the service, the service was quite unreliable. Even though they were giving people extreme discounts, free trips, and they were paying drivers a lot of money, they were not able to deliver a reliable service. What would happen was, you ordered a ride and would expect a car to come, and the driver would not be able to get to you reliably because he didn't have your accurate location. Other times, he would be coming to you, but on the way, he gets a call from his other client and then he cancels the booking and goes on to his other client. Something or another like that would happen because they did not build their service based on this environment, so they weren't familiar and ready with the reality of this region.

Whereas our service, even though we had a very basic app, we were totally reliable. When we said we would get you a car, we would get you a car. It would come to your exact location. It would take you where you needed to go, and when things didn't go well, we would compensate you with amazing customer service.

So, in the first year of competition, we were winning because of our reliability and because of our customer service. We figured we got another year on them because they were still learning the region. By the time they had learned, we would be able to raise some more money as well, and we would be able to compete a bit more equally. Today, we have raised much, much less money than they have raised, so we still have to be very scrappy. We really had to fight a guerrilla war and be very creative in order to compete with them.

How did you go about raising those funds?

Along the way we found some very strong supporters. The first round of funding was with Saudi Telecom Ventures, who were very helpful when we launched in Saudi. Then we got Al Tayyar Group on board as a second-round investor. Again, a very strong family group in Saudi that was able to support us and help us develop that market. The first round was Saudi-led, because that's where the battle was being fought.

Then after we had captured Saudi, we wanted to expand a bit broader in the region. We wanted to go to North Africa, Egypt in particular. We wanted to go to the Levant. We wanted to go to Pakistan. At that point, Abraaj Capital, the private equity group in Dubai, saw that as an opportunity to help us expand to those markets. They came on board as an investor, and they were instrumental in us going into North Africa and Pakistan. Then we became big enough that we were able to attract international investors' interest. Up until then we were so small, and the region was such a low priority for global investors, that every time you would talk to them, they would not show interest. They were like, "You guys are small, and your region is small."

Around 2016, we became quite sizable. We were mostly growing 20-30 percent month on month, and at some point, the scaling charts slid up, and we became big by global standards. Not only did Careem as a platform become interesting for global investors, but they also started realizing the opportunities in the region, in overlooked places like Egypt. They started thinking that if a Careem could come out of the region, this meant that the regional investment opportunity was not to be dismissed. That's when Rakuten, the Japanese e-commerce company, came on board as a lead investor for our last round. Since then we have received investors from Daimler, the car maker, and from many other global investors. During the last twelve months, the profile of the business changed from being completely region-owned to now having an A-list of global investors, and we continue to grow rapidly.

What do you feel was Careem's greatest differentiator against Uber?

I think that growth has happened despite competition as a result of us being hyper-local. We understand the region better than the competition, and we prioritize the needs of the region. When we go to Saudi and find out that most people in Saudi don't have a credit card, we are very quick to launch a cash-favored option, and that gives us a big edge of nine or ten months over the competition. When we find out that women in the region would not like their phone numbers to be shared with strange men captains, we launch a feature that hides the phone number of these women from captains in order to protect their identity. The competition doesn't do that, and since they don't pick up on that, they are not able to prioritize it along with many other requests that are unique to local consumers.

It's really been a story of us being closer to the needs of the market and prioritizing those needs before the competition can catch up. Sure they learn, and they copy, but typically with everything that we do, we get a three- to six-month leap, which always keeps us ahead as the better overall product in the region. That allows us to compete with Uber with even less money. If they sold 100 million dollars in the market, we're able to compete with them with just 20-30 million, because our product is just a better fit for the market, and it's more mass-oriented than their product. That's where we are today, and I think in total we are now in thirteen countries.

> TODAY, WE ARE IN EIGHTY CITIES, AND HOPEFULLY WE'LL CONTINUE TO GROW 20-30 PERCENT MONTH ON MONTH. WE HAVE ALMOST HALF A MILLION CAPTAINS THAT ARE WORKING WITH US, AND WE FEEL QUITE RESPONSIBLE FOR PROVIDING THEM A LIVING AND THEIR FAMILIES A DECENT QUALITY OF LIFE. WE HAVE ALMOST 16 MILLION CUSTOMERS THAT HAVE SIGNED UP TO USE THE SERVICE.

Our last market very proudly was Palestine, so we are really excited to be in Ramallah and making it in that part of the region, which is very close to our heart. Today, we are in eighty cities, and hopefully we'll continue to grow 20-30 percent month on month. We have almost half a million captains that are working with us, and we feel quite responsible for providing them a living and their families a decent quality of life. We have almost 16 million customers that have signed up to use the service.

Luckily, all this has grown much faster than we ever imagined. We are grateful to have been in the right place at the right time. We are grateful for competition, which fueled us to become more aggressive and more ambitious. We are very grateful for the support that everyone in the region has given Careem, with all the support that came from our investors who believed in us and saw opportunity in the region. We are very grateful to our captains who supported us because of being local. We are very grateful to our customers who continue to support us because we are local and they find the story inspiring. It's really a blessing to have come this far with that kind of support. We're quite grateful.

What's your advice to aspiring entrepreneurs?

I think the first advice is finding the right partner. It's a tough journey, and it has its trials and heartbreaks. I think it would have been extremely difficult to do it alone. My first advice to entrepreneurs is to really find someone that they're aligned with on the vision, mission, and whom they get along with socially to do this with. Find someone whom you have some common history with, ideally, that would complement you in some way, that is aligned with you on values. Look up into your past and search for people that might be looking to do something similar. Don't do it just by yourself.

Another piece of advice: I think sometimes we are quite obsessed with what is happening in other markets, and we think that this is working in Germany, this is working in the U.S., what can we bring into the region that's going to work? Often, what happens when we try to bring those ideas to the region, we find out that the region may not be ready for them yet. I strongly advise entrepreneurs not to think that way.

If your focus is on understanding and solving local problems, then you can feel free to get inspiration and learning from solutions that might be applicable that may have worked in other markets, but don't make those solutions your focus. Even in the case of Careem, even though we may look similar to Uber or other foreign solutions, if we had obsessed over bringing, let's say, our competition to the Middle East or that exact solution to the Middle East, we would have been wiped out after the first year of business.

The only way we were able to really compete successfully was because we focused on understanding the local problems. We had solved mapping. We had solved privacy. We had solved driver education. We had solved customer service. All of these things that we had solved to deliver a reliable service that is tailored to the region were the real reasons we survived. If we had just blindly copied and pasted foreign solutions, we would have been out of the market by the second year.

TALK TO CUSTOMERS. TALK TO OTHER STAKEHOLDERS, NOT JUST AT THE BEGINNING, BUT AS A CONTINUOUS PROCESS. CONSTANTLY UNDERSTAND THE PROBLEMS AT HAND.

So, talk to customers. Talk to other stakeholders, not just at the beginning, but as a continuous process. Constantly understand the problems at hand. Constantly learn how your product is doing or not doing, and everything about the experience. Make sure that it's a realistic, good experience, and make it fit the needs of your customers.

The third advice, which is not region-specific and is more general on how you build startups and technology: Sometimes what we used to do before is we would have an idea. We would then take six or twelve months to build a product and then go to market. Unfortunately, that's how many people still approach product development today.

When we were starting out Careem, fortunately, we had read this book called *The Lean Startup,* which also reflected some of the recent methods of early startups in the Valley. The idea was you go to the market with what they call an MVP (minimum viable product), which is basically a working prototype that you could develop very quickly that would add some small value to some customers, launch it as soon as possible, and use the feedback that you get from customers to learn from and tweak the product.

That book was quite valuable for us, because when we launched, we said, let's do an MVP. We gave ourselves only six weeks from the day we started to do the first trip. You can only develop so many things in six weeks. We had to go to market with a product that was very basic. There were many things that we wanted to build, but we just didn't have time to build, because we gave ourselves a time deadline of just six weeks to launch it, and it's been six years since that launch.

There are some cool features that were on our initial wish list that we still haven't implemented, because when we went to the market and launched the service, people started asking for different things than the ones that we felt the market needed. The third advice is to be quick to market and use feedback to refine the product and keep learning and refining until you hit what they call "product-market fit." You will know you've hit product-market fit, because things will click and you will start growing automatically without you doing a lot of hard work.

The fourth advice is about the team. It's quite difficult in the beginning to hire people, because you don't have the money to pay them well, and good people are generally employed at good places and paid well. Also, in the region, we don't have a culture of inkling to work at startups. In Silicon Valley, on the other hand, everyone wants to work at a startup. In fact, the better you are there, the more you want to launch your own startup or work at a startup. Whereas here, many people still want to work at multinational companies, and if they don't want to work at multinational companies, their families want them to work at multinational companies. It becomes quite difficult to attract top talent at startups in the region. Hence, we had to do a few things differently to get people on board.

First, we decided we wanted to attract the best people we could find. Given the experience we had at McKinsey and others, we felt that with our profile, we should be able to attract top talent. It wasn't easy, though; in fact, what we realized very soon was that we would not be able to hire employees, or at least the caliber we were after. We stopped looking to hire "employees" and started looking for "business partners." This was our recruitment pitch in the early days. We said, "Look, I don't want you to come in and work for us. I want you to come in and become a partner in this business. We'll give you equity. This is your company just like it's ours. Just come in, and let's build this thing together."

So first, focus on top talent, because in a startup you don't have a lot of cross-functional systems, so smart people can really make or break your business. Second, use equity and an open approach to attract top talent. Third, don't give up. Sure, it's going to take time to onboard top talent, but when you find someone that you think will make a big difference in the trajectory of your startup, please don't give up on them. Knock on their door ten times until that person stops answering your phone calls and make sure one way or another that you get that person on board. For example, Abdulla Elyas, who is our third co-founder, rejected us at least three to four times before we got him on board. So if you feel that someone is going to add value, you owe it to yourself and to your startup to keep trying. Having said that, a lot of our leads came through referrals, people that we knew directly or indirectly that came on board, which was quite helpful.

How is the work dynamic between you and Magnus?

Magnus is such an amazing guy that it's very easy to work with him. I think what has really worked for us, and I suppose there are two things that have made it easy—I think the first thing is mutual trust. We trust each other blindly. There was trust before we started Careem. It has just become even much stronger since then. We don't second-guess each other. Even though we have divided things between us, with Magnus focusing on technology, operations, and experience, whereas I'm on commercial, marketing, branding, business development and fundraising, we jointly discuss many topics that are important for the business overall. There is a very healthy problem-solving dynamic between us. We like to find solutions together.

When we disagree, the person that owns that area tends to decide what to do.

We also go to each other with quite regular feedback, and this is something that we learned at McKinsey. It had a very strong feedback culture. So from time to time there are things that I might do, or that Magnus might do, that don't seem right. It can create some emotion or tension, and then we try to make sure that we don't let that linger. We discuss everything openly and use constructive feedback so that we can re-address those things. It's always a team effort. We especially help each other out when we are down. We are brothers before we are partners at this point.

Another thing that has really helped us is discovering the purpose behind Careem. As much as we came from different places, we were aligned on the big picture. We both were striving to create a big impact, though we didn't articulate it in the very beginning. Though everyone that has interacted with us would know in loose terms what our purpose was. It wasn't until the second year when we realized we were growing rapidly, we undertook an exercise to discover the essence of that purpose and figure how to articulate it well.

How would you describe the mission of Careem?

The mission of Careem is to simplify the lives of people in the region and build an awesome organization that inspires. There are two parts of the mission. There's the simplifying of lives, and this is based on the premise that living in the region is difficult. You know many of us had visited or lived in many parts of the world, and there is just more friction in daily life here than elsewhere. Friction basically is a lot of overhead and wasted energy that pushes people down and does not allow them to realize their full potential. We wanted to simplify people's lives so that they can actually focus on things that really matter and realize their full potential.

The second part of the mission is to build an awesome organization that inspires. This comes from the perspective that the region hasn't had huge successes. We believe that if the region gets to building great big companies, it will lead to many more. So we would love to become one of the few companies in the region that becomes so awesome that it inspires the entire ecosystem of entrepreneurship in the region. It also means that we do things in a way that inspires.

> Everyone will have their own reasons for creating a startup. If you, an entrepreneur or founder, can figure out its purpose and articulate it well, it will be a motivator when things become challenging. It will attract like-minded people to support the mission, and it will manifest itself much more easily than it would have otherwise. I truly believe that this has been "the secret sauce" behind Careem's success.

I truly believe that the mission of Careem is the real differentiator. It has attracted people who are aligned with this mission, who are passionate about this mission, to come and work with us even though they might be earning 30 to 50 percent less money than they would working elsewhere. It really gets the best out of them, because they're not doing this for money; sure, they will make a lot of money over time, but they're doing this for the wider purpose of improving the region.

Everyone will have their own reasons for creating a startup. If you, an entrepreneur or founder, can figure out its purpose and articulate it well, it will be a motivator when things become challenging. It will attract like-minded people to support the mission, and it will manifest itself much more easily than it would have otherwise. I truly believe that this has been "the secret sauce" behind Careem's success.

Any resources you recommend for entrepreneurs to continue learning?

If you're an entrepreneur and your business begins to do well, it really needs you to play different roles at different stages, and it is critical for you to develop with the startup. I remember listening to the founder of Dropbox speak, and he basically said, "The things that you do really well in one phase of a startup are the things that become your biggest handicap in the next phase." He gave the example of himself, where he was an amazing coder at the beginning. He did the initial source code version of Dropbox and did really well. As the company grew and he was entering the second phase of the startup, he realized that he was such a good coder that it actually became a huge handicap, because no one could code as well as him. He would literally be micromanaging everyone who was developing codes for Dropbox. Whereas when he was in the second phase, he had to step up and provide leadership, especially tech leadership, to the people that were writing the code, versus micromanage them at that level. I think the same is true for other areas as well.

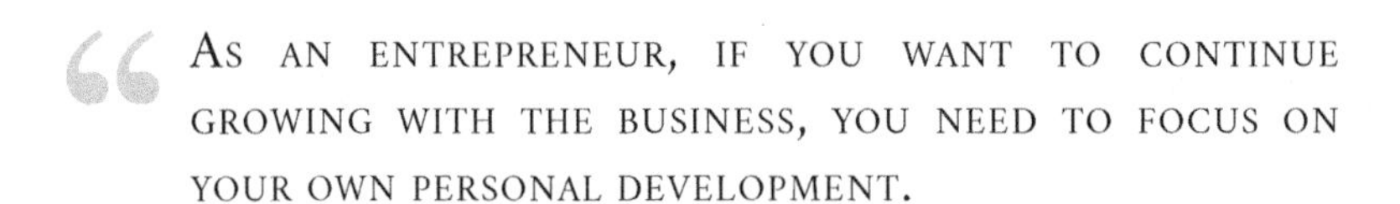

> As an entrepreneur, if you want to continue growing with the business, you need to focus on your own personal development.

As an entrepreneur, if you want to continue growing with the business, you need to focus on your own personal development as well. What I do personally is, I listen to a lot of podcasts. So every time I'm traveling or on the road driving, I'm typically listening to podcasts. The ones that I listen to are more tech-oriented, like "Masters of Scale" with Reid Hoffman, the founder of LinkedIn. Andreessen Horowitz also has a good podcast, and it's keenly insightful. *Harvard*

Business Review's podcasts are quite interesting as well. *McKinsey Quarterly* I also listen to from time to time.

You also have to read. I try to focus on biographies and autobiographies of entrepreneurs. The one I've read and really liked is *Made in America* by Sam Walton, which is an incredible story of this entrepreneur from the middle of nowhere in the U.S., starting Walmart with such humble roots and creating a global retail empire. It's quite inspiring. More recently, I read the book about Amazon, *The Everything Store* by Brad Stone. There are a few more insightful books like this that are on my reading list. The advice here is, as an entrepreneur, you never should stop learning.

What do you feel is working and not working in the region's startup ecosystem?

Let's start with what's working. Dubai itself is a huge success story, because up until recently we had a brain drain from the region, where a lot of the top talent from the region would go abroad to the west. I think Dubai has created a valuable position that is enabling a bit of a reverse brain drain and is attracting talent from within the region as well as global talent. Dubai is really the best of both east and west for many people like me. It has a very solid and a very compelling social and physical infrastructure. I'm very excited about what Dubai has done and continues to do for the region as a whole.

The second thing that is working is the collaborative spirit of the ecosystem is quite amazing. Even though we're a small ecosystem, everyone is aligned in that they want to make something happen and share the sense that if you promote entrepreneurship, this will lead to incredible things from the region. From the Fadi Ghandours of the world, to Dani Farha, to Mohamed Alabbar, everyone is excited to put entrepreneurship on the map for the region.

The third thing that is working, and it's ironic, is that there are a lot of problems to solve in the region. You have the fact that there are problems, and this means that things are not working, but these problems are also opportunities. The bigger the problems, the bigger the opportunities. There are all sorts of opportunities in the region, which is exciting. You find an industry, you find an area, and you will see that things are not working as seamlessly, as efficiently, as effectively as they can, and that poses an opportunity to improve things. So, in some weird, twisted way, this is also working.

Now things that are not working so well: The fragmentation of the region is not helping. The region is unlike the U.S. In the U.S., you have 300 million people that live in one geographic boundary. When you register a company or open a bank in California, you can immediately target the entire United States of 300 million purchase power. It's quite remarkable. That's not the case in the region. There are 22 countries that make up the region, and these countries are quite different when it comes to their stages of development. They have different currencies. They have different laws. They have different border patrols and different frameworks. The challenge then for a technology business is how do you scale across an entire region, when the investment that's required to build some of those smaller or less developed markets cannot be justified. The enormous complexity that you have to tackle to operate in the region as a whole makes things quite tough.

For many parts of the region, except for maybe the UAE and to some extent the Gulf, we don't have a lot of the required infrastructure to build these internet businesses. For Careem, our business requires accurate maps for us to operate, and I remember in 2011, 2012, when we were developing the first version of our app, we realized that Google Maps in the region is neither always accurate nor complete. Many locations don't exist, and some locations are purely incorrect. We had to build our own maps for the region.

We also recognized that many people in the region don't have credit cards. We had to figure out a way to work with cash. Similarly, we realized that there are no messaging services alike in even two different markets, so we had to build our own uniform messaging services, migrating with various telecom operators throughout the region. Unlike the west, these basic things don't exist consistently in the region, and as a result, a lot more time, money, and effort need to go into development just to build the base infrastructure that is taken for granted, say, in the U.S. or Europe.

The second thing that's not working, though is changing rapidly, is the lack of funding for startups. There is no shortage of money in the region. As a region, we are a net exporter of capital to the rest of the world, but that capital from the region does not always flow into the local startups. The big money in the region is being invested abroad away from the region. A lot of our entrepreneurs and startups in the region don't make it just because they aren't able to raise money. You know there's not enough money to go around to fund the ideas that are being developed locally, and it's a little bit torturous, a vicious cycle. Since there is not enough money, there are not enough successes, and since there aren't enough successes, a lot of top talent that would have built local startups seek refuge in working at multinationals to have a good career and to do well for themselves. We really need to solve the funding issue.

The last thing that's not working is talent. I mean, to build internet businesses, you need a lot of technical talent, and unfortunately, we still don't have enough amazing engineering colleges and universities that are producing strong engineering, computer science graduates, and it's a very big issue. Not only do we not have enough, the best ones that come out of our colleges, after spending a few years working in the region, also often get offers from abroad from Microsoft, Google, and Facebook and end up moving away from the region.

Now, for Careem, we are enabling a little bit of reverse brain drain of this tech talent, where we are actively doing recruiting roadshows in the U.S. looking for people that are from the region that may be working at good companies in the U.S. and would like to move back to the region. It's actually going well. Our head of engineering is ex-

Facebook. Our head of product is a Y Combinator executive. There are many other people that have joined Careem from companies like Google, Facebook and others that left the U.S. and have moved to Dubai with their families and are now developing the business.

What's your future vision for Careem?

We are the largest internet business in the region today, and the internet in the region is quite small. Less than 2 percent of what consumers spend goes through the internet. That number in places like China is almost 30 percent. There is going to be a huge shift from traditional retail to the internet in the region over the next five to ten years, and we want to make sure that as the largest internet platform in the region today, we are able to enable the region's move to the internet. What we have done over the last five years is build a lot of the building blocks that are required to build an internet business in the region, and we would like to prototype these building blocks and enable others to scale much faster to all parts of the region.

Imagine if you can create a business in Casablanca, Morocco, and other countless cities across the region—without having to register twenty legal entities, twenty bank accounts, twenty offices, and God knows how many integrations with favored platforms and otherwise —with just one legal entity, with just one integration with Careem. We should be able to enable you to operate in the entire region, just like you're able to operate from one legal entity in California to the entire U.S. We literally want to build the United States of Middle East as far as enabling the internet for the ecosystem is concerned. In the next ten years, Careem should be the dominant internet platform of the region that has played a key role in moving the region to the internet. Of course, ride-hailing and mobility will be a big part of our business, but the business will be a broader internet business than just the ride-hailing business. That's the hope and the broader vision.

At Careem, our vision is, first and foremost, to build a lasting institution that impacts the lives of everyone in the region. So we should, over time, impact the life of every single person in the region. There are 400 million people in the region, and God willing, we will impact each and every person's life. Secondly, we should be building amazing products and services versus substandard or non-world-class products and services. Third, we should be doing things in a socially meaningful way, not just focus on profits, but focus on social good. Lastly, we eventually become the leadership factory for the region so people that work at Careem learn things from us and then they go out and do their own startups or assume other leadership positions in the region. So just like places like PayPal had this "PayPal Mafia" (where the founding team went on to launch such companies as YouTube, LinkedIn, Yelp, Tesla, SpaceX, 500 Startups, etc.) and a lot of entrepreneurs and leaders in California come out of places like Google, we would love to be the leadership factory for the region. We have a functional vision, which is to hopefully develop an internet platform in the region, but on the more organizational part, we would love to build a lasting institution for the region that does these four things. We want it to be a part of the region for centuries to come, even after we are gone, and be a source of welfare and prosperity for the region.

5

OMAR SOUDODI

Building a trusted brand for online payments

Co-Founder and CEO of PAYFORT
Former General Manager of Souq.com, Egypt
WWW.PAYFORT.COM

Omar Soudodi is the co-founder and CEO of PAYFORT, one of the leading online payment service providers in the Arab world, with thousands of merchant clients and billions of dollars in annual transactions. Omar successfully launched Souq.com in Egypt to become one of the top twenty most visited sites and the number one e-commerce site in Egypt. Prior to Souq.com, Omar co-founded Accelarabia.com, the first online loan comparison website in the Middle East, in late 2005 and sold a majority share of the company to Orascom Development in 2006. Omar initially started his career in the U.S. in various capacities with such banks as Bank of America, California Bank and Trust, and Sunwest Bank, after studying financial management at California State University and obtaining a Financial Adviser Certification from the NASD. He also completed Stanford Graduate School of Business in Innovation & Design Thinking in 2018. Omar is actively involved in the Arab world business community, serving as an advisory board member for American University in Cairo, as well as a mentor at Flat6Labs, In5, and Injaz Middle East.

Tell us a bit about your background and early influences.

I was born in New Jersey in 1974. I have an identical twin brother, Ahmed. He is a huge influence on my upbringing and who I am. If you are a twin or if you have any twins in your family or friends, you can relate to growing up with a twin, a play buddy. So, from a young age, we shared a lot of experiences and aspirations together. I also have an older sister as well, who's always been very supportive to us.

Both of my parents are Egyptian. When I was two years old, we moved from New Jersey back to Egypt and lived in Alexandria until I was eighteen years old. My parents were very influential on us. They were both entrepreneurs, and they got us involved in all of their business dealings from a very young age. I remember my dad getting us involved in his import/export business, which we didn't understand much of. He always kept taking us to the office, to the warehouse, to the factory, where we were always doing something. My parents always gave us anecdotes of how business is run and instructions as to how to get things done and at times even got us involved in their actual businesses.

That influenced us quite a bit, being that close to the business. When we were nine years old, we actually had a candy stand right in front of my mom's restaurant in Al Ajami, a popular summer resort in Alexandria back then. We would go buy candy from the wholesale market of candy in Alexandria. We would actually go to downtown Alexandria to the market and buy the candy once a week. We would then sell it to the kids and the families coming to my mom's restaurant so they could have candy after their meals.

My dad moved to Greece when I was thirteen years old. We started visiting him in the summertime. Although everybody thinks that it is glamorous to spend summers in Greece, my dad had a different idea. He would put us to work in his textile clothing factory the entire summer. We really had crappy jobs. We would clean, stock trucks in the warehouse, jump on the truck and drive for two or three hours to unload them by selling in street bazaars. It was exhausting.

When I was a young kid, I really hated to do all this work, because I would always look at my friends and say, "How come I have to work and everybody else doesn't have to?" My dad always said, "You're going to thank me for it one day." He was right. I do, every day. I think this upbringing has really shaped me to this day. Unfortunately, he's not with us anymore.

Every summer, my father used to promote us. Every summer when we'd come back, we didn't do the exact same job. We did something different. Toward the later years, we were actually running the books and doing the accounting. We were making orders for supplies. I even trained in a textile factory in Alexandria for a few months so I could get the hang of it. I wanted to understand the technical aspects of the end-to-end process of the textile business.

When I was eighteen years old and living in Greece, I wanted to go to university there, but it didn't work out. So I came back to Egypt. I ended up studying at the University of Assiut, because when I applied for Alexandria University, I couldn't get in, as my grades were not all that great. I had to take a train and stay in Assiut for four weeks at a time during my exams. The University of Assiut is in upper Egypt, so is quite far from Alexandria. I was away from my family and friends and didn't know anyone there. It was a difficult period, but I think it was one of those experiences where you say to yourself, "OK, this is what it is. It has to work. You have to go through it," and you learn to tough it out.

I actually did quite well. The first year in university, I studied business. It was in Arabic, which was a bit tough for me since I came from British school. The content of the subjects was very interesting, though. I took business law, human resources, economics, and accounting. I really liked those subjects, but I didn't like the learning experience, which was practically nonexistent. You pretty much read a book, you memorize most of it, then you go and try and answer as many test questions as you can, and that's basically it. There was no application to what we were learning whatsoever. So I always aspired to go beyond Egypt to the U.S. and get my education there.

When was your first real business experience?

Ironically, it happened during those back-and-forth trips on the train from Alexandria to Assiut, where I always ran into an acquaintance of the family. He was a much older gentleman, an established businessman. He also happened to be friends with Yasseen Mansour, a well-known Egyptian billionaire businessman who was bringing McDonald's to Egypt at the time. Meanwhile, Arby's (large American restaurant chain) had just started in Egypt. On one of those long train trips, I ran into him, and he asked me how my mom's restaurant was doing. I answered, "Oh, not so good. There's not enough staff, and business has slowed down." Then I lied to him and told him, "We're talking to

Arby's to maybe take over the restaurant." He replied, "No, no, don't do anything. You should talk to Yasseen first before you proceed with that." "Sure, OK," I said.

He tried to connect me to Yasseen. Of course, back then, there was no internet, there was no email. This was 1994. I was nineteen years old. After a month, nothing had happened. So I called him and said, "You know what? Things are getting serious with Arby's. If Yasseen Mansour is really interested in partnering and converting our restaurant into McDonald's, then the time is now." He said, "OK, I will reach out to him." A week later, he called and said, "Yaseen is actually very interested, and he wants to meet you."

I was leaving Egypt with a huge sense of pride. I remember the first day I got my class schedule from college in southern California, I cried. I really felt it was the first step to getting a great education, one that I wanted, and one that I earned because I paid for every penny of it.

We went to meet Yasseen Mansour and his lawyers. Three months later, they inked the deal and partnered up with my mom. They converted the location into a McDonald's, which actually became one of the first McDonald's in the Middle East. I made $30,000 commission. I received $15,000 from my mom and her partners and $15,000 from McDonald's as a finder fee, because I was the one who orchestrated the deal. I took that money and moved to the U.S.

I was leaving Egypt with a huge sense of pride. I remember the first day I got my class schedule from college in southern California, I cried. I really felt it was the first step to getting a great education, one that I wanted, and one that I earned because I paid for every penny of it.

How was life like in the States, attending college and starting a career?

I worked full-time while I was going to college. I was lucky to land a financial services representative position at Bank of America. In spite of not having any banking experience, I had scored high in their assessment, so I was offered the position.

I worked really hard while trying to learn the ropes in this new role. After six months, I was promoted to become business loan officer. It was a really fun job, because you get to analyze businesses' financial standing and base your recommendation on that. You're constantly working with data and problem-solving, which I really enjoyed.

Whenever I would call a small business owner, I always said, "At Bank of America, we have a $10 billion budget to loan to small businesses this year. Do you want some of it?" They would laugh and say, "Yeah, sure." I'm like, "OK, Bob, I'll write you a check and send it to you." It helped me break the ice.

Rather than do business over meetings as other loan officers did, I did everything over the phone. I took the application over the phone. I FedEx'd it or faxed it to them to sign. I was always trying to work smarter in terms of time management and being efficient. I was actually signing up six or seven loans a day. My results didn't go unnoticed; I got promoted to become the youngest assistant vice president at just 24 years old.

This experience at Bank of America was foundational for me. It taught me a lot about the finance side of business, as well as helped me hone my relationship management as well as my sales and presentation skills. This served me well as I moved to take on bigger roles at other banks, like California Bank and Trust and Sunwest Bank, and practically everything I did till today.

At what point did you decide to make the move to Dubai, and what did you do there?

In 2004, my twin brother, who was also living in Southern California with me, decided to leave and go to Dubai. For a year, he was always calling me and telling me that I needed to move there and how promising things were looking there. On August 6, 2004, I left the U.S., which is the land of opportunity, and I came to Dubai, which to me is the new land of opportunity. When I landed in Dubai, I had never seen so many cranes in my life. Between every crane and crane, there was another crane. They were everywhere. I remember the one area where I moved to in Dubai, there were only four buildings that were complete. Meanwhile, there were 200 or 300 being built!

For a while I was looking for a job. Then I realized, I didn't leave the U.S. and everything I had accomplished to come here for a job. My brother said, "Forget the job." A lot of my friends were becoming entrepreneurs, and I had just turned thirty years old. My brother said, "I'm making good money. I'll take care of you"—not just in terms of personal support. He also offered to finance me to go through this process of starting something of my own. He was very encouraging in terms of pushing me into actually going down that path.

I became very motivated to start my own company. The only problem was, I didn't know what kind of company to start. Then it hit me! I was a banker in the U.S. for some time, though I never obtained a credit card or any type of a lending product from the bank that I worked for. I always did it on the Lending Tree website in the U.S. I realized, wait a second, with all this real estate boom happening in the UAE, and all the mortgage plans being offered, it was a nightmare just to try to understand what interest rate the bank was offering.

I decided to adapt the Lending Tree model, which is basically allowing customers to apply for a real estate loan online. I didn't know anything about technology. So I asked an old friend of mine who is practically a genius computer science engineer, Ahmed Moussa. I had picked his brain a few times about how to build a product. He was very helpful, so we kept meeting more and more and having more discussions. After two weeks, I asked him to co-found the company with me. We co-founded AccelArabia in 2005. This was six months after I came to the UAE. I recall the first thing we wanted to do was go after the banks, but we didn't have a plan or know how to pitch our offering to them.

> I used to get very discouraged when people would tell me, "It's not going to work." Then I started asking them, "Why?" Then I realized that 90 percent of the time people didn't have a good reason why it would not work. The other 10 percent, they had a really good reason.

I searched various books about entrepreneurship for clues. They were really helpful; they gave me a framework of how we could build the roadmap of the project. We decided we were going to bootstrap and build a prototype. We then showed banks and partners what we were building and got their feedback. I also spent four months putting a business plan together. I needed to figure all the pieces to this puzzle. What was the size of the market? How long did it take for customers actually to go through the lending process? What was the profile of all the properties that we'd finance? How many developers? How many banks? How many products?

I remember back when I was really strapped for cash after I had used all my U.S. savings, my computer had suddenly died. So I had to wait every day for my brother to come home from work at 6 p.m. to borrow his computer. I shifted to work all night, starting work at 6 p.m. and not going to bed till 7 a.m., when he was going to work in the morning.

The only asset that I had at the time was a USB flash drive that was given to me at a conference I attended. I kept using that until my sister actually bought me a laptop as a birthday gift. Those are the little things that keep you going, especially when you're broke and you're thirty years old, while everybody is looking at you and saying, "Go get a job. Go get a job." These little gestures really make a difference. It felt as though the hand of God was reaching out to me and giving me a hand.

We approached investors, but everyone was saying, "People will not apply online. Banks will not agree to it. Banks will not pay the costs." As an entrepreneur, you have this eureka moment, but you hardly have any data or proven business case to validate your hypothesis. You're naturally insecure about your thinking process in the initial stages, let alone what you are able to build and articulate a solid business case for.

I used to get very discouraged when people would tell me, "It's not going to work." Then I started asking them, "Why?" Then I realized that 90 percent of the time people didn't have a good reason why it would not work. The other 10 percent, they had a really good reason. They would say, "Oh, because this is how banks operate here. They have what is called a directory of agents. They go on and get the loans." I incorporated the good feedback into the business plan and tried to solve the challenges based on the good feedback I was receiving. I kept thinking, how would I solve that problem? It made our business even stronger having gone through this exercise.

After a few months, we were ready with the prototype. We kept knocking on banks' doors for five months until one bank finally said yes. The problem was, we still didn't have any funding or money to market our service. So we continued to pitch the opportunity to investors. Finally, Samih Sawiris, CEO of Orascom Development and one of the top businessmen in Egypt, gave us the half million dollars, and we started AccelArabia. That was really timely. In the two years that followed, we took over 900 million AED (approximately $255 million) in loans. We also had ten banks go live with us in the UAE. We were definitely turning the corner.

Of course, in 2008, the credit crunch crunched us, in the midst of the process of getting our second loan. So the company became insolvent, and there were no new jobs for someone in real estate or a finance background anywhere in the world. I had to liquidate everything. All I had left was my car.

How did Souq enter the picture?

One of our partners at AccelArabia was Souq. When the business folded, I sent them an email that basically said, "I am moving to Egypt, and we won't be able to support you." Then five minutes later, they called me and passed the phone to Ronaldo Mouchawar, the co-founder and CEO of Souq. He said, "I want someone to launch Egypt for me. I'm in Saudi today. Why don't you come up with four PowerPoint slides on how you're going to run Egypt, then we can meet when I'm back?"

Of course, I could hardly sleep. I worked four days straight on the four slides, and then I met Ronaldo. He is one of the most visionary and charismatic leaders you'll ever meet in your life, the kindest person. He was very excited to launch in Egypt and so was I. Though his board of directors at the time had decided not to launch in a new country and they wanted to continue to grow the UAE and Saudi Arabia markets.

Then I got another call from Ronaldo in 2009. He said, "I'm ready to launch Egypt, but we need to do it right away." I said, "I'm in." I joined Souq in August of 2009. I was thrilled but a bit nervous at the same time. I had zero retail or e-commerce experience. I was quite a bit insecure about what was going to happen. I think being insecure is good as an entrepreneur. It keeps you on your toes and makes you work harder. Inadequacy is good if you still trust yourself, and you say that this is something that I need to put more effort into.

As I joined Maktoob Group, which owned Souq at the time in Egypt, they said, "We're being acquired by Yahoo!" The business ended up getting split, so Yahoo! would acquire the Maktoob.com portal and leave the e-commerce division, Souq, intact. Nevertheless, I got to experience the last thirty days before the exit, all the stuff happening with the deal, revising contracts and establishing new accounts as the company was being split. I was very lucky to experience that while I was learning and putting the Souq product together.

We spent five months building the product, setting up the company legally, hiring people, getting an office and thinking about the marketing plan. Who should we bring on board? What are we going to do? Are we going to launch auctions? No, let's not launch auctions. How are we going to get the word out and get customers? There was a lot of discussion about how we were going to do things and how we were going to launch.

I recall when we launched, it was quite a rush. The traction was much higher than we had anticipated. We literally had no time to breathe; we had to run fast. During the few months the followed the launch, we had done a lot of promotional campaigns to build momentum and grow the business. We were pleased with the progress we were making when the unexpected happened, the dawn of the Egyptian revolution, January 25, 2011. The day that changed Egypt forever.

Here we are really going in the right direction, and suddenly there is no internet! The moment they cut the internet on January 28, we asked amongst ourselves, "Now what are we going to do? We're going to send catalogues to people and take orders over the phone?" Of course, this was not an option but just to give you an idea of the mindset that we were all going through at that point. The revolution took us by surprise, to say the least, and we now needed to figure how to deal with this new reality. The team actually stuck together and became quite agile and focused on problem-solving and staying resilient. The attitude of the team was like, "Bring it on! We've seen it all." "If there's blood in the street, fine. We're still going to go to work."

This was a very difficult time. A lot of essentials went missing; sometimes we didn't have gas or electricity in the country; and one time our fiber optic router was stolen. After the revolution, many people were unable to come to work or unable to leave the office building. It wasn't easy and quite challenging to keep up morale. I think, for a while, I was the court jester. I was working every day, trying to cheer up our team. Meanwhile, out in the street, the news was morbid. So I had to defuse the situation and try to normalize things in the office as much as possible. Our customers didn't care. They ordered that product and they wanted that service. It was quite challenging, but Souq was there every morning. I think it's one of the lessons that I learned. Even when things are tough, as a leader, you should always stay calm and strong.

THIS WAS A VERY DIFFICULT TIME. A LOT OF ESSENTIALS WENT MISSING; SOMETIMES WE DIDN'T HAVE GAS OR ELECTRICITY IN THE COUNTRY; AND ONE TIME OUR FIBER OPTIC ROUTER WAS STOLEN. AFTER THE REVOLUTION, MANY PEOPLE WERE UNABLE TO COME TO WORK OR UNABLE TO LEAVE THE OFFICE BUILDING. IT WASN'T EASY AND QUITE CHALLENGING TO KEEP UP MORALE. I THINK, FOR A WHILE, I WAS THE COURT JESTER. I WAS WORKING EVERY DAY, TRYING TO CHEER UP OUR TEAM.

We learned to work through it and leverage the situation to our advantage. One of the most successful promotional campaigns that we ever had back then was actually the January 25 campaign. We had a campaign selling all of the T-shirts and all the calligraphy stuff that had to do with the Egyptian revolution. A lot of people that came to know Souq remember it as, "This was the campaign that made me think of Souq and made me buy something from Souq," because a lot of these products you couldn't find on the street.

There was hardly any customer awareness about e-commerce in Egypt at the time, so every bit of campaigning we did helped. We tried to educate the consumer on the benefits of e-commerce. The challenge was there was no clear incentive or motivation for people actually to make online purchases. Usually, you use e-commerce to find online value, but we didn't have enough of a product selection or product variety. So, no selection, no variety, no value, and therefore no promise in terms of whether you're going to get the right item, at the right price, at the right time.

It was really challenging in the early days to get people to shop online in Egypt. We did our research just by asking friends and family and people that we knew, "What do you think about e-commerce?" A lot of people didn't have an answer to that. They talked to us about online shopping from eBay and Amazon. There was no expectation or trust to shop online from local sites.

We understood that it wasn't going to be an easy ride when launching a new market, but we also understood the brand and the success Souq built in the UAE and Saudi Arabia. We knew we could duplicate some of that success and learn from the mistakes that Souq made in both markets. We had to think hard about how to introduce the service, how to get customers, how to earn their confidence, how to onboard merchants and marketplace sellers. How do you earn the trust of consumers in all the products that are bought and sold on the website?

We focused on offering deals of popular items, starting with mobiles. I recall one campaign we did which featured spectacular deals on Blackberrys, where we did over 700 percent of our goal registration of customers. Our primary goal initially was to get as many buyers as possible to register on the site. We did similar campaigns for iPhones and iPads, which were quite successful as well.

Then a couple of months later, we started looking at a growing segment in Egypt, the rise of offline entrepreneurs. A lot of Egyptian entrepreneurs created or sold their own products on Keystroke (a retail point-of-sale software). Scarves, a lot of textiles, beanbags, pens, and phone accessories were all being either built, made, or customized in Egypt. Of course, there were other entrepreneurs that were just buying wholesale and selling retail. We reached out to them on Facebook, typically where they sold their products. We onboarded many of them, of which fifty or so became top sellers on Souq very quickly.

I think the success of Souq in Egypt had a lot to do with those early sellers. It was a match made in heaven. Souq benefited from their presence on the website, and they benefited from the online exposure Souq gave them. A lot of them have scaled their businesses to big companies since then, many to tens or even hundreds of employees. So they really got into it.

Then, of course, we continued to add retailers. I think that was a big challenge for us to have retailers in the beginning, especially established brands. They really didn't see any value in selling online. A lot of the ones we approached, in the beginning, were very skeptical. They said, "We already tried this strategy in Egypt. We sold like two or three orders in six months, and it didn't work out, and Egyptians don't buy online."

With all the campaigns that we were doing, we had to prove to them that we could get them the customers that they were looking for and the sales that we were looking for. Slowly but surely, we were able to build their confidence, too. Of course, we weren't selling thousands of units. We were selling hundreds of units. But 100 this week and then 200 the following week and 300 the following week.

We actually had to walk the walk, not just talk the talk. So we actually bought some Puma stock. We were selling the national jersey of the football team. We did a video on YouTube, and every time the team played a game and scored, we edited that video and made it into one big video. We found that people would watch the goals from that match and then go watch goals from other matches that they played in the tournament. Every time the team scored goals, we just added those goals into the video, and in a couple of weeks, that video had over 150,000 views. Back then, 150,000 views on YouTube was like 2 million views today. It was quite significant.

Customers were really engaged online, on the site, on YouTube, on Facebook. We did a lot of user activations. We ended up selling more Puma jerseys than Puma in Egypt. Even Puma was actually quite shocked with the outcome. I believe that was one of the highest moments where we felt like we were on to something. This was the recipe that we wanted to use moving forward.

Campaigns became extremely important, whether it was a holiday or a football game or back-to-school. We really started to pay attention to those events and their relevancy and campaign around them, and get supply and sellers and develop volume in terms of product selection and deals, which in turn attracted more customers. It was a winning formula.

We paid special attention to customer service during that time, knowing that for both sellers and customers alike, this was probably their first experience with e-commerce and Souq, so we couldn't afford to make a bad first impression. For the first few months, in fact, every order that went out, we gave a Souq notepad and hand-wrote a personal note congratulating the customer on making his or her first online purchase. Meanwhile, every time sellers reached a milestone like 10,000 orders or, say, selling 1,000 iPads, we would actually give them a call or send them an email to congratulate them on their achievement. We wanted to add that personal touch and show them we really cared and were there for them.

We invested a lot in customer education. We would call customers and tell them that we were shipping their order. We had to tell them that the couriers would call them and then deliver the product, that there was a chance the courier might be running late, and to make sure their cash was ready (since most of the orders were made using COD or cash on delivery). We were also calling the customer after they made the purchase for follow-up. So, every week we had like pizza night and a few more calls for new customers. Then, of course, customers would come back and say, "You called me, I wasn't available, so you should send me an email." So there was a lot of learning for all of us as well.

Of course, there were mistakes being made, and we wanted to make sure that we learned from them. The team was very young and very willing to make mistakes and learn from them and apologize in the hopes that the customer would then be happy. They would volunteer to say, "I was wrong," to the customer. "I will take care of it." Then, figure a way to make it right with customers. I think that was critical to Souq success in Egypt.

ONE OF MY MOST FULFILLING EXPERIENCES I FOUND THROUGHOUT MY CAREER WAS ALLOWING UNDER-PRIVILEGED CANDIDATES TO ACTUALLY GET A DREAM JOB.

We also put a lot of effort in finding great talent and bringing on board the right team. We partnered with an organization called Education for Employment (EFE), and we designed an eight-week course to teach university graduates about e-commerce together with EFE. We covered management, marketing, social media, customer service, and logistics. In eight weeks, they took a lot of classes on the fundamentals, and those processes were actually given by Souq members.

It allowed the Souq team to also step up and teach. The best way to learn is to actually teach, because people continue to ask you questions, and you have to come back and answer those questions. Plus, we were identifying the people that we wanted to hire from those classes. I think over the years, we had 1,000 individuals in the program, and we ended up hiring 100 to 150 of them.

We would actually identify potential talent right then and there. After class, we'd be saying, "You see what he said?" "Oh, I'd like to hire him." "I'd like to hire her." "We need to get them on board." Thus, we never had to ask people to submit their resumes. By the end of the program, we knew exactly which people we would hire.

One of my most fulfilling experiences I found throughout my career was allowing under-privileged candidates to actually get a dream job. Today, I see that some of them have actually grown with the company from Egypt, while others went to Dubai and continued to grow with the company as managers within the organization.

That lasted for two to three years, learning on the job how to scale a company, how to increase our supply and how to fine-tune our supply. What was missing in our supply? How could we add more value here? How could we give customers better value? How could we save money? So all of these factors started to excite not just me, but everybody in Souq about what we were doing and how we were going to move forward.

Eventually, we became one of the most visited websites in Egypt. The team had grown to 300 or so people. Things got a lot more mature with very healthy growth every single month. The company has become quite stable.

How did you get started with PAYFORT?

In 2013, Ronaldo called me and said, "Now we want to solve the online payment problem in the region. I want you to move back to Dubai," because building the online payment component of the business was now a top priority for Souq. We recruited Omar Elsahy, who is an exceptional leader, to take the helm as GM of Souq Egypt, so I could now focus on the online payment business. I packed and headed back to Dubai. That was really the birth of PAYFORT.

PAYFORT first started in the UAE, and then we launched in Egypt a couple of months later, then Saudi Arabia the following month. In the following years, we launched in Lebanon, Qatar, Jordan, and Oman. We kept launching new markets to help our merchant base expand in the region, because a lot of the big brands and retailers said, "We don't have a payment partner in all the markets, and that's important for us." We felt like this was one of the competitive advantages we had over everybody else in our sector, coupled with the department leadership site that we built early on by pivoting from performance marketing to content marketing. We still have performance marketing, but it's very small; maybe 10, 15 percent of our total lead generation comes from performance marketing, versus content marketing.

When I say content marketing, I'm talking about the *State of Payments* report that our marketing team put together every year. The report has become the definitive annual industry resource on all aspects related to online payment in the Arab world. It covers such topics as sizing up the market from different verticals to consumer insights into trends to what are people buying. What are they buying with? Who's buying it? How old are they? What's their income level?

We give a comprehensive view and a lot of data for startups and even for companies to work on their business plans or work on their annual budgets. You can check at www.stateofpayment.com, and you can download all of these reports for free.

Of course, we continued to develop our product, based on our understanding of what merchants want, but we felt we were still not helping startups enough. So we set up something called Fintech Capital for investment in cutting-edge payment startups. We launched START in the UAE over a year ago, and today over 50 percent of our merchants are actually on START, which takes companies from applying to going live, to integrating, to doing their first transactions. We're not there yet in the product we're offering, but we're very happy with the performance and milestones we have achieved. We also started looking at other areas in terms of alternative lending, the blockchain, and investing online.

How did you keep a startup culture as the company grew?

As PAYFORT kept growing, with seven markets and 120 employees, we talked about becoming even bigger. Meanwhile, we started to face some internal and operational challenges. Communication was becoming an issue. A lot of people were operating in a silo and not informed. A lot of people started seeing that their job was mundane, and they didn't feel like they were being well-utilized in the organization.

So, for two months, I started doing a lot of research about organizational behavior and structure. What works, what doesn't work. What are the trends in terms of how to scale a company and how to make people happy? Then I looked at what many tech companies do, and I stopped looking after I came across Zappos, because it's one of those companies focused on happiness and customer-centricity.

This is where I started to learn about "holacracy." Holacracy is a new school of thought in organizational management. Rather than having a hierarchy and a manager and people reporting to that manager, you have a self-managed circle. Everybody in that circle is equal. They do have what they call a "lead link," someone who leads the team in terms of getting things together, agreeing with the team on certain things, organizing them, but the team would actually break into different roles.

Basically, the way holacracy works is that you start with a purpose of an organization, a department or a circle. You state your purpose, and then you start asking questions about what are the responsibilities that would lead to achieving that purpose. From those accountabilities, you carve out certain roles, and those roles are assigned to people that circle you. Then an action plan is set in place as well as a weekly tactical meeting. This circle would come together to discuss what happened and who is doing what and how the work went, what went right, what went wrong. What were the highlights, what were the "low lights"?

The beauty of this management methodology is that it adapts fast and well to change. There is no need for reorganizations or realignments in holacracy. It's a constant evolution of the individual, of the circle, of the department based on the specific demands of the business at any given time.

At PAYFORT, everyone is empowered to make decisions. You don't have to get approval. Rather than approval, we go through an advice process. So our people would seek advice from different other stakeholders that would get impacted by the decisions, whether it was financial, performance or operational. We started to see that people were actually talking more to one another, listening more to one another, spending more time at the office voluntarily. There was much less friction. A lot of challenges that we faced were actually being addressed.

Of course, as with everything else, it has its pros and it also has its cons. Some of the cons were that people were sometimes getting involved in too many circles. That took them away from their core responsibilities. Sometimes if people didn't like their primary job, they were escaping the job by going to other circles. When we found that out, we just sat down and talked to them individually and said, "If you don't like your role, fortunately, you can re-create yourself. The question is, how can you re-create yourself and still add value that is equal or more to what the company is paying you in salary?" Some people were actually able to create a greater value, and some people were unable to create that value and left the company. Not right away, of course. They left the circle first, and then if they couldn't find a way to re-create the value, they did leave the company.

Then, of course, a year later, we started to look at going public as part of Souq Group, and that discussion evolved into a few interested investors. Of course, that is the history of the acquisition by Amazon of Souq Group, including PAYFORT. Today, PAYFORT has been rebranded as "PAYFORT, an Amazon company."

> YOU HAVE TO BE A DREAMER. EVERYTHING STARTS WITH A DREAM, BUT IF YOU DON'T ACT ON THE DREAM, NOTHING IS GOING TO HAPPEN. I COME UP WITH IDEAS EVERY DAY, BUT I DON'T ACT ON THEM. I FORGET THEM AFTER TEN MINUTES, UNLESS OF COURSE I WRITE THEM DOWN AND MAKE IT A POINT TO FOLLOW THROUGH ON THEM.

What are the most important characteristics of an entrepreneur?

I would say that you have to be a dreamer. Everything starts with a dream, but if you don't act on the dream, nothing is going to happen. I come up with ideas every day, but I don't act on them. I forget them after ten minutes, unless of course I write them down and make it a point to follow through on them.

It's kind of like the ignition of an entrepreneur is getting this Eureka moment and saying, "Aha!" Then if you get that aha and that aha keeps coming back to you, you should listen to it and be curious. It should lead you to the research, to industry experts, to figure out where are the problems that you can solve with your idea. If it doesn't solve a problem, then it's not really a business idea, and if the problem is too small or infrequent, then it is not an idea that anybody is going to get excited about.

Then, of course, when you start crystallizing the idea and you believe that you have something to go with, then this is where resilience comes into the picture. Not giving up, but really leaving everything behind if you really believe in your idea. Sometimes it's very difficult, because we all have responsibilities. We all have to pay the bills. We all have to pay the rent. Sometimes that is quite challenging to achieve: sticking to the idea, day in and day out, until you stand on solid ground or fail.

As a matter of fact, you initially fail so much that in the morning you wake up and feel that you are tired and exhausted and think, "What's the point of making calls? What's the point of taking meetings? What's the point of even going to work?" Then one day, someone will say, "Uh-huh. That sounds interesting. Let's try that out." Then failure from that point on moves on to small success, and again persistence comes in to make that small success into another small success. The next day, another small success and another little bigger success, and so on. It's a process but not without its fair share of missteps and frustrations, which is normal for an entrepreneur.

You're going to have some failures, and that's how you are going to continue to learn. Entrepreneurs have to be very pragmatic with no ego. If you have an ego, forget it, because the ego shuts down people, it shuts you from listening to people. If someone has an ego, I would urge them to keep doing what they're doing and not quit their day job.

You also have to be resourceful. You have to learn a lot of things. You have to consider how and when to get a logo, how to write a business plan, how to model your business, how to get a five-year financial forecast, do wire framing of your product, use your experience, maybe even do a prototype.

What's your view on work-life balance?

Entrepreneurship is not a sprint; it's a marathon. Unfortunately, a lot of entrepreneurs think it's a sprint. Think they're going to run 100 meters and they're going to get to the promised land, which is more like 100 kilometers.

Work-life balance is quite tough as an entrepreneur, but it's quite essential that you escape to re-energize yourself, to de-stress. If you have a family, spend time with your family, spend time with your friends, even if it's just going to the beach with a book. Just jump into a pool and enjoy a couple of hours every day.

It's quite important to keep a positive mindset. You have to get used to dealing with the pain. Any person who runs marathons, they're usually tired by the second mile, and they've got another twenty-five miles to go. You've got to learn to deal with the pain, and you have to enjoy it as well. Sometimes the struggle is the glory, as they say.

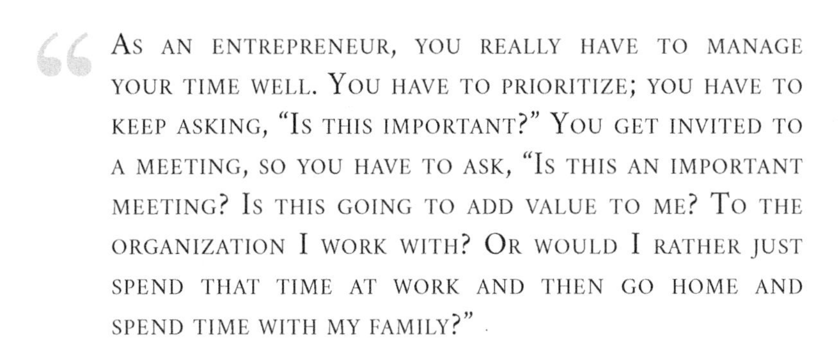

> As an entrepreneur, you really have to manage your time well. You have to prioritize; you have to keep asking, "Is this important?" You get invited to a meeting, so you have to ask, "Is this an important meeting? Is this going to add value to me? To the organization I work with? Or would I rather just spend that time at work and then go home and spend time with my family?"

Can you touch on the role family plays in your success and for entrepreneurs in general?

The silent partner in my entrepreneurial journey has been my wife. I met my wife in 2010 in Egypt right before the revolution. She is Turkish and was working on a project in Egypt at the time. For the three years we were together in Egypt, she was extremely supportive while I was launching Souq. I was putting in long hours, and it was not easy for her, especially being a foreign woman in a post-revolution Egypt. I will always cherish and never forget that she made that sacrifice for me.

Basically, your loved one, your girlfriend, your fiancé, your wife, or your husband, boyfriend, whoever, they really play an important role in terms of putting you in the right mindset, supporting you and always believing in you, because you doubt yourself all the time. Having them by your side in tough times when you feel down and you feel like this is not going to work, they can remind you why you are doing this and how you've done it before. They provide you with support and an emotional safety net. On the other hand, if you have a partner that is always telling you, "This is not going to work" or "Why don't you just go get a job?"—that can be detrimental. Having your partner on board is extremely important, because if they're not on board, it's going to be a very difficult journey at home.

Fortunately for me, it was a very pleasant one. We were blessed with a baby girl two years ago, and that really changes your perspective significantly and your priorities as to how you provide for your family. Given the stakes being higher, you probably take less risks or, should I say, make much more calculated risks. When you're single, you can sleep hungry at night, but when you have mouths to feed, your mindset completely changes.

As an entrepreneur, you really have to manage your time well. You have to prioritize; you have to keep asking, "Is this important?" You get invited to a meeting, so you have to ask, "Is this an important meeting? Is this going to add value to me? To the organization I work with? Or would I rather just spend that time at work and then go home and spend time with my family?" Of course, unwinding on the weekend is also important. Sure, I still work at night and during the weekend, but you definitely have to make time for your family, for your kids, because you don't want to succeed in business but fail at life.

It is extremely important for me to make sure that this work/family balance exists. Of course, sometimes that balance gets thrown out of whack. When that happens, which it inevitably will from time to time, you just need to tell your loved ones, "Right now work is a little demanding, but this is how I plan to make it up to you." Communication at home, just like at work, is extremely important.

What are your future plans for PAYFORT?

PAYFORT started in 2013 by wanting to solve the online payment problem in the Arab world, and in spite of becoming the largest online payment processing company in the region, we still have many areas to tackle. I believe we've set the scene to solve a lot of the challenges associated with paying online for both merchants and customers alike. I think we're very well positioned and set to tackle these problems, and now we have Amazon behind us. It's quite exciting!

6

MAAZ SHEIKH

Creating the ultimate entertainment platform for premium and affordable video content

Co-Founder and CEO of STARZ PLAY

WWW.STARZPLAY.COM

Maaz Sheikh is the co-founder and CEO of STARZ PLAY, a Dubai-based cutting-edge video-on-demand platform servicing the MENA region. He brings more than twenty years of experience in the media and telecom sectors, spanning technical, operational, sales, and marketing functions at Fortune 100 as well as early-stage technology companies operating in the U.S., Europe, and the Middle East.

Maaz started his career with Sprint Corporation, where he developed a passion for innovative technologies designed to improve the consumer experience. After Sprint, Maaz held consulting positions with Ernst & Young's San Francisco office, where he provided technology and marketing consulting services to media and telecom companies. Maaz has also held various positions in U.S.-based technology and communications corporations, including product manager at Concentric Network (now XO Communications), vice president of sales and marketing at Virtela Communications (an NTT Communications Company), and vice president of worldwide sales and marketing at StorePerform Technologies (now JDA Software).

Maaz spent part of his childhood growing up in Dubai and returned to the region in 2006 to join Showtime Arabia (now OSN). As chief sales and operations officer at OSN, he was responsible for regional growth, customer service, and spearheading overall customer operations across the Middle East.

Maaz holds a B.S. in Electrical Engineering from Oklahoma State University and an MBA from The University of Kansas.

Tell us a bit about your background.

I grew up between Pakistan and Dubai. I was born in Islamabad, Pakistan, but moved to Dubai in 1976 for my father's work—he was an engineer who would set up big developments. Funny enough, I actually grew up on a construction site in the heart of Dubai. I moved to California in 1989 to attend college, where I received a bachelor's degree in electrical and computer engineering before working a few years as an engineer with Sprint in Kansas City. I guess I was smart enough to know that I am not smart enough to be an engineer for the rest of my life, so when I was offered an opportunity to move into consulting with E&Y (Ernst & Young), I jumped at the chance. This was my first step in transitioning from an engineer to more of a sales and marketing role.

Following my time at E&Y, I both launched and worked at two startups, both with successful exits. The first was Virtela Communication, which subsequently got acquired by NTT—I was the VP of sales and marketing there. I held a similar role at the second startup, which then got acquired by JD Edwards. After that exit, I moved to Dubai in 2006 to work for what was called Showtime (now OSN, one of the largest media companies in the Arab world), as well as for personal reasons, to be close to my aging father.

As VP of sales at Showtime, it was a very exciting time, and being in the right place at the right time, things went my way, and I was often promoted. When Showtime acquired Orbit and the combined entity became OSN, I got promoted to COO, and I stayed in this role until 2013.

How did you decide to leave OSN and start STARZ PLAY?

I was at OSN for almost eight years, and even though I took on many different roles during that time, I felt that I had stayed there long enough. It was my lifelong dream to become founder or CEO of my own company, and at that time I felt that it was now or never—if I was going to start my own business, I needed to make that jump. I was reaching my mid-40s, a point where it becomes more and more difficult to be a startup CEO, so I decided to just make the jump.

In many ways, it was a leap of faith. When you start on a journey like this, nothing is in your control. You're leaving a stable job, you have kids and family to look after, you have a home to pay for, you have school fees you are dealing with, and you have bills to pay. You take that burden and add to it with the risk of pursuing your own dreams and ambitions to start a new journey, and it's scary. You really cannot control or plan what's going to come your way.

On the other hand, I had a general sense that there was an opportunity in our region to make premium television affordable to the masses, so at the same time I was confident in the new venture. You have MBC, which is extremely successful in what they do in terms of providing content to the masses, and you have OSN, which is extremely successful in providing premium content to a very niche, high-end audience that can afford it. Then there is a whole big gap in between—the idea that came to mind was how to fill that gap with a new product or a service. When I left OSN, I wasn't 100 percent sure exactly what that would be, but through some networking and a lot of luck, I met a gentleman called Peter Ekelund who later became my cofounder. He helped me get things on the right track right from the outset.

Peter is a private equity Swedish investor, and when we met, he had already launched and built HBO Nordic before selling it back to HBO. He became an early investor in STARZ PLAY, and we went on to set up this company together. We used the early seed investment to develop the technology and the platform, but it wasn't until this was in place that we realized how capital-intensive this business is. It was then that we turned our attention to fundraising, signing up institutional investors like Starz and Lionsgate, as well as financial investors like State Street, Global Advisors, and a local investor from the UAE called Delta Partners.

How did you get started, and what kind of challenges did you face early on?

We started building the platform with our own money until October 2014, when we closed our first round. However, it wasn't paid in one tranche and was contingent on meeting certain conditions before the funds were to be released. There were several technical conditions, including performance and security standards associated with the platform, so that was the first hurdle we had to overcome.

The next challenge we faced was securing the content rights. We were dealing with the likes of Disney, Warner, Sony, and CBS, and all those big content guys who were working with MBC and OSN already. Meanwhile, we were just a young startup with an unproven technology and market, so they really had to believe in what we were doing in the long term to take a chance on us. Obviously moving their content or starting a relationship with a new player poses a risk to their existing established relationships, so the next three months for us were all about content acquisition, getting their buy-in and locking those deals while aiming for a launch date of April 2015. If we failed, we risked losing our funding.

Our top priorities were first fixing the technology platform and then securing the content rights while dealing with all the regulatory and compliance approvals in the region. We worked closely with the National Media Council and Dubai Media City to get all the right approvals and company structure set up, so there were a lot of administrative requirements and legal paperwork. Nevertheless, we managed to stay on track and launch the service in April 2015, as originally planned, which was a huge relief for us.

Even after building the platform, fundraising and securing the content rights, it was the next phase of the company's growth that was perhaps the most challenging for us—online payment. We underestimated how big of a challenge it can be in this part of the world, and as we initially launched payment only by credit card, we just didn't get the uptake we expected in terms of volume of subscribers.

We also underestimated the complexity of digital marketing in the region, and it took some time to unravel and understand how to execute. As much as we are an online entertainment TV service company, we are equally an e-commerce company, and it was important to recruit folks with a strong background in that field to help build our internal skill sets.

We realized quickly that issues with credit cards are a huge hurdle to scaling our business, as once you go beyond the UAE, Saudi, and the GCC, credit card penetration is relatively low. Meanwhile, mobile penetration is extremely high, so we had to come up with innovative ways to work on carrier billing and payments through prepaid or postpaid mobile phone billing. Solving some of the payment problems in our platform was a big part of our technology, and we also had to address the varying degree and consistency of broadband networks in the region with some unique content and load distribution methods within our platform.

As you can see, there were a lot of technology aspects of our service that we designed and built for the region that we needed to fix before we could start talking to the studios in Hollywood. While we engaged with several studios, ultimately our vision and chemistry aligned really well with FOX and STARZ, so we ended up re-engaging with STARZ in a more formal way. They agreed to come on as a strategic investor in the business, and in return we would be using their brand to launch the service.

The next six to nine months were extremely challenging for us, as while we had built a great product and invested a lot of money in content and technology, we needed to be doing a thousand subscribers a day based on our projections. In reality we were doing only twenty-five subscribers a day, which was way off our plan. Fortunately, we have a team in place that does not give up, so we managed to adjust and adapt to the market realities quickly. That was critical in such a difficult time.

To tackle the issue, we began by solving the methods of payment, which involved launching carrier billing solutions with Etisalat. Next, we expanded to Kuwait and then to Saudi. We also launched with Saudi Telecom Company (STC) before expanding to Morocco with Maroc Telecom and to Egypt with Vodafone. One by one, we kept on doing our telco integrations, and now we were working with all the major companies in the region on carrier billing and mobile payments, in addition to having other methods of payments.

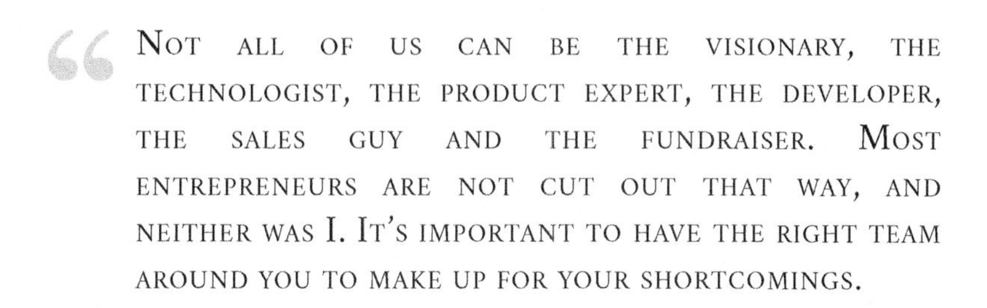

> Not all of us can be the visionary, the technologist, the product expert, the developer, the sales guy and the fundraiser. Most entrepreneurs are not cut out that way, and neither was I. It's important to have the right team around you to make up for your shortcomings.

During this phase, you also realize that we are not all Steve Jobs or Bill Gates—not all of us can be the visionary, the technologist, the product expert, the developer, the sales guy and the fundraiser. Most entrepreneurs are not cut out that way, and neither was I. It's important to have the right team around you to make up for your shortcomings, and this was where, with my company, I have been very fortunate.

Can you describe your consumer offering and differentiator against competition?

We started with the proposition that we wanted to make the latest Hollywood blockbusters and TV shows more affordable in this part of the world. Now they are being delivered in a digital way, in an on-demand form, because that's what the market and consumers are looking for.

When we initially started, we launched with around 2,000 hours of content, including 700 movies and 1,000 episodes of popular and current TV shows. Over time, we have grown to around 5,000 movies, and we've also added over 1,000 hours of Arabic content, including some current TV shows, as well as 1,000 of the latest Bollywood movies.

As we serve the North African markets, including Morocco, Algeria, and Tunisia, we make French and French-dubbed content available for all our Hollywood movies and TV shows as well, so altogether we have grown from 2,000 to almost 10,000 hours of content in the past two and a half years.

Our mindset is that when it comes to solving local problems and tailoring to the local consumer, where Netflix sees problems and challenges, we see opportunities and hope. That's the reason why Netflix didn't launch in MENA four years ago and instead chose to focus on the U.K. and Western Europe. They passed on MENA because they saw the lack of credit card penetration and the complexity that revolves around scaling and distribution in twenty or so countries as prohibitive. Meanwhile, those are all the regional-related challenges that we turn to our advantage.

The audience tastes and demographics are also very fragmented in this part of the world, which can be very daunting to an outsider. From Hollywood preferences and Arabic requirements to Egyptian content popularity—even now you have Gulf or "Khaleeji" content that's becoming increasingly more popular in Saudi, UAE, and Kuwait —there is a lot to account for. Not forgetting the expats diaspora, the Arab expats throughout the region, those from the Indian subcontinent who are looking for Bollywood movies, Emiratis, Saudis and even North Africans—the list goes on! We subtitle our Bollywood movies in Arabic, along with popular American movies and TV shows, and we also stream popular animated content from Pixar and Disney, among others.

Over time, we have been able to adjust our content offering to the various needs of the segment here, and today we are fortunate that we are dealing with every major studio in the industry, including Disney, Warner Brothers, 20th Century Fox, Sony, CBS, Showtime, STARZ, Lionsgate and Universal Studios. We work with all major studios, and in 2018, we will show thirty-five to forty new TV shows that will be made available at the same time as the U.S., which is also a big differentiator for us. In short, everything that, to a global platform, might seem like a black-box kind of challenge that requires additional regional and market-specific customization, we see as opportunity. That, I would say, is our biggest differentiator.

If we look back now and you say: "Hey, what are some of your competitive advantages in addition to content and digital marketing and brand?" I would say it's that we are integrated with seventeen telecom operators, while Netflix is not integrated with a single one. Even back-end and billing capabilities start becoming your competitive advantage, which are all the lessons in terms of things that we evolved into along the way, rather than were evident to us from the very beginning.

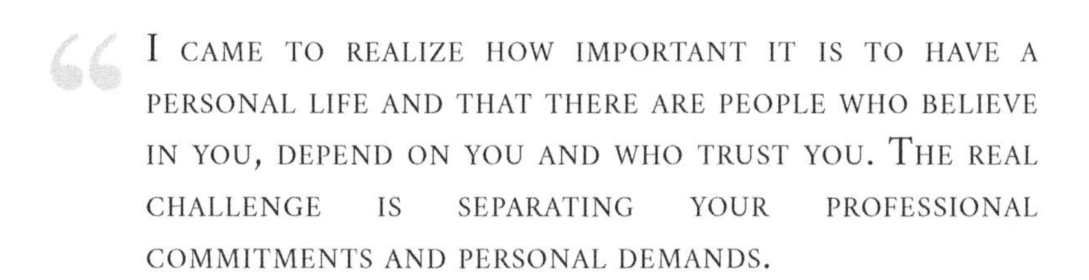

> I CAME TO REALIZE HOW IMPORTANT IT IS TO HAVE A PERSONAL LIFE AND THAT THERE ARE PEOPLE WHO BELIEVE IN YOU, DEPEND ON YOU AND WHO TRUST YOU. THE REAL CHALLENGE IS SEPARATING YOUR PROFESSIONAL COMMITMENTS AND PERSONAL DEMANDS.

Can you recall a difficult experience and lesson you learned from it during this journey?

My father was always a constant source of strength and support for me; I looked up to him both professionally and personally. He was very supportive of my decision to leave OSN and start STARZ PLAY, counseling me throughout, before and after.

As I was constantly on the road, it meant I was often away from my family. I was traveling internationally for meetings when I got the news that my father had passed away, and I immediately took a flight from New York back to Pakistan to make it in time for his funeral. However, at that time, it felt that this was too big of a price to pay. Being on the road for six to nine months a year and sacrificing time with my family, I felt I had given up too much to make this business successful.

It was then that I came to realize how important it is to have a personal life and that there are people who believe in you, depend on you and who trust you. The real challenge is separating your professional commitments and personal demands, so when something like this happens, you continue to show commitment to your co-founder, your team, and your shareholders. I think that's perhaps the most difficult experience I have encountered, but fortunately we closed our first round of funding two months after my father passed away, and I was able to normalize things with family and personal life. It was a very tiring period but helped put things in perspective.

Was there a turning point when you started seeing the light at the end of the tunnel?

There was one specific moment about two years ago, as well as another around two weeks ago. However, for me, I never feel like I'm quite there yet—there's always something you can improve on. Your job as an entrepreneur is never finished, and you never get an opportunity to say, "OK, this is it; now we have made it!" I do believe there are certain standout moments and breakthroughs, though, and these are truly brief moments where things do click.

For me, this was when we hit the 100,000-subscriber mark. We knew that no one in the MENA region had done this before in our industry with this kind of platform and service, and it was a big achievement for us to reach that critical mass.

The other moment was only two weeks ago when we announced a five-year partnership with E-Vision—a fully owned subsidiary of Etisalat, which was recently named the number one brand in the region. This was important for us for lots of reasons, not just commercially and financially, but in terms of further establishing our credibility in the market. It was further proof that we're doing something right, since Etisalat could have chosen any other platform globally. It's a five-year commitment that includes not just licensing our service and content, but also working with us on taking advantage of our technology and our capabilities.

WE HAD OVER A BILLION SESSIONS ON OUR WEBSITE AND MOBILE WEB, AS WELL AS APPS ACROSS ALL OUR PLATFORMS, IN 2017. WE ALSO HAD 3.2 MILLION APP DOWNLOADS AS OF DECEMBER 2017. THAT WAS ALSO THE YEAR WE ANNOUNCED 700,000 PAYING SUBSCRIBERS, AND SINCE THEN WE HAVE BEEN GROWING.

So where are you today in terms of milestones?

According to some independent, third-party web companies who monitor traffic stats, we had over a billion sessions on our website and mobile web, as well as apps across all our platforms, in 2017. We also had 3.2 million app downloads as of December 2017. That was also the year we announced 700,000 paying subscribers, and since then we have been growing, so we will announce our next milestone on the current number of paying subscribers soon.

If you also look at SimilarWeb rankings, we are consistently ranked as one of the top twenty websites in Saudi and the UAE in terms of volume. In terms of traffic share we are neck-to-neck with Netflix, and we are outperforming them in many markets that we operate. Overall, we are holding our own in the region and are certainly the leading platform for online entertainment video in MENA.

What's your general advice to aspiring entrepreneurs?

This is the same advice I give to my kids, which is to embark on an entrepreneurial journey as early as you can. I think doing so later in life is a little more difficult because you have more commitments. When you are young you can learn so much, and you will have a lot more time ahead of you to make your vision a success.

I think the biggest hurdle is convincing yourself to take that risk. In many ways, I'm a very cautious person, but I also know when it's important to take a risk. Whatever your spiritual or religious orientation is, you have to just dig deep and find that faith and trust in making those bets. I think Steve Jobs said it best: "You have to trust that the dots will somehow connect in your future."

I THINK THE BIGGEST HURDLE IS CONVINCING YOURSELF TO TAKE THAT RISK. IN MANY WAYS, I'M A VERY CAUTIOUS PERSON, BUT I ALSO KNOW WHEN IT'S IMPORTANT TO TAKE A RISK.

The other piece of advice would be to stay humble and realize that no matter what your virtues and strengths are, you're imperfect. You're not going to be the perfect founder, and you're not going to be the perfect CEO. This forces you to gather the right team around you and build a strong network of advisers and a support network that can help you, especially through difficult stages. It also allows you to admit when you're wrong and to learn from your mistakes.

What are some takeaways you'd like to share with entrepreneurs regarding fundraising?

In the context of this region, the number one thing is to show local investors that the investment opportunity is sizable enough. You also have to prove that you have a unique ability to navigate the inherit complexity in the region and create meaningful shareholder value.

Second is to reduce investor risk around execution by taking some of those risks on yourself initially by getting some traction on your own. We built the technology and the platform well before any major investors came in the picture, so those risks were off the table, making our investment opportunity a lot more attractive to investors. If you can show something that you have done on your own or organically before you start seeking any institutional or major funding, you will be at an advantage. You also have to show that you have the right skill set within the team and your team is execution-ready. Investors don't back a single executive; they back a team.

Having said that, fundraising is never a straightforward process, no matter how big your market or how good your product and your team are. We were in active talks with over a hundred investors that turned us down initially, and it's important not to give up. You have to keep adjusting your pitch and fine-tuning the product and the strategy. Learning from one investor meeting and taking that adjustment to another investor meeting is extremely important.

What's your advice to tech entrepreneurs regarding marketing?

If you are entering an online business, think of online experience and online marketing as a very core product of what you will be doing. Don't think of marketing as traditional brick and mortar businesses do. It's not a support function; it's a core product of your overall offering and needs to be part of your internal capabilities and internal skill set from the very beginning.

What are your general thoughts on customer service, especially for a digital media startup?

While all the basic, traditional customer service principles extend in the digital world, there's one principle that is strikingly different—that the power of social media, especially in this part of the world, is extremely strong. While social media can be your best friend as a marketing and customer acquisition channel, it can also be your worst enemy. Sure it can help you gain new customers, new subscribers, and new visitors to your website, but it also cuts both ways in terms of bad customer experience.

This is why it's important to maintain those customer-centric strategies and capabilities. Hopefully you won't have product-related problems or technical issues that affect your user experience, but if you do, you need to be able to respond immediately, across all social media channels—Facebook, Instagram, Twitter, and Snapchat. This region is very young in terms of population demographics, and all social media are actively being frequently used. Every entrepreneur in this part of the world needs to be very careful and very sensitive to the social media customer experience and customer service angle in general.

Similar to marketing, entrepreneurs also need to view customer service as a core offering rather than just a support function. You need team members that are empowered and know your service and the user experience inside out. This is why we chose to have our customer service team in-house, as opposed to outsourcing it remotely somewhere else in the world—they literally sit next to the core product team, and that way they can learn from each other. The product and core development team can learn from the customer service team on all the issues and the problems that the customers might be facing, while the customer service team can learn from the core product and development team on the newest features and the newest improvements and how to respond to more challenging and technical customer questions.

How do you go about continuously learning and staying on top of the industry?

I am a big believer in networking and learning from in-person experiences, and I make it a point to attend industry events. For example, I attend IBC (International Broadcasting Conference) in Amsterdam every year, and I also frequent regional events as well, which are especially important to meet our potential B2B clients. Events are something I highly recommend to stay on the pulse of your industry, as well as for networking and learning purposes.

What is your future vision of STARZ PLAY?

It's always difficult to predict the future, especially in such an extremely dynamic industry. We need to keep growing our clients and keep fairly fluid. We started in the MENA region, but global expansion is a top priority for us.

We also feel that having based ourselves in the UAE gives us very unique access to different parts of the world, both in terms of logistics and physical access. Dubai is also a very unique place to start from because you have a hub for entrepreneurs, technology and investors. More and more we are seeing opportunities from Asia, Africa, and Eastern Europe that are being served out of Dubai. The fact that we're based in Dubai is a unique advantage in terms of our international growth strategy.

7

DELPHINE EDDÉ

Building an online fashion and lifestyle publishing empire

Co-Founder, Partner, and Publishing Director of Diwanee

WWW.DIWANEE.COM

Delphine Eddé is co-founder, partner and publishing director of Diwanee, a digital media company that creates Arabic content primarily for women and distributes it through its several Arab websites, including Yasmina.com, 3a2ilati.com, AtyabTabkha.com, Mashaheeri.com, and Mayzun.com. The websites she has co-created attract millions of users across the Arab world, offering lucrative advertising solutions, ranging from display banners to branded content, to consumer brands eager to penetrate the Middle Eastern market. She co-founded the company with her husband, Hervé Cuviliez, in 2006. Prior to Diwanee, Delphine was digital director at Condé Nast, an American mass media publishing group and the publisher behind *Vogue, Glamour, GQ* and *Architectural Digest*. She was born in Beirut and grew up in Paris.

Tell us a bit about your personal background.

I was born in Lebanon, and because of the civil war, my family quickly fled to France when I was just a toddler. I was raised and educated in Paris. Growing up, I never thought about becoming an entrepreneur or was interested in it or even in the internet, or digital media for that matter, all of which came at later stage.

I had a normal, very happy childhood in Paris. I grew up with my parents and sister. I traveled a lot with my family back and forth from France to Lebanon, but Lebanon was always a holiday destination for me, whereas Paris was my home.

Although my parents were Lebanese and they were bringing up two girls, they were always quite modern in how they raised us and in their teachings. They always told us, "You have to be independent. You have to work hard."

I studied communication in college. I then went to New York. At the time, I still didn't know what I wanted to do in life. I loved communication and marketing. I also loved working for brands. I was always more or less in the luxury sector. I worked in advertising, and I think this was the best school for me, because you're exposed to a lot of different industries. I was working literally day and night, and I loved it. I worked in advertising for about eight years before moving to media.

At some point, I had the opportunity to work in DDB, which is a worldwide marketing communications network owned by Omnicom Group, one of the world's largest advertising companies. I knew nothing at the time about the internet in 2000. I mean, I had an email, of course, but that was about it. They wanted people who could understand brands, and I wanted to learn about this new thing that was the internet. So I got hired at their digital branch, and I was helping them on the branding side, like understanding a brand, while I was learning from them about the tech side. It is also where I first I met my husband, Hervé Cuviliez. He had already been an entrepreneur.

Eventually, the CEO of DDB left the agency and went to Condé Nast, an American mass media publishing group and the publisher behind *Vogue, Glamour, GQ* and *Architectural Digest.* He called me a few months later and said, "Listen, you want to join us? Because I am looking for a digital director at Condé Nast." The idea was to be the link between the print and digital. He had picked me because I deeply understood brands. I also understood how to run old media brands digitally and how to develop digital assets.

I joined Condé Nast, and this was practically where I learned everything about media and content creation. This was an extremely important experience in my professional life, because it led me to Diwanee a few years later.

In early 2006, my husband, Hervé, and I decided that we were too young and too much stuck in an unhealthy comfort zone to continue our careers along the same path. We figured, the way our lives were shaping up to be, unless we made a drastic change now, we would probably be in the same place five or ten years from now, and we really didn't want to do that. We knew in our hearts it was time to move on.

How did Lebanon and Diwanee come into the picture?

We decided to leave everything we had behind in Paris and move somewhere new. At the time, we were living very well, yet we decided it was time to start over and find a new opportunity. We looked at Brazil, Dubai, the U.S., and few other places. We said, "We must go, we don't know exactly where, but we need to start over and create something new, or we'll forever be stuck in the same spot." Eventually, we decided to come to Lebanon. I don't even say return to Lebanon, because I never lived here, since I left when I was two years old. Beirut was definitely a big adjustment from Paris.

WE LAUNCHED THE VERY FIRST VERSION OF DIWANEE IN JULY 2006, THREE DAYS BEFORE THE WAR WITH ISRAEL. SO I GUESS WE PROVED WHAT PEOPLE SAY, THAT ENTREPRENEURS ARE CRAZY (LAUGHS), LEAVING OUR COMFORTABLE LIVES IN FRANCE, PUTTING ALL OUR LIVELIHOOD AND SAVINGS ON THE LINE TO LAUNCH THIS WEBSITE, AND NOW A WAR BREAKS OUT!

We wanted to come to Lebanon to make a difference and to have an impact on the economy and to participate in the country's growth. At the time, we felt that something good was happening, and we felt it was now a more stable country. So, we thought, let's give it a try there and see how it goes. We opened a small web design and web development agency in 2006.

Shortly thereafter, we launched the very first version of Diwanee in July 2006, three days before the war with Israel. So I guess we proved what people say, that entrepreneurs are crazy (laughs), leaving our comfortable lives in France, putting all our livelihood and savings on the line to launch this website, and now a war breaks out! Perhaps that's where we get our drive and tenacity from. From knowing that the odds are stacked against you and you're facing all these challenges, yet you have this vision you wholeheartedly believe in, and you have the sense of obligation to not let yourself or your employees down. We pressed on; we never once hesitated. We didn't lay off anyone, nor did anyone quit. We kept our heads down and worked, and continued to work. We never, ever thought about stopping. It didn't cross our mind, even in the darkest hour of Diwanee.

We had a lot of ambition from the get-go and knew what we wanted to do from day one. We wanted to create digital media brands, along the lines of what I was doing at Condé Nast. We wanted to become the leader in the space in terms of digital media assets. We had high expectations and standards and pushed our team hard to deliver and build the right foundation for the business from the very beginning.

Shortly after we started, we quickly realized that while Lebanon was a great base, its market size was just too small, especially for digital. We were already starting to think more regional, especially since we noticed there was hardly anything for women in the region. All the websites were for men, like news, finance, or sports at the time. Yahoo! was still there, and so was Koora, the popular football website. Meanwhile, there was nothing specifically for women that comprehensively addressed local women's interests, especially in the Gulf. We said, "You know what, let's create something around women in Arabic, and let's address Saudi Arabia, being a key market, and the Gulf countries, and see if we can still create jobs in Lebanon and keep our company in Lebanon while we develop business outside of Lebanon into other bigger markets." Eventually, we decided to open an office in Dubai, where most of the international brands operated their Middle East business from, as well being home to most of the largest media and advertising agencies in the region.

Tell us more about the Diwanee business model.

Diwanee is a publishing company. We create digital content, and we distribute that content for different agencies. I can also describe it the other way around; we try to develop agencies and create the right content for them. We have one side of Diwanee that works directly for our media brands and magazines. We create content for Yasmina.com—that is our fashion, beauty and luxury portal. We develop content for 3a2ilati.com, a family-oriented parent education portal. We develop content for AtyabTabkha.com around food. We also developed our first male-oriented website, called Mazyun.com. These are the portals we have today, with each having its own social media platform, so from YouTube, to Facebook, to Instagram, to Twitter, etc.

We develop a different content strategy for each platform, but it's all under one umbrella brand. For example, on Yasmina.com, what I have on the website is not what I have on YouTube, and what I have on YouTube is not what I develop for Facebook. Same for Instagram and other social media outlets. It's all under Yasmina, which has its own scope and editorial line, but the way we express the content or the way we execute the content is different per platform. This is important, because the audience expectations on each platform are not the same. What works on one social media platform may not work on another, and vice versa.

The other side of Diwanee is the work we do directly for clients and partners. For a long time, we worked, for example, with Saudi Telecom, the top telco (telecommunication service) in Saudi Arabia. We also worked with L'Oreal, the premier cosmetic and beauty brand in the world. We were actually the first digital department of L'Oreal in the Middle East. When we started, they didn't have anyone for digital, so my team and I would go there every day, and we had our desks at L'Oreal and managed their entire digital operation from there till they developed their team in-house.

We also worked with a lot of brands that are relevant to our publication. It is a natural fit, for example, for a brand or a group like Tefal to work with people who know everything about cooking, who know about their audience, expectations of the audience around cooking, etc. Tefal was attracted to us because we have AtyabTabkha.com, our food portal, and because we knew how to create content and audience around food, cooking, and recipes.

We quickly grew to become a leading women-focused portal in the Middle East. Back then, no one was looking at traffic or user engagement figures, and many publishers were lying about their numbers anyway. There was no independent third party to validate the numbers online publishers were reporting or publicizing. Of course, today, we have lots of tools and data management systems to accurately track our numbers. It was really messy back then and unreliable.

Today, we have grown to approximately 180 employees between our main offices in Lebanon, UAE, and Serbia. The story of how we ended up setting our technical operation in Belgrade, Serbia, is quite interesting.

One of our co-founders is Ivan Petrovic, who is our tech director or CTO. He started with us here out of Lebanon and very quickly realized that the type of specialized tech skills we needed in the company cannot be found in Lebanon. So one day, he went to Belgrade and found some developers in a small boutique tech shop and decided to test them. We eventually ended up buying and integrating them in Diwanee. Since then, that operation has grown quite a bit, where now all of our tech team is based in Belgrade. So that's how the Belgrade operation became an integral part of Diwanee.

Do you recall a specific lesson you learned in your journey?

Yes, I remember in the first few years of Diwanee, we were quite shy in terms of external communication. Given my husband and my personalities, we're not people that go out that much; we're just like work, work, work. So, it's not in our DNA to speak out or talk much about what we're doing or what we're accomplishing. We generally prefer to keep to ourselves and stay low-profile in terms of PR and the media.

Then, in 2013, we became part of Endeavor, a global entrepreneur organization, and they really pushed us to talk (laughs). They pushed us to communicate our story, our milestones, future plans, etc. They had to convince us that our story can be very inspiring to others, rather than thinking we were just bragging. They convinced us that opening up about our experience can help reinforce the message that success, for a tech startup like ours, is possible in Lebanon. We had to shift our thinking and be more proactive about sharing Diwanee's story with the world, and this has become important in our development on many fronts the more we did so.

You almost cannot let a day pass without looking at your numbers and other metrics in your business. You need to make sure you always know everything about the business today, where you are going, and why this is not working and going into the details, being very specific and granular at every level.

What's your advice to aspiring entrepreneurs?

My advice, and it is probably quite common but is an important message to restate, is to be obsessed with what you do. You need to live it, eat it, sleep it, especially in the first few years, because if you don't do it, no one will do it for you. Every aspect of your startup, your numbers, your people, your customers, everything needs to be your daily obsession.

You almost cannot let a day pass without looking at your numbers and other metrics in your business. You need to make sure you always know everything about the business today, where you are going, and why this is not working and going into the details, being very specific and granular at every level. You need to have this 360-degree view of the business at all times. People don't realize how much work it takes to build a company, and it's not just because you are talented, it's because you are talented and obsessed with what you want to achieve.

What's your advice to entrepreneurs regarding finding the right partner?

One of the most important things for entrepreneurs is to have a tech partner, if you're developing or building anything based on technology, if they're not all that tech savvy. As you always want to own the technology. If you don't, then you really have nothing. Anyone can copy what you have, or you are too dependent on another agency who is developing your product, which may not necessarily turn out the best, fastest, or cheapest results. It's critical to master or control the tech aspect of your company if you are a startup that needs tech elements, hence why you need someone from the founding team who is at least very well-versed in the technology, if not a developer themselves.

What's your advice on team-building?

In terms of team-building, when your team is just ten or twenty people, it's quite easy. You go out for dinner. People know each other. They work together. They are more or less on the same page. The challenge always comes when your team grows to, say, 50, 100, or 150 people in few months; then things start to get a bit messy.

In our case, we started doing all those extra things to help the team bond and build team spirit, often small things like distributing ice cream for everyone on Thursdays, arranging manicures for all the ladies, team breakfasts, Christmas parties, etc. Then little by little, it all come together.

Another thing we do that's quite helpful in terms of team-building is organize what we call Diwanee Day once or twice a year. We basically gather all top managers to present for ten minutes each what they are doing. Since we do so many things, we want to make sure everyone is updated on what's happening in the company, whether we have a new client, developed this latest innovation, implemented a new process, or have a new edition to our CMS (content management system), etc. Then we organize a small workshop and get people to work together. Last time, I gave the managers a challenge to develop a new product within Diwanee. It's a great event for team bonding and generating new ideas and new solutions to problems, especially in tough times, with the team coming together from different parts of the world, from Beirut, Dubai, Belgrade, and now Iran.

As a side note, speaking of Iran, we launched there two years ago, and it has already proved to be quite an amazing market, both in terms of a population size of 80 million people and consumer digital consumption. So today we have an office of about seven people there, where we host Yasmina.com's "little sister," which we call Yasaman.com, that also focuses on women-related interests, including beauty, art, wedding, lifestyle, food, etc. for the Iranian market, and it has done quite well so far.

What has been your experience with fundraising?

When we started, we funded the business ourselves from our own savings, as well as from any revenues we generated which we would reinvest back in the company. That lasted for about two years. Then at some point, we started having some cash flow issues, mainly because clients were paying late. We never had revenue problems; it was always cash flow issues that we needed to resolve to pay our employees and grow the team. We said, "Listen, we need to fix this. We need to grow. We need to go and raise capital."

We went around to investment banks asking for money. No one wanted to invest in us or lend us money. Banks in Lebanon would not lend us money unless we would put some kind of guarantee. They were like, "I can lend you $100,000 if you put in my bank $100,000." And we were like, "If we had a $100,000, then I wouldn't need you in the first place." So that obviously didn't work out too well.

Then we figured we needed a different kind of investor than banks, ones who appreciated the needs of a startup. They needed to understand what it took to build a digital company and how difficult it was, and how cash-intensive it can be for it to scale. We tried different avenues and ended up raising $6 million, half of which came from friends and family, which wasn't what we originally intended, but we had no choice at this point.

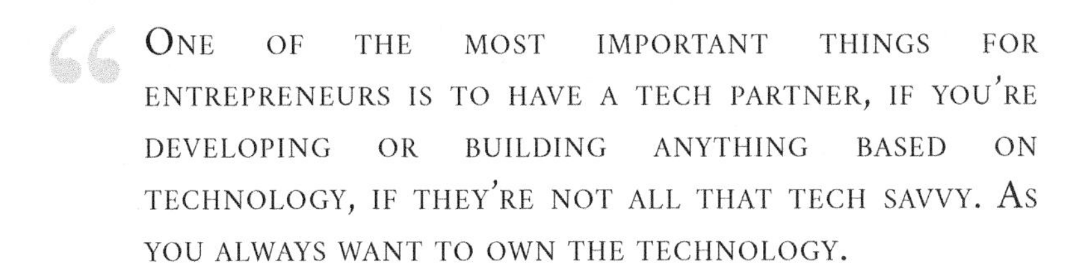

> "ONE OF THE MOST IMPORTANT THINGS FOR ENTREPRENEURS IS TO HAVE A TECH PARTNER, IF YOU'RE DEVELOPING OR BUILDING ANYTHING BASED ON TECHNOLOGY, IF THEY'RE NOT ALL THAT TECH SAVVY. AS YOU ALWAYS WANT TO OWN THE TECHNOLOGY.

That's how we initially got funded, and then we had Lebanon-based MedSecurities invest with us. They were looking to test digital.

Eventually, Webedia, a large Paris-based digital company, came in the picture through a mutual friend we had who introduced us to them. We were at MIPCOM, the premier annual tradeshow for entertainment content held in Cannes, France, when we met with their co-founder. Upon learning what we do and how we go about our business, I remember him saying we were like a mini Webedia. That's how it all began. They eventually acquired a majority stake in Diwanee. It was a natural fit for Diwanee in terms of helping us accelerate our growth, expand into new verticals, as well as being able to share knowledge, data, tools, and resources. We were quite excited about the potential of this partnership then, as we continue to be today. Not to mention, their investment was quite large, one of the largest in the region of its kind, in fact, so needless to say, all our early financial investors, backers, and stakeholders came out extremely happy with their very positive ROI (return on investment) in Diwanee.

What's your perspective on innovation in a startup?

Every year we try to reinvent the way we work and the way we are organized, and I think this is very important and quite refreshing to think like this. So, every year, I take a blank piece of paper and I ask myself, "What if I was to re-create Diwanee today—how would I do it?" I also do this exercise with my team or during Diwanee Day or during brainstorming sessions.

It's particularly important to do this, because we live in a dynamic world, especially the digital world. When we initially launched, for example, Instagram and Twitter didn't exist; YouTube was nowhere as big as it is today. The external environment is constantly evolving, which is why our business model and the way we're organized need to constantly evolve as well. This simple exercise of rethinking our business from scratch has done wonders for our business. It forces us to think outside the box and find new ways of seeing things, all by simply asking, "If we had to rebuild Diwanee or do it all over again today, what would it look like?"

Of course, it's difficult to just throw everything out the window and really start from scratch; nevertheless, there is always one or two new innovative ideas that create a fundamental shift in our strategy that come up as a result of this exercise.

What are your thoughts on the startup ecosystem in Lebanon?

I always say I wish I started Diwanee today, because today it is so easy to create a startup in Lebanon, and the ecosystem has really evolved a lot since then. When people ask me, "What are you most of proud of?" I answer, "I am proud of being one of the first tech entrepreneurs in

Lebanon and hopefully leading the way for others and showing that it can work from Lebanon." Since when we started, there was nothing. There was no infrastructure. Internet connectivity was quite weak. There were no recruiting agencies. There was no talent in the universities, which were very poor. Digital media and tech talent in general were rare to find. Banks did not understand what we were doing nor our business model. There were hardly any VCs (venture capitalists), if any.

Fortunately, Banque Du Liban or "BDL," as we call it here, the Lebanese bank, and the central bank lobbied for a new law to support what they refer to as "the knowledge economy," so they implemented Circular 331 in 2013. Basically, this law ensured that any bank investing in the knowledge economy or in a startup, up to 75 percent of their capital would be guaranteed. This was a major initiative to de-risk investing for banks in the space and to develop the ecosystem, and because of this new initiative, some VC funds were created.

So banks would put the money into the VC funds, and the VC funds are reinvesting into startups. This had a profound impact on the ecosystem here, so much so that many Lebanese living abroad began to see the changes in the country and decided to return back to Lebanon.

This all also triggered new startup-oriented forums, conferences, and events. New investments into startups were being made as well. Of course, we now have Beirut Digital District, where our office is, which is a great hub for tech startups in Lebanon and now hosts around 2,000 employees in the tech sector. There is definitely a growing interest in the tech economy, with politicians starting to see the economic potential in this sector and starting to focus on growing.

Are there any regulations that you'd like to see change in Lebanon?

Yeah, definitely. I think attracting talent is a key, and sometimes you need talent that is not Lebanese, and you can't hire. For example, by law, Lebanese women cannot pass on their nationality to their kids.

Sometimes you have people who are of Lebanese origin that cannot come back and live here, because their mom is Lebanese but not their dad.

Another example that comes to mind—I remember when we launched an e-commerce initiative in Diwanee, I could not find anyone in Lebanon who was experienced enough in the field. I found someone I wanted to recruit from Dubai who was originally from Tunisia and was qualified for the role. There was no way I could; it was nearly impossible. I was never able to get her visa, never, ever. Obviously, that delayed our plans and hurt our business. I would also change that visa/work permit regulation in those two regards.

If you look, you can see this in action perfectly in Silicon Valley, where a big portion of the talent is not American. That is because American companies are in fact able to recruit personnel from overseas, and the local regulations support that, rather than block. If it works for some of the largest companies in the world—Apple, Google, Microsoft—surely it's something that we need to take a really hard look at in Lebanon. I would love to see such an open system implemented in Lebanon that invites and draws talent from everywhere. I think that would do a lot of good for the ecosystem and the economy at large.

What impact do you seek to create with Diwanee?

Beyond meeting business objectives and milestones, one thing that is dear to my heart and which we always strive to do at Diwanee is to help create jobs and train people in this new digital era. We even want to create a school for developers. I would like Diwanee to be somewhat of a hub for creative and talented people in Lebanon and utilize it to drive innovation in all kinds of areas.

Anything else you wish to add?

Thanks for the opportunity. I also want to thank you for one thing that I really appreciate, which is that you didn't ask me anything about being a woman in business. At some point, we are so tired of answering questions like this again and again. You are just an entrepreneur, and you just have to compete against everyone else, and they are not all women, and it does not really matter. There's really no noticeable difference I ever felt in my entire professional journey. So thank you for this!

8

IDRISS AL RIFAI

Disrupting pickup and delivery

Founder and CEO of Fetchr

WWW.FETCHR.COM

IDRISS AL RIFAI founded Fetchr in 2012. Fetchr attempts to disrupt the retail market with technologies and customer-centric shipping services that enable the growth of e-commerce in the Middle East and beyond. Fetchr helps local merchants and global brands build, launch and grow profitable e-commerce businesses. Fetchr app pickup and delivery software takes the hassle out of online shopping. Before founding Fetchr, Idriss was director of operations at MarkaVIP and a consultant with the Boston Consulting Group. He earned his master's degree at Institut d'Etudes Politiques de Paris (Sciences Po) and his MBA at the University of Chicago, Booth School of Business.

Tell us about your background and early career experience.

I was born in Iraq in 1979 to an Iraqi father and a French mother. My family fled to France due to the political turmoil in Iraq when I was just three years old. Growing up in France, I was a huge basketball fan. I played my fair share all throughout my teenage years and eventually played for the French junior national team. I completed my A Level at Lycee Bellevue in Toulouse, followed by my master's studies at Institut d'Etudes Politiques de Paris, which is the French Ivy League for anything with regard to international relations, economics and social sciences. I then joined the Ministry of Defense, where I became the special adviser to the head of HR (human resources) of the navy, a four-star admiral I had a huge respect for. I also started learning Arabic around that time, which was something I felt was missing from my education and something I was missing as a person. I attended Arabic classes at night for three years and slowly started speaking formal Arabic or "fusha."

After the navy, I joined the French Special Forces. I was in operations for three years on a request basis, as a reserve officer. I just loved this experience, the discipline and just the excitement of trying new things. It was a fun opportunity to travel the world and have broader experience. It was thrilling to be in new countries and get exposed to new things. I then joined the Delegation of Strategic Affairs, which is a think tank for the Ministry of Defense. I did that for two years in Paris before pursuing my MBA at the University of Chicago, Booth School of Business. Afterward, I moved to Dubai and worked two years with the Boston Consulting Group (BCG). I wanted to learn the ropes of consulting. I think consulting teaches you a lot in terms of how to develop a clear message, build a story, put together a presentation, be analytical, and make good decisions. That type of business training early in my career was very valuable, and I still use what I learned there every day. It also allowed me to be exposed to multiple industries and businesses across the Gulf.

I was then recruited by a top executive at MarkaVIP, which went on to become a leading online fashion retailer in the Middle East for many years. However, at the time, I was just in discussion with one of their leading investors to start a new venture from scratch. We all knew e-commerce was nascent in this part of the world, and we just needed more supply of quality e-commerce platforms. However, after a few discussions, I was told, "Look, we have this great, fairly late-stage startup, it's growing rapidly, and we're looking for a head of operations, with the potential to be COO." So I decided to jump ship. I ended up staying at MarkaVIP for a short while before deciding to start Fetchr.

What did you learn at Boston Consulting Group and MarkaVIP?

As I mentioned, consulting was quite valuable. It teaches you four things basically that are helpful with regards to entrepreneurship. First, as an entrepreneur, you need to be able to raise money, and raising money is about building stories and having presentation decks and financial models to support them.

Second, consulting gives you exposure to top people. It's not so much about whether those folks are going to become your investors down the road or not. It's more that you start understanding how top decision makers make decisions. This is especially the case in any B2B company, as Fetchr is a B2B2C (business to business to consumer) type. You need to understand what the decision cycle within these organizations is, in order to have the right material for the right people at the right time so that, as an organization, they can decide to, say, switch to another provider like Fetchr.

Third, and probably one of the biggest lessons I learned in consulting but even more so at MarkaVIP, is that I was under the impression that big companies were working very well, like clockwork. Like they're well-oiled machines. Then when I was working for a fast-growing startup like MarkaVIP, I was exposed to other big companies and saw firsthand how inefficient some of these organizations were: how inefficient they were in pursuing markets and pursuing opportunities, as well as making decisions internally within the organization. It was a key moment when I realized that you don't have to be perfect to disrupt large organizations who think they have it all figured out. We create our own mental barriers.

When I was at MarkaVIP, for example, we were working with Aramex, which was the leading shipping provider in the Middle East. I got to see firsthand Aramex internal operations and how their service was nowhere near to being e-commerce ready at the time. I was thinking, "You are not ready to tailor to my e-commerce needs at MarkaVIP while we're one of your biggest clients." There was a problem, and I knew somebody would come and disrupt them with a better service.

It was one of those key insights that told me, "You need to and can do this. Your product is not going to be perfect from day one, but you need to get going because nobody is perfect anyway." So that was a very important realization that encouraged me to take that first step and start Fetchr. I would not be deterred or intimidated as a startup, taking on the big guys so to speak. Maybe you're a mosquito up against a giant, but you have your strengths, too: You can fly, you can poke, and you can bother. Meanwhile, the giant is often big, slow, and clumsy. So you can make a lot of noise and impact no matter how small you are. That was also a valuable lesson.

Where did the idea for Fetchr come from?

Back at MarkaVIP, we weren't happy with the level of service we were getting from shipping companies. We tried about twenty different companies, and it just never worked. So we decided to handle shipping in-house and build our own delivery system and operation. I was put in charge of this and built it from the ground up with the help of Omar Yaghmour, who later became a co-founder of Fetchr; we developed the software, the operations, the legal setup, and everything else related in six countries. Once I saw that the results were better than our main shipping provider, Aramex, I realized right there and then that there was a missing gap in the market. We all knew that e-commerce in the region was growing fast, between 30 percent and 40 percent year to year, but there was no specialized, go-to player in the industry for e-commerce shipping, nobody that fully understood the huge tech requirement to build and sustain such an organization.

That's when I decided to leave MarkaVIP and launch Fetchr in 2012, with the aim to provide an end-to-end shipping solution for e-commerce companies. Since then, we've grown quite a lot. We now have more than 2,300 staff and are present in six markets. We are growing at about 15 percent month to month. There is a tremendous momentum we're building here.

What was the biggest challenge you faced in the early days of Fetchr?

It's very tough to fund a company in the Middle East. I put all my money, my wife's money, my mom's money into the business when we had no clear end in sight. I went out to raise about $1.2 million in seed funding. But the process hadn't been a smooth one by any means. After putting all of my and my closest friend's money in, I started raising a couple of hundred thousand dollars from angel investors and friends. Later in the process, we got traction from a prominent VC at the time. He renegotiated the deals that already took place, restructured the company so that it was "VC ready." They had decided to put a fairly large chunk of the remaining $600K we intended to raise to close the round. Everything was going along great. We then started gathering additional investors under these terms. I still remember September 27, 2013, when this VC unexpectedly decided to pull out last-minute. The whole ground crumbled. Obviously, as your lead—and only institutional—investor pulls out, everyone started getting cold feet. No blame on them to start questioning whether there was something wrong that they missed seeing. As a result, everything fell apart, and I was left with no money at all and a broken dream.

THE MOST SIGNIFICANT LESSON THAT I'VE LEARNED FROM THIS WHOLE ORDEAL IS THAT IF SOMEONE BEGINS SHOWING SIGNS OF NOT FULFILLING A PROMISE AS AN EMPLOYEE, OR AS AN INVESTOR, YOU NEED TO CUT THAT RELATIONSHIP LOOSE AS SOON AS POSSIBLE.

During the four following months, I tried everything. I really struggled. I took loans and scrapped for money to be able to sustain and keep the company afloat and make payroll. We had a handful of employees at the time. It was just me, Omar, four developers and a few other people on the payroll. I had to start taking personal loans because I could not take business loans here in Dubai, having zero in the bank and no revenues. So that was extremely tough. Then eventually things got better. I managed to close the seed fund, and things got back on track, but up till now this period was probably the most difficult one because of the level of uncertainty we had.

Then the next challenge was to raise the next round of finance, series A. We wanted to raise about $10 million. That was the target. The ecosystem was not and is still not fully developed in the region with regard to series A financing. It was tough to raise any money here while having the risk profile we had in the business. Also, everybody was questioning whether we could compete with the big guys, being Aramex. Eventually, I went to Silicon Valley and was able to find our lead investor through the critical help of Joy Ajlouny. More recently, we closed $41 million from a number of players. We're also growing exponentially and have exceeded all our targets so far. We have recruited 400 people just in the last eight weeks. Things have moved along quite a bit since those early fundraising nightmares, but I still remember those were quite tough days.

What did you learn from this whole experience?

The most significant lesson that I've learned from this whole ordeal is that if someone begins showing signs of not fulfilling a promise as an employee, or as an investor, you need to cut that relationship loose as soon as possible. It's one of my mistakes as a human being, as an entrepreneur. I tend to give second and third chances to people, thinking that they deserve it, but statistically speaking, it's just rarely the case. I tend to wait too long to be able to make decisions on cutting loose people that promise the moon and obviously don't deliver. I tend to get stuck too long with these guys. I think I've changed a little bit, but it's still one of my weaknesses, which I'm working on.

What are the key ingredients for becoming a successful entrepreneur?

There are three key ingredients for becoming successful. You must have the drive. The drive. The drive. First and foremost, the essential quality to have, as an entrepreneur, is relentlessness. You're going to be told "no" hundreds of times by clients, by investors, by employees that you want to recruit. It's all about giving the same pitch or "spiel" day after day to ensure that some of it is going to convert into positive outcome. It's also similar to the fundraising game, especially early stage and in this part of the world, where it's a numbers game. You need to talk to lots and lots of people if you want to make it happen. You also need to be able to get knocked down, get up and get back to work. That's the most important quality that you need to have as an entrepreneur. Obviously, if you don't love what you do and the impact you're making, and believe that it all will work out, it will be difficult to stay driven and keep on fighting the next morning.

The second ingredient would be the ability to pitch the story, convey the message quickly and in a crisp manner. You need to be able to have a 360 view of your business and be ready to articulate clearly what you're doing, and how you're going to win market share and even to disrupt your industry. You will need to convey a consistent and effective message to potential clients, investors, and employees. This is extremely critical.

Third, you need to be able to assemble a team that works together. Building team chemistry is also a big part of success. Your team has to live and breathe the business literally. They have to be extremely passionate, take full ownership in everything they do, and infuse that same spirit among each other. There are a lot of entrepreneurs that believe that they are taking ownership, but then they outsource and let someone else make critical decisions. The ability to grow through pain, get your hands dirty, and learn to do it yourself from A to Z is critical. Having said that, you also need to understand your strength and weakness. If you're not technical, for example, I would first start looking for a co-founder who is technical. You need to make sure that you're going in the right direction and hiring the right people who make up for any shortcomings you may have. Having a very strong CTO/technical co-founder that goes through this journey with you and whom you can fully rely on is very important.

What are some of the best practices you found around hiring?

You need to test people well before you hire. You need to put a minimum requirement, for example, for any engineer to join your company through an actual test. There are some online tests out there that help define and identify the right candidates. We are having a lot of people, a lot of techies, applying to the business. The first thing we have them do is take an online test, because it helps weed out the unqualified candidates. There are a lot of average folks, even ones coming from top companies applying. No offense, but a lot of those e-commerce and tech-ish type of companies have a lot of B-players. So I recommend testing everyone for every position. That way you ensure you're recruiting top talent and A-players as much as possible.

How important is building the right culture in a startup?

Culture is critical. If you define company culture by the ability of a group of people to work together and to enjoy the work they're doing, then it's everything. If they don't like working with each other or if they are not excited about coming to work, then obviously it's going to impact the business.

> If you're releasing something that you're not entirely proud of, you're probably on the right track. If you're waiting to build something that you're totally proud of, you're never going to release or it's too late. I'm not saying to release faulty products or be sloppy. What I'm saying is you need to be willing to release products in the market with stripped-down features.

It's particularly difficult to keep startup culture or "DNA" when you're growing fast, but we're trying damn hard to make sure that we do that and recognize people for what they're doing. I think that's one of the key problems within a lot of organizations, that they only recognize the boss. As a CEO, I need to have an understanding of who, within the company, can make any given success, big or small, happen. We try to make the pyramid as flat as possible, because we believe 99 percent of the innovation comes from the frontline people. We realize we need to empower every employee to make decisions and give them the space they need to feel valued and trusted so that they can innovate. That's a critical piece to keeping a startup culture. We're really trying hard at this. It's never an easy thing.

What's your approach to product development?

Always remember, if you're releasing something that you're not entirely proud of, you're probably on the right track. If you're waiting to build something that you're totally proud of, you're never going to release or it's too late. I'm not saying to release faulty products or be sloppy. What I'm saying is you need to be willing to release products in the market with stripped-down features. The concept of building a prototype or MVP needs to be more embedded in the mind of every entrepreneur. You need to get out a product that incorporates only essential features and is not perfect, because your definition of "perfect" is not the market definition of "perfect." You need to test it out with the outside world, with real paying customers who are the driving force of your product. Being able to test it out, battle it out with customers as early as possible is extremely important. It reduces your time to market, builds momentum, and motivates your tech team as well.

How do you decide which customer feedback goes into product development and which doesn't?

You have to base that on business impact. Every time you have a customer feedback or request, you have to think as to whether you're building that feature for one or a few specific customers or for a lot more. You have to make that call based on how many customers you think this feature would be a valuable add-on for. You need to go through a lot of discussions with customers, especially in the early stages of your product. You also need to have a very close feedback loop with your customers, because you constantly need to improve the features based on what customers say. That's why early on, the CEO of the company should be very involved in that process and not limit the discussion to just tech or the product development team. It's very important to stay involved and steer development in the right direction and make sure it doesn't go off track.

AT SOME POINT, EVERYTHING IS TELLING YOU THIS IS NOT GOING TO WORK, AND YET YOU'RE STILL PURSUING IT. SO THERE IS DEFINITELY AND SHOULD BE A BIT OF THIS REBELLIOUSNESS, LIKE, "I'M GOING TO MAKE THIS WORK AND SHOW THE WORLD THAT EVERYONE IS WRONG."

As an entrepreneur, when do you know when to press on, change direction, or quit?

That's a great question and extremely difficult to answer. There is no right or wrong answer. This is where entrepreneurs are a little bit crazy, me included (laughs). At some point, everything is telling you this is not going to work, and yet you're still pursuing it. So there is definitely and should be a bit of this rebelliousness, like, "I'm going to make this work and show the world that everyone is wrong."

Having said that, in the early stages, a lot of things naturally don't work. It is about trying to define opportunities rather than problems and sticking to the big vision. The line between craziness and relentlessness is thin and blurry. Maybe we all have cognitive biases, one of them being the winner's fallacy. Winners always write history. So maybe there is no line. We only build an imaginary line because we only talk to the winners. The examples we have in multiple industries of leaders that displayed tremendous ability to stick to their vision, to be relentless, are numerous. What the stories don't show, though, is how many of these opinionated, hard-nosed people did actually fail. It's extremely difficult to draw a line between the required relentlessness to make every business succeed and the sheer stubbornness displayed by startup CEOs that is just counterproductive.

What's your view on work-life balance?

I don't know if I'm old-school, but the work-life balance was a serious problem for me for the first three years, and even now it's difficult. Personally, if you're thinking about work-life balance in the early days, I think there is definitely a problem. I put all my savings and all my family's savings in the business. I couldn't cheat half a day or a Friday afternoon break or go watch a movie. It's just impossible. There was just too much at stake and too many people who trusted me with their money. So I don't think you should aim for balance necessarily in those early days.

Obviously, after the company matures, you should be able to balance things out a bit better. I still think that work-life balance is overrated, because if you love what you do, you're happy to be there. It's like the old saying, "Choose the job of your dreams and you never have to work again." I really believe in that. If you're passionate about the business, it's no longer "working," so to speak. You know you can still go out and have a drink with your CTO and work. For me, this does not feel like work, and it's fun. It's more like building something that is cool—with friends.

How crucial then is working after hours in startup success?

I wouldn't go as far as what Elon Musk says about putting in 100 hours a week and outworking everyone. If you hear his speech, he says something to the effect that, "I don't believe I'm smarter than anyone, I just work harder. And if I work six hours per week more than my competition, which is 10 percent more, then I'm going 10 percent faster by definition."

I do agree with him about the importance of working hard and long in a startup. As an entrepreneur, you are always catching up with either the big competition or the other new startups in town. You always need to produce faster. There is obviously a lot to be said about working smart and being efficient with your time and resources and being able to produce the maximum output within the same amount of time and under the same budget. At the end of the day, though, there's a lot of work that needs to be done all at the same time. There's no way around working long, hard, smart, and fast.

What are some of the misconceptions of entrepreneurship you come across?

One misconception a lot of aspiring entrepreneurs tell me is that "I want to start a business because I want to be my own boss." It always makes me laugh, because, for me, this is one of the worst reasons to be an entrepreneur. Being your own boss doesn't mean anything. You have a lot more responsibility for all the employees that made the jump to join you and took a pay cut on their salaries, as well as to all the investors who trusted you with their money. Not to mention customers who rely on you to provide great service and solve their problems. You're in fact always accountable for what you're doing to a lot of people. So being your own boss and having this feeling of not being accountable for anything is just extremely unrealistic.

The other misconception is entrepreneurs who are afraid to share their ideas because they believe that someone is going to steal it. It's a massive false belief of what startup is. Ideas are worth 1 percent, whereas execution is the other 99 percent in a startup. You have to have a good idea, sure, but the ability of a company to deliver a product, a viable value proposition, and fulfill a promise, that's 99 percent of the business. The 1 percent is interesting, having a good idea, but it's of minimal value, and it's not protectable.

What is missing from the startup ecosystem in Dubai?

There are two main problems I see. First, we tend to think that Dubai is a tax-free place, but that's not entirely true. Now in the U.S., you pay about 30 percent on profits. You're being taxed on profits as a company, whereas here you're being charged pre-profit. You actually have to pay when you start, so it's extremely difficult. For example, in my business, the two things that are killing me is that I have to pay everything up front. I have to pay employee visas up front. I have to pay my warehouse lease up front. We're talking about a lot of money being up-fronted here, like hundreds of thousands of dollars, that could've been invested in the business. This is regardless of whether you're running a profitable business or not.

The second problem is employee visa regulations. As you know, a startup is a lot like a big experiment. It's a lot of trial and error. So, often, when you recruit someone, if they are not a good fit, they end up leaving, whether it's the person's own choice or the company's. In Dubai, it's just extremely difficult and extremely expensive to do this. Most of the time the people you are recruiting are coming from outside the country. You have to apply and pay for their visas. Then they realize they don't like Dubai after one week, or they don't like the company, or they're not a good fit. There is a lot of money spent up front, with no ability to ever recoup.

I would love to have something like a startup visa where you hire someone from abroad, and you pay say $1,000 for the first few months or until you're profitable, or whatever, just something that makes this scenario a lot more feasible and practical.

The other option is if the new hire departs or gets fired within the first three months, you're allowed to still use that visa again without paying a second time for someone else to come and fill that position. That would help tremendously, especially in regards to expanding the pool of tech talent.

What are some promising changes you noticed regarding UAE regulations?

There are also a lot of positive things being done. Bankruptcy law was just introduced in the UAE. So, that's something that is good, because the law used to hold individuals responsible and liable for the business, which was extremely worrisome. As an entrepreneur, you sign lots of checks, and you always have to worry about having enough money in the bank. From an entrepreneur's perspective, it is difficult to take on the personal risk of going to jail for business shortfalls.

What role do schools play in prepping youth to be successful entrepreneurs?

School can definitely play a bigger role in advancing this type of education. I also think that students need to have more exposure to startups.

For example, one idea is to have a program where students have to join a startup for, say, three months. The other is promoting the journey of a startup for students at university or having more startup founders speak at universities. Anything that can help students and young adults understand the challenges and rewards of entrepreneurship is a step in the right direction.

We also need greater subsidies with regards to teaching youth how to write code and become great developers. It would put a lot less stress on startups in regard to having access to good talent. Tech talent here is extremely expensive, which in turn would create a lot of value for the economy as a whole. Everybody, every startup, every single retailer that is going online now is looking for tech, so anything that will help expand the local tech talent pool is very helpful.

What are your views on the region's future prospects?

I think there are a lot of promising opportunities in the region. Danny Farha, from Beco Capital, recently wrote a post to the effect that "now is the best time to invest in Middle Eastern startups." Why? Because we have a population that is relatively wealthy on average. They all have smartphones, and the smartphone usage in the region is as high as it is in the U.S. There are also tons of services that are missing, tons and tons.

You can disrupt so many industries here. There is so much to disrupt. This is definitely the right time. There are a lot of segments that are being disrupted right now—the shipping industry, the banking industry is another, and so is healthcare. There are a lot of models where you can make a difference.

Are you satisfied with where you are in the business and how far Fetchr has gone?

I'm actually very unsatisfied and frustrated with where we are. There is so much in store that we have yet to tap into. I think we are barely scratching the surface; meanwhile, everybody is telling us how great we are, and we're not. For me, the glass is not half full, half empty. It's more like 10 percent full and 90 percent empty. Everybody is ecstatic that we got some water finally in the glass, but there is still so much more to do. So I think I'll be proud of what we're building only in a few years when I'll be able to look back at it and say, "OK, we achieved what we set out to do."

What is your vision for Fetchr?

I believe that the whole shipping industry is going to go through a complete shift. For one, the entire industry is based on an address system, which is irrelevant for two-thirds of the world. There are four billion people who don't have addresses. Even for the other two billion people who have an address, many are not necessarily at home when a package arrives or prefer to receive it somewhere else. An address-based pickup and delivery system was never optimal across the board. I think that whether Fetchr succeeds or not, the whole shipping space is moving to that type of service model. You receive your package anywhere you want and any time you want. That way people who don't have addresses don't have to be stuck at home for multiple hours to receive anything. Hopefully, we can change this once and for all and make Fetchr a verb and the norm for sending and receiving everything. Then I can be proud of the impact we created.

Ultimately, our goal is for Fetchr to be used in all the major markets, where a customer's mobile phone will merely replace their address. I want people to laugh when they remember the old days when you still had to give an address to receive a package. We started in the Middle East because this is the territory we know, both regarding e-commerce and market knowledge, but we don't want to stop here. There are a lot of other markets that need our solutions. We are aware of this. We're talking about different larger markets like India, Pakistan, China, Nigeria and so on, where people want to have a better customer experience with regard to receiving packages.

> SUCCESS, TO ME, IS MEASURED IN THE QUALITY OF YOUR PRODUCT OR SERVICE AND THE DEGREE WHICH IT IS FIT-TO-MARKET. SUCCESS IS NOT DEFINED BY HOW BIG YOUR COMPANY IS, IN TERMS OF NUMBER OF EMPLOYEES OR ITS RADIUS OF OPERATION.

What's your definition of success?

Success, to me, is measured in the quality of your product or service and the degree which it is fit-to-market. Success is not defined by how big your company is, in terms of number of employees or its radius of operation. All of this is like "whatever." Success is a moving target. When you start sprinting, if you do the 100 meters, you want to beat the 11 seconds, like 10.8, and bring that number lower over time. Your definition of success continually changes as you get better, and that is the same in business. The idea of success changes as you grow. Whatever you are proud of and whatever you are building that you're proud of is the true definition of success, from my perspective.

9

KUNAL KAPOOR

Making buying and selling luxury apparel seamless

Founder and CEO of The Luxury Closet

WWW.THELUXURYCLOSET.COM

Kunal Kapoor is the founder and CEO of The Luxury Closet. It was founded in 2011 and is currently the largest online marketplace for buying, selling, and consigning pre-owned luxury items at discounted prices in the Middle East. This unique and successful venture sees luxury products from Louis Vuitton, Chanel, Rolex, Cartier, Louboutin and many other top brands sold for up to 70 percent off the original price. Kunal strongly believes that the ability to buy luxury items should be available to everybody. Prior to founding The Luxury Closet, he built a successful sportswear brand in India. He subsequently landed in Dubai, working for the French fashion empire Louis Vuitton. He received a Bachelor of Arts degree from the University of Wisconsin at Madison in the U.S. and an MBA from INSEAD in France.

Tell us about your background and when you first became interested in technology.

I was born and raised in New Delhi, India. I became interested in technology at a very young age. I remember growing up and all my friends had computers, so I would just go to their homes and play with them until I got my own. That began my lifelong obsession with computers and technology.

When I finished high school, I wanted to study abroad in the U.S. I applied to a few schools there, and I received a scholarship to a small college called Knox in Galesburg, Illinois. In 1998, I got enrolled to study computer science and economics at Knox, which was a small liberal arts college. One of the great things about going to a U.S. liberal arts school was that you could really study whatever you wanted. There was a basic core curriculum, but otherwise you were free to literally choose whatever you wanted to study on top of that. This was very different than the colleges in India, where my friends attended.

I double-majored in both computer science and economics. On the whole, I attended all kinds of classes I wouldn't have been able to attend had I gone to college in India. I took music classes, voice class, and even an Indian history class. I became very interested in photography; I think I ended up taking every photography class that was offered there. I learned how to use 35mm, SLR cameras, and I printed all the photos by myself. Having the opportunity to attend a spectrum of different classes and get exposed to many things in college really broadened my education and interests.

I think I always had this obsession with computers and art. I was very much into black and white photography, so I spent a lot of time in the darkroom. I was also assembling my own computers, which I found fascinating.

I was the type of student that if I liked a particular class, I would do really, really well. On the other hand, if I didn't like a class, I would put the least effort in and just try to pass it. After college, I was worried I would not land a job with a good company doing interesting work. Not so many companies were recruiting on the Knox campus. I had this scary thought that I would get a mundane job in a company that makes mosquito repellent. I was afraid I would end up there, and I was like, "Oh my God, I'm just going to die here fighting mosquitoes" (laughs). So I transferred from Knox to the University of Wisconsin at Madison, which was a much bigger school with 40,000 students.

I also wanted to graduate early because I was just excited to get out and actually go to work. I finished college in just three and half years by dropping my computer science major and just finishing with economics. The University of Wisconsin had all kinds of companies and recruiters on campus. I ended up taking a Microsoft job test and found that I was the "right kind of nerd." I submitted my CV for their review and got a call back. I went through several interviews at Microsoft headquarters in Redmond, Washington, and unfortunately got shot down.

While I was in Washington getting shot down from jobs, my dad, who owned and ran a footwear manufacturing company in India, said, "You should come back and run the footwear company." I was always wildly ambitious, though sometimes too wildly ambitious for my own good. I decided to go back to India and join my dad's company. Right before I started, he said, "Listen, if you're going to be a shoemaker, you will need go to shoe school." So I went to shoe school for six months. I learned how to manufacture shoes. Then I went back to work with him at the company.

We started off as a footwear manufacturer. He developed a brand named "Portland" and made leather shoes and then distributed them. I really learned from the ground up what his job was. It was really a very father-to-son type of apprenticeship and a very dynamic small-business kind of learning.

I worked at the footwear company for a few years until I decided I wanted to do more than that. So I tried my luck launching a women's shoe brand called Skin Footwear. I had no clue how to make women's shoes. I also didn't listen to my dad, who said, "It's completely different. We don't have the machines to do it, and you will not be able to make it." Nevertheless, I went out and tried to get some orders and went to some fashion designers to make some shoes.

I went to some really famous Indian fashion designers, and I offered to make some shoes for them. I was able to make only a few samples to show them. Then they said, "OK, give me a few hundred." I would make them but end up ripping or breaking all of them. I remember one time, I was backstage at Indian Fashion Week. There was a model who wore my shoe. She went out, came back, and the heel broke. So it was really a very hard realization. I think it was a huge failure, and I said, "This is crazy. I should stop doing it." So I stopped. I guess my dad was right in warning me about women's shoes, after all (laughs).

As difficult as this experience was, I think it was important. It forced us to pivot and shift focus from selling leather shoes to selling sports shoes. We realized that we could bring in sports shoes from China and sell them in the mid-price range. In India, there were very cheap, low-quality local shoes and very high-quality shoes, like Nike and Reebok, and only a few options in between. That's where we thought of filling the gap.

We started and specialized in that space. We went from selling 2,000 pairs a month to selling 20,000 pairs a month. This is where I'd like to say that every business I've been engaged in has this mathematical element to it, versus a designer element to it, which I really liked. What I would do is go to China and come up with all these new sports shoes. I would make sure that there was a very strict quality control process, and we were always adhering to strict manufacturing techniques that were on par with some really large factories in China, which would custom-manufacture according to our specs.

We also opened a retail store, which worked out well, so we added a few more. I did this for five years before I decided I wanted a change. I always thought about going to business school, and it was good timing to do so. I applied to a few business schools and got accepted into INSEAD (Institut Européen d'Administration des Affaires) in France. It is considered one of the best business schools in the world. So I went to France to study. INSEAD was a brilliant experience. Afterward, I decided I wanted to work at Louis Vuitton to better understand the luxury business. So I applied and I got a job there. They put me into a management training program. This means you go to the store. You learn how things work. You become on-site manager in the store, manage a team, manage revenue; this was my introduction to the luxury business. I did that for a year, after which I realized I wanted to spend more time with my family business.

Then I finally decided I wanted to start something of my own. My dad was pretty encouraging. He kept on saying, "Don't become a shoemaker. It's too complicated. Do something else. Go start your own business. I'd be happy to put up the initial capital."

I went to Dubai and started looking for business ideas. I was discussing with all my friends and practically everyone I knew and kept asking "What do you think is a good business to get into?" I was getting all kinds of answers. Then, one day, my girlfriend at the time, who is now my wife, came to me and said, "You know what? You sound very confused." She was right. So I thought maybe I should try to get a consulting job at McKinsey. I prepared really hard for the interview and went all the way to the final rounds, where the guys there said, "Man, you should not be a consultant. We're going to turn you down for your own good. You're better suited to doing your own thing." So they shot me down right then and there, and I was back at square one looking for business ideas.

MY GIRLFRIEND FINALLY CAME TO ME AND SAID, "LISTEN, YOU NEED TO PUT YOUR LIFE PURPOSE IN ONE SENTENCE." I WENT AND THOUGHT ABOUT IT, AND I CAME UP WITH, "I WANT TO BUILD A COMPANY, A SCALABLE COMPANY THAT SELLS REALLY COOL PRODUCTS THAT I HAVE SOME BACKGROUND IN." I THINK THAT REALLY DEFINED ME.

How did you get the idea for The Luxury Closet?

After this initial trial and miss in Dubai, my girlfriend finally came to me and said, "Listen, you need to put your life purpose in one sentence." I went and thought about it, and I came up with, "I want to build a company, a scalable company that sells really cool products that I have some background in." I think that really defined me. It had to be a company that could become big and scalable. It had to sell a product, and I had to think that the product was cool. It also had to be in a field where I have some background in doing something similar so that I could leverage my experience.

One day, I was having a conversation with a friend, and we were bouncing around business ideas. Then a resell idea came up. We were like, "You can buy and resell stuff." I saw similarities with reselling luxury cars. In Paris, for example, you can buy a recently pre-owned but well-maintained BMW at 50 percent off, and you can resell the BMW for a profit. I figured, why can't I do the same with Louis Vuitton? It was like a flash of light went off, "Yes." Actually, in many countries, you can do that. I did some research and found Milan Stations, a company that had gone public selling. I viewed it on the Hong Kong Stock Exchange. I was like, "Wow, you can actually hyper-sell used bags. This is great." I worked for Louis Vuitton and wanted to resell Louis Vuitton products.

That's how the idea started. As a matter of fact, looking at the model, there was always a very small number of retail companies doing that. There were other online companies in the U.S. and retail companies across the world already doing it. We actually looked around at all these competitors doing it on a very small scale. I actually almost gave up, thinking others were already doing it. Then I came to realize, "If they can have such a few items to sell and still get that many people viewing and buying them, in spite of the less than optimal way they're conducting, then there sure is a big opportunity to do it properly." This is still a luxury business, so you have to brand the business in a certain way, treat the customer in a certain way, sell the product in a certain way. It needs to be done right, and I realized it wasn't. So that was really the big concept behind The Luxury Closet.

How did you begin to implement the idea?

I built the first version of the website with WordPress by myself. I found a programmer, started with a few basic features and just showcased two or three bags that came from my sister. The funny thing was that when I was at Louis Vuitton, I bought my family a lot of shoes and gifts. So they were donating all these gifts back to me so I could start my website! (laughs)

Then I began to display items one by one on the site without actually selling them per se, just to clarify value proposition to customers. That worked out well. I also outsourced an office where I would go just to meet clients. In July 2011, when I had fifty actual bags, I launched the website. The next morning, I was surprised to wake up with an order. It was for a bag that my sister gave me to list on the website. I remember thinking, "This is really an ugly bag. Who would buy this thing?" (laughs) The bag was an outdated Burberry bag, a British brand, made in Italy, sold in New Delhi for like $200. It was hard and not pretty to look at all. The original price of the bag was $1,000, and I sold it for $500. I gave her more money than she had paid for it! Then, I was like, "Wow! This is crazy!" A customer bought it in Bur Dubai. We couldn't believe it. I was like, "What's going on? Why would a buyer in Bur Dubai come to my sister's address, take this item from her, pay cash, and be thrilled buying? Why couldn't you find it in the mall or in a specialty shop?"

That is the essence of the model. Beauty is really in the eye of the beholder. There is also a huge gap between what items brands were giving the customers and what the customers actually wanted. The question was, "How big is the gap?" Well, as it turned out, it's a huge gap. It's a massive gap between what the customer really wanted and what was available.

As I mentioned, I started with fifty bags, then items started rolling in. It became 100, 200, and so on. We started selling $5,000 bags, $10,000 bags. We were up to $15,000-$20,000 in monthly revenue. My friends told me, "There is a lot to get done here and to keep doing all this work yourself. Find investors for your capital so you can hire and scale the business properly." That made a lot of sense to me.

One of my earliest investors was MEVP (Middle East Venture Partners). They came in and they were very, very quick. They discussed with me for a week and closed in a week. Then Walid Hanna, their founder and CEO, came down, greeted me for half an hour, shook my hand and said, "You'll have the money tomorrow." I just raised $200,000. They literally had the money to my bank account in two days. It was great! I found a small office, hired a few people on board, and just started from there.

We raised a few hundred more thousand dollars, moving us from Series A to Series B. We grew the business from the initial fifty items we launched with to nearly 20,000 items online we have today. We are now collecting more than a million and a half dollars per month.

Were there any challenges you faced during this time?

The challenges we faced were trying to figure out how to build an e-commerce business. How do you set up a company in Dubai? It was more complicated than I had anticipated. You spend way too much time trying to set up some really basic stuff because the ecosystem was practically nonexistent back in 2011. There weren't any answers out there. How do I incorporate a company? Do I incorporate a bigger company? A Cayman Islands company? How does it make a difference? What is going to happen in the future if people are not going to be funding because of it? I was doing the M&A (mergers and acquisitions), and I couldn't find a decent lawyer. So I decided to write down the agreement myself. It was just chaos. One investor dropped out. He said, "This is a Dubai entity. It makes no sense for me." So it was very confusing in the beginning.

With any new startup, there's a certain level of minimum frustration you go through. Hopefully, it stays minimum, and that's normal. You have to just go through it till things get better, though you can't really eliminate problems altogether. In a way, if you don't have problems, you really don't have a business. Having said that, over time, I think that my brain has become completely immune to frustrations. It's like when mothers go through childbirth, and it's a traumatic experience, yet they forget about it and move on afterward. I think I have become more like that (laughs).

Did the business turn out the way you had expected?

I think that in many ways the business turned out a whole lot better. I remember looking at revenue numbers of our competitors and admiring them. We're much bigger now than all those companies. However, I think that it has taken us much longer to get there. It has been much more complicated to get there. There have been a lot more challenges than I expected. When I started, I was like, "I'll do what it takes." Now, what I estimated would need to be done was like one-tenth of what actually needed to be done. In the middle of that was just people management, recruiting and execution, execution, execution. Just boatloads of execution.

Any missteps and lessons that come to mind?

In terms of lessons, I think that what I learned most is that you have to choose a business that has a large market. You hear this all the time, but if there wasn't a large market, then people just wouldn't list their bags and other luxury products. In the beginning I also remember thinking that revenue would come from everywhere: Dubai, Saudi, Qatar. So I immediately decided, "Let's just pick up and run there and put all the stuff out there." It wasn't that simple. I ended up wasting energy. Learning how to prioritize was probably the biggest thing. I don't think I did it as well as I should have.

The second lesson was creating the team. Recruiting many A-players or what I call "hits" but also having way too many subpar ones or "misses." I think that you really have to find folks with experience. Think through what you want for your team. It needs to be lean and combine great skill, experience and motivation.

The third lesson is about technology and the need for top tech talent and technology process. When we started, I think we drastically underestimated how complicated it was to build a consumer-focused marketplace. It needs a complex back-end system. Initially, I started with a WordPress website, then we changed our developer and added a process, eventually adding one content person to this team who was a genius, thank God. Then we had to change our CTO and eventually went from one developer to six developers to now like twenty developers. There's a lot there to think about. I think we now have a very well-thought-out technology process, but it was quite an evolution and a lot of trial and error early on.

Finally, I think the data and finances must be very clear. Like, "What are you building? How will you build it? What will it cost? What is the budget and timing? You have to think about your assumptions, your forecast. You need to be on top of all of those things at all times.

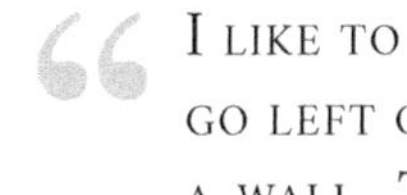

I LIKE TO TELL PEOPLE, DON'T PUSH A WALL. YOU HAVE TO GO LEFT OR RIGHT. THERE'S NO POINT IN TRYING TO PUSH A WALL. THE QUESTION IS, WHEN DO YOU REALIZE THAT YOU'RE FACING A WALL? YOU GET BETTER AND BETTER AT KNOWING AS YOU GO. THE FIRST CLUE IS ALWAYS DATA.

As an entrepreneur, how do you decide when to persist, shift, or quit?

That's a very interesting question. I like to tell people, don't push a wall. You have to go left or right. There's no point in trying to push a wall. The question is, when do you realize that you're facing a wall? You get better and better at knowing as you go. The first clue is always data. You just have to read data to see what is actually happening in the business and whether you need to go left or right.

You really have to get granular, to break it down, break it down, break it down. Understand the problem in-depth. The root cause of the problem might be three levels down, so you have to keep probing and removing layers to get to the bottom of it. Then you have to make quick decisions. That's also really important. Agree to disagree at times and then execute, and then measure again. This is the bread and butter of startup learning: analyze, execute, measure, tweak.

Do you have any marketing insights from building The Luxury Closet?

I would say the biggest realization is that in our business, there is no point in finding more customers until you know how to treat your current customers extremely well. We've had the same website traffic level for two years. There's just no sense in trying to grow the number of website visitors unless you can ensure an awesome customer experience. That's where the magic needs to happen, when they visit the website—having the right product catalog, which matches what people actually want and making sure they have an all-around awesome experience. It will bring returning customers. All those things are critical.

I also think content is very important. You have to learn to speak the language of luxury, if that's the business you're in. That's been important for us. That entails everything from branding to UX (user experience) to messaging, recognizing that your target demographic is different and thus needs to be treated differently than you would ordinarily.

Finally, data. Even though we're not a large company, we have one guy who is dedicated full-time to data analysis and feeds his findings to the marketing team. Everybody needs a formal data guy. Otherwise, the manager will have to spend X amount of their time doing data and calculating, worrying about greater turnaround time and backlog on every single step and so on.

Can you describe briefly your recruitment methods?

I think we have a very good recruitment process. If we're recruiting a hundred people, out of that, five will come from recruiters. The other ninety-five will come from our own internal recruitment process. I think we're kind of unique in that sense, in that we're able to be self-sufficient when it comes to recruiting. This entails creating a great LinkedIn page. More people follow us on LinkedIn than on Instagram, which is ironic, being a fashion company. The other thing is writing great descriptions, having A/B testing of names of jobs to see which one gets more applicants, headhunting on LinkedIn, even using recruitment software, which is very beneficial. So it really worked out very well for us where others have struggled.

Any learning resource you recommend for entrepreneurs?

Yes, my favorite now is a podcast called "Masters of Scale" by Reid Hoffman. It's amazing and just brilliant and invaluable to entrepreneurs. The show sets out to describe how some of the most successful entrepreneurs out there managed to take their business from zero to gazillion.

I WOULD SAY THE BIGGEST REALIZATION IS THAT IN OUR BUSINESS, THERE IS NO POINT IN FINDING MORE CUSTOMERS UNTIL YOU KNOW HOW TO TREAT YOUR CURRENT CUSTOMERS EXTREMELY WELL.

Do you feel that schools are doing enough to prep entrepreneurs?

I went to the University of Sharjah in the UAE once to speak to some students. It was a shocking experience for me, I have to say. I was at a fashion conference. I turned around and asked the students, "Listen, how many people here have had mathematics courses in the last three years?" Few people raised their hands. "Statistics?" I asked. Even fewer raised their hands. I was like, "OK, engineering students. Any engineering students here?" Like one person raised their hand. I said, "Really? How many students want to do social media?" 90 percent of the audience raised their hand. I was like, "Wow!" Schools are outputting students who all want to be social media managers, but are they really prepared?

Obviously, you need to have flair for content as a social media manager. However, social media managers also need to know how to convert audiences and do basic math. We see all these new graduates, many who went to school in Dubai, who are sorely lacking Excel experience. I mean, the conduit itself. I feel like sometimes we are a country full of people who can't do Excel presentations.

So I think in terms of the education system, it really lacks some fundamentals. I only wish that schools would produce more engineers. India, for example, is full of engineering talent. So often, when you start building a startup in the region and you need 100 engineers, you have no choice but to go to India and find your 100 engineers who will essentially build your company.

Do you think leaders have a responsibility to give back?

I think they really do. I think the best example out there is Fadi Ghandour. He's really an icon. He really understands what it means to be an entrepreneur, and given what he had to go through to build Aramex, he's very empathetic with other entrepreneurs. He really understands the journey, and he really gives back. That's what it's all about. Somebody becomes successful, and then they, in turn, become a mentor and an investor and start more companies. Then it just makes the entire ecosystem go around and gets bigger.

There are other examples of people out there that help everybody else. Then I know people who don't tell anything. They're extremely secretive. Of course, that's not conducive to the ecosystem. I really wish there were more people like Fadi.

Anything you've come across that you feel is counter-productive to startups?

I think that startups are unique. They are in a unique space. I don't think that many people understand that space. My biggest shock has been in people who are at high-level positions in the corporate world who are advising entrepreneurs. I'm personally very scared of people who think that their corporate know-how is necessarily great for startups. I think this can kill a startup.

Startups are so different from large corporations, in terms of risks involved, your past experience, how far you see, how fast you move, how quickly you have to react, your priorities, and your budget. People need to better understand what it takes to build a company at this stage of development and tried and proven methods involved, and not blindly follow corporate footsteps.

What is your definition of success?

That's a great question! I think, as a business, my aspiration is to build a company that customers really obsess about and they really love, and with a fair number of customers; that also has great DNA, from a brand and culture perspective; and that lasts 100 years.

If you ask me personally, I think it doesn't matter what I do, as far as personal success goes, as long as I always focus my effort on one thing that I do really, really well, and combine that with a bunch of other things that I do pretty well. Among these things, my family comes at the very top. You need to take great care of your family, but otherwise, your "one thing" is completely flexible.

BANA SHOMALI

Making finding and booking home services easy

Co-Founder and CEO of ServiceMarket

WWW.SERVICEMARKET.COM

Bana Shomali co-founded ServiceMarket in 2013 with Wim Torfs to innovate the home services industry in the UAE. After realizing that many residents struggled to find and hire professional home services companies, Bana set up ServiceMarket, where customers could get free quotes for any home service they required and book the service online. Before founding ServiceMarket, Bana worked as a consultant for McKinsey & Company in Dubai. She is also a Fulbright scholar and has an MBA from Vanderbilt University in Nashville, Tennessee, in the U.S.

What's your background, and how was your childhood experience?

I was born in Amman, Jordan, in 1980 to a Palestinian father and a Jordanian mother. Soon after, we moved to Kuwait. My dad owned and ran a software company there, building customer relationship management (CRM) solutions for businesses who wanted to digitize their processes.

My early childhood was in Kuwait. As an expat child, I lived a relatively comfortable life and studied in a very good private school, Kuwait English School. Every summer, we would go back to Amman for the holidays.

In the summer of 1990, we traveled to Amman for the holidays as we did every year. Little did we know that our lives would take a completely different turn that summer. On August 2, 1990, the Gulf War broke out. I remember being glued to CNN in those days, watching what was happening in Kuwait. This was a very seminal point in our lives. Our lives were uprooted because our family could not return to Kuwait. We had nothing but our suitcases and our summer clothes in Amman, and that's how we started over. At the age of 40, my father and mother had to start from scratch in a new country while raising my three brothers and me.

It was a very stressful time for us to say the least, but I think it played an important role in forming our perspective early on. In a way, my brothers and I felt that our backs were against the wall and that we had to learn to work hard and depend on ourselves. As a result, we all ended up being straight-A students and graduating at the top of our class. It might not have happened if we didn't have to face this sudden change and challenge in our lives.

Even though I was the only daughter, I never felt that my parents had different expectations and aspirations in terms of my education and career than my brothers. My loving parents and the great mentors I had in my childhood presented life to me as an opportunity as long as I worked hard for it. They taught me that life didn't owe me anything. I would only be successful if I studied hard, kept my grades up and stayed focused.

Any remarkable experiences you had in school?

When I was 16, I applied for a scholarship program to the United World College in Wales, U.K. The program allows youth from more than 150 countries to apply. The students selected from all over the world get to complete the last two years of their high school at the United World College and earn an International Baccalaureate.

I went through a series of interviews and exams before I was the one selected from Jordan that year. I was just 16 when I left the comfort of my hometown, my family, my school, and my friends in Amman and moved to the U.K.

Looking back, those two years at United World College were probably the most incredible two years of my life. It's a school where every student was hardworking, high-performing, and ambitious. Though many came from challenging environments, all of us were on equal grounds financially, since everyone was on the same scholarship. We were all there to succeed, while learning about each other and our cultural backgrounds. There were over a hundred countries represented by students in the program. For example, there were students from Pakistan, Uganda, Trinidad and Tobago, the U.K., France, and Norway. I made friends from all over the world.

My experience was exceptional. I moved from the small city of Amman, where everyone looks the same, speaks the same language, does the same things, to a culture which was hyper-international and extremely open and liberal. It was a fantastic experience for me to have at 16, as it also shaped my perspective on life. I realized how big the planet is and how the whole world is essentially one giant opportunity.

Where did you land your first job?

After university, I got my first job as a marketing analyst at the only mobile telecom player in Jordan at the time, Fastlink. In hindsight, I was very fortunate to have worked with the great people there so early in my career. I didn't realize at the time how lucky I was to have remarkable managers. They were fantastic coaches. They taught me how to think, how to analyze and how to present myself. They also gave me a lot of room to grow. I learned how to be a very secure and open leader from them and focus on building the team around me.

A few years after that, I decided to pursue a master's degree. I applied for the Fulbright scholarship and got accepted. I was very happy to be awarded the scholarship since I was among the fifteen candidates that were selected from Jordan each year to pursue a master's or Ph.D. degree in the U.S.

I enrolled at Vanderbilt University to pursue my MBA from 2005 till 2007. During that time, I applied for the summer internship program at McKinsey & Company in Dubai. I was selected, and at the end of the program, I was offered a full-time role.

What skill set did you develop at McKinsey?

I worked for McKinsey for six years. As you can imagine, it was very demanding in terms of the hours, the travel, and what was expected from you. You come into an environment like McKinsey, having historically been the top five percent of your class at school, only to realize you are average in that environment. You have to work exceptionally hard to inch your way up to be in the top 20 percent, then the top 15 percent and finally in the top 10 percent, which is incredibly challenging when everyone around you is as hardworking and ambitious as well.

Looking back at my career in McKinsey, it strikes me how exceptional of an organization it was to work for. Problem-solving is what McKinsey is known for, and rightly so. That was a very important skill set I learned at McKinsey, which comes handy in my business today. You learn how to take a very complex problem, break it down into components and then, one by one, slay the beast. It's a lot easier said than done, and it takes years of training to get to that point where you can take any problem, figure out how you would attack it and crack it.

That's a daily skill that you have to practice as an entrepreneur, because every day there are dozens of problems that are pushed your way from the tiniest issues to the very big ones. You need to be able to know how to think on your feet.

The second thing McKinsey stresses, a core to its approach, is once you have figured out the problem, ask yourself: "So what? What's the answer?" They teach you to have an opinion or perspective. The CEO of a client company, for example, doesn't want you to list the pros and cons of the problem or run a SWOT (Strengths, Weaknesses, Opportunities, Threats) analysis. She wants your opinion, your answer to the question, "What should I do?"

Besides everything I had picked up at McKinsey, it is also where I met my co-founder, Wim. When I moved to McKinsey Dubai, he had moved to Dubai from their Belgian office, where he was initially based. We ended up doing a lot of work together in the telecom sector. He was a senior McKinsey partner that I learned a lot from. I worked on his projects because he was known for being an exceptional leader and a great people person.

How did you decide to leave McKinsey?

I realized at the time that although I was moving along the ranks at McKinsey, it wasn't the right career for me in the long term. Although I was working with exceptional people, I just felt that there was more to life than crunching numbers, making slides, presenting and hoping for the best that your ideas would be implemented.

If I was going to be working eighteen hours a day, then why not do it for myself? The personal ROI on the number of hours spent on building something for myself was much higher than the ROI on hours spent working for someone else. I knew I had to get out and find a different path for my life.

I also thought that if I was going to be working eighteen hours a day, then why not do it for myself? The personal ROI on the number of hours spent on building something for myself was much higher than the ROI on hours spent working for someone else. I knew I had to get out and find a different path for my life.

On New Year's Eve 2013, I was out with a good friend, complaining about being stuck in my job and not knowing what to do. She said something like, "Sometimes you just need to take the first step. You don't necessarily need to know what comes after that, but if you take that first step, the rest will follow."

What she said resonated with me, and I decided to leave McKinsey at that point, even though I wasn't sure about what I was going to do next. As soon as I got back into the office on January 3, I walked into Wim's office and told him that I was going to quit McKinsey. Even though I had just been promoted to associate partner, I didn't want to stay any longer.

He asked me if I had a backup plan or knew where I was going. I said, "I have no idea. But if it means if I have to sit for a year and search for the meaning of life, I'm going to do it, because I think it's the right time." So just like that, I quit McKinsey.

How did ServiceMarket come into the picture then?

I had a conversation with Wim a few days after I resigned. He said, "You know, if you're leaving, I've always had this idea that no one has launched yet in the UAE. I have seen this concept of service market-places just start and scale in Europe and the U.S. Why don't we try to do something together? I'll be the investor with a couple of other people. Why don't you help us out?" That's how the idea of Service-Market was germinated.

I think back to the advice that my friend gave me: how taking the first step allows other things to fall in place. Well, ServiceMarket was born when I took the first step to leave McKinsey, and I allowed it to come my way.

How did you and Wim start implementing the idea?

In 2013, Wim and I started bouncing ideas off each other on which service we would launch with. We would say, "Listen, let's start with one service. Do we start with laundry? Do we start with cleaning? Do we start with moving? What do we start with?"

We prioritized based on the size of the opportunity and ease of implementation. We ended up choosing moving services, because we realized that there was a lot of demand for it. We thought it was going to be much easier to implement because people plan moves a few weeks in advance. We could make a very straightforward website and wouldn't have to do anything on-demand like cleaning or laundry, where people need it right away and where the necessary logistics could be tricky.

From the day we decided to launch with the moving service till the day we went live was a grand total of six weeks! We launched with a website that was a total of three pages long, that's it. We called it MoveSouq.com. It had a form that people filled if they needed to move. Once the form was filled and submitted, the screen said, "Thank you very much. Someone is going to contact you shortly." Everything we did after that was manual. The data we were processing, every single request that we were getting, was in Excel.

Our plan was to launch with just one service in the simplest, most basic way possible and test to see if it works. We have adopted that approach with everything else that we have done since then. We try to launch concepts as fast as possible and then see if they work, and if they don't, we tweak them. If it doesn't work after two or three tweaks, we kill the idea and move on.

We went live the first of May 2013. That was the beginning of what is now called ServiceMarket. Ironically, my first day outside of McKinsey was the first day the website went live. Going live that day was great, because we started seeing requests come in right away. Soon after, Wim also handed his resignation to McKinsey. We were now officially partners in this new business.

What were those early days like?

The early days were thrilling and exciting. The experience of going from something as specialized and hardcore as consulting to something as broad and rich as running a startup was great. Suddenly, you are involved in everything from choosing the color scheme of your website, to designing the logo of your business, to dealing with the movers, etc. For me, leaving corporate and a very specialized career to do this felt great, because it activated parts of my personality and skills that I hadn't utilized for a while.

I was able to tap all of those hidden skills and exercise muscles that I had a long time ago. I got a chance to brush up on my accounting skills, for example, from my early days at university. It felt refreshing to be involved in all the different parts of running a business.

In those early days, we were glued to our site. I remember monitoring the number of requests coming in obsessively. One day, it would be one request. Another day, it would be ten. Then, it would be five, and the next day, it would be zero.

I also remember when we first broke through ten requests a day. We bought a cake, and we went out for dinner to celebrate. No one realizes how long it can take to cross ten requests a day. Those were the early fun days that made you realize how much the small things matter and how much effort can go into making them happen. Before, at McKinsey, we were talking about millions of dollars of budgets with our CEO clients. Then suddenly, we were solving for how you go from nine to ten requests and from ten to eleven requests and celebrating them like they were big client deals.

So as an entrepreneur, you exercise a lot of aspects of your personality and skills that you probably won't when you are working in corporate. You celebrate the small things much more, because you realize how challenging it is to get those things to work completely from scratch.

What did you decide to focus on in the early days?

We focused on the moving services line for the first year or so, just trying to perfect that model of being a marketplace for moving services. Then we started, obviously, moving toward our ambition to become a marketplace for all services. We started taking on more and more services. We added a cleaning service, followed by a handyman service, then painting and then all these different services. We hired more people.

What were some of the challenges you faced in those days?

The earliest challenge that we faced was that we threw ourselves into this thing not knowing the first thing about digital businesses. As a result, there was a massive cost to learning. We made a lot of mistakes. We even got scammed a few times! Looking back, there was no other way to learn. I don't think we could've called anyone or talked to anyone who knew any better. There weren't a lot of people in the digital industry we had access to who knew what the right answer was. Thus, we had to learn everything on our own, and sometimes we had to learn the hard or expensive way.

Basically, figuring out the right answer for a digital platform was very hard. We had to read a lot, learn a lot, watch a lot of YouTube videos ourselves. We also learned that it's better to do it ourselves than use external providers, because then we could experience it and figure out what works the best for us rather than take a chance by outsourcing it.

It's a lot easier for startups today to figure out this stuff, because the industry is much more mature. In 2013, however, when we asked someone how to do SEO (search engine optimization), we would get ten different answers. That was challenging.

Another big challenge we faced was in 2015 when we went out for our first round of funding. Up until then, we had funded through friends and family. Our first attempt to get institutional funding through VCs was very difficult. Going out into the markets, presenting what we had done, going to meeting after meeting, and then getting a lukewarm response was challenging. We had to take it all in and keep at it. I think we met fifteen different VCs that year. We didn't get any yes's, and we didn't get any no's. It was very difficult being in the gray.

We were fortunate that someone finally introduced us to an angel investor who decided to put in a tiny amount of investment. Then the minute this person said yes, because of his influence and his network, we were able to get additional funding from other sources. Other angels came in and topped up the original investment. Luckily, a VC jumped on board in the final hour, and they ended up being the VC that, a year later, would fund our entire Series A investment.

Looking back at 2015, it was really touch and go when we first started to fundraise. Those were tough days, because there were days when I didn't know how I was going to pay salaries that month. All the while, I had to walk into the office and greet my team with a big smile regardless of how stressful the situation was.

Hiring was also very difficult. It was quite a challenge to excite people who were high performers, to tell them, "Come take a risk with us. Leave your very comfortable career, take a pay cut, work for longer hours and join me and Wim in our little office, because this is where the big things are going to happen."

How important is having a business partner?

I don't think I could've done this alone. The sheer amount of responsibility that you have toward your customers, employees and investors in a startup is massive. Everyone's looking at you to be the person who's going to make everything right and somehow find or have all the answers. Bearing that responsibility on your shoulders without having someone else to bounce ideas off is very difficult.

Having Wim by my side and me by Wim's side has been extremely important for the both of us. There are days when it's tough and we just need to vent and talk to each other. There are days when I'm feeling particularly low, and he's feeling stronger. There are days when he's feeling low, and I'm feeling stronger. We pick each other up, and we keep moving forward.

I was very lucky that I worked with Wim for six years before we decided to do this together. He was my mentor when I worked at McKinsey. I knew that I could count on him. It is important to go into business with someone whom you fully trust.

Having said that, don't just jump into partnership with anyone just because they share the same idea. It's not enough. More important than believing in the same ideas, you have to have the same values and perspective. I think that is very important for making such a partnership work.

Wim and I also complement each other. Our approach has always been divide and conquer. In the early days, Wim and I split our work more toward our natural strengths. Wim had a year of coding experience back in university, so he raised his hand and said, "I'll deal with the technology." I took operations and sales, which were more suited to my strengths.

So, partnership is like a marriage in the sense that it takes a lot of hard work to keep it going. It's not something that you can breeze through. You have to be dedicated to it. It takes actual work. If you have someone who will be a great support, that you fully trust and are willing to work with, then by all means, don't do it alone.

Did you always feel you were cut out to be an entrepreneur?

Funny you ask. I think if I looked at myself back in 2013 and who I knew myself to be, I think being an entrepreneur was the last thing on my list. I never saw myself as an exceptionally innovative person, nor was I ever a risk-taker. I'm just a hard worker. My reputation was that if you gave Bana something, it would get done and it would get done well. I'm also very sensory in that I like to do my homework and read the facts before I make any decisions, not the kind of fly-by-the-seat-of-her-pants person, so it's quite interesting to see where I ended up in my career.

Even though I didn't initiate the idea for ServiceMarket, the reality is that I ended up utilizing the same strengths I already possessed, from my ability to work hard and focus, to assess risk, to crunch numbers, and making sure everything works.

What lessons would you like to share with aspiring entrepreneurs?

What I found here in the Middle East is that there's very little investor appetite for ideas that cannot be monetized quickly. VCs here prefer investing where the business will be monetized from the first transaction. So that is something to keep in mind when you are starting out.

My advice here is to start meeting with investors early. Don't be afraid to talk to them openly about your idea. Get input early; allow them to follow your business and get some excitement built so by the time that you do need the cash, they know you, they've met you, and they trust you.

Another thing that we learned is that every time we had to launch a product, we spent too much time designing it, and in hindsight, we should've just launched the draft version, seen how it worked in the market, and then tweaked it afterward. Launching things quickly and seeing how they work is much better than spending hours and days and months trying to spec the Mercedes Benz version of the product.

The idea is to accept that you don't know what you don't know. You don't know how the product is going to perform in the market, so just launch it and then fix it as you go along. We use this saying a lot in the office: "You've got to fly a plane and build it at the same time."

MY ADVICE HERE IS TO START MEETING WITH INVESTORS EARLY. DON'T BE AFRAID TO TALK TO THEM OPENLY ABOUT YOUR IDEA. GET INPUT EARLY; ALLOW THEM TO FOLLOW YOUR BUSINESS AND GET SOME EXCITEMENT BUILT SO BY THE TIME THAT YOU DO NEED THE CASH, THEY KNOW YOU, THEY'VE MET YOU, AND THEY TRUST YOU.

What's your approach to marketing at ServiceMarket?

Marketing for us is essential. We focus predominantly on digital marketing and marketing activities that generate the biggest bang for the buck. For us, this is search-based marketing. So if anyone is looking for a mover or a cleaner or a painter, they should find us in their search results. We've not spent much on offline marketing yet.

We find that spending an extra dollar on AdWords from a revenue point of view gives us more returns than spending a dollar on a billboard or offline marketing activities, so we stick to what works for us.

Do you think creativity and flexibility are very important in a startup environment?

Absolutely! I think over time every company can build a bias to stop trying new things and just say that things have always been done this way. I think that being challenged by either new team members who join our company or new investors who join our board is very important. I remember that we had a big dilemma because of the way we had set up our system in the early days. Our tech team was saying, "It takes six weeks to launch a new service on ServiceMarket." With typical delays in development, this meant that it could take eight to ten weeks to launch one new service. As a company, our fundamental business case relied on us growing laterally by adding more services. With competitors starting to nip at our feet, such a delay was a massive issue. We would go back to our tech team hoping for a faster process, but the tech team had no way around it because they were dealing with our system, and that was the way we had built it.

Luckily, we got some blunt advice from one of our board members to "screw the system" and launch a new one from scratch. He was right. We realized it would take us less time to build a new platform that could scale easily than to try to adapt the existing one.

While the decision was risky, integrating this new system completely from scratch now allows us to launch a new service every week. As a startup, your agility and responsiveness are crucial for your growth and success in the long-term. You always have to challenge the way you do things and break the legacies or traditional ways of doing things. This is especially true when working with technology. And to do this, creativity is critical, and challenging the way things are being done is also very important.

What's your perspective on work-life balance during the startup years?

I think for the first time in my career, the word "work-life balance" bears no meaning for me. Every other time in my life, and especially when I was a consultant, it was something that I was continually optimizing for. But somehow when it's your own company, it's the last thing on your mind. There's such a joy coming to work every day when you know that it's something that you've built. The only reason you're there is because you want to be there.

I think it's still important to have the things that allow you to de-stress, whether that means retaining important connections with your family or your friends or traveling every so often. Working out is very important for me, for example.

That being said, I do get burned out sometimes. I think it is important to make sure that when I'm feeling burned out, I take my day away from the office and work from home, which helps.

What are your views on the startup ecosystem in the UAE?

Dubai has been very good to us in terms of the sheer amount of investment the UAE has put into the telecom sector and the kind of internet connectivity that everyone has here. Every single home is fibered up with high-speed Internet, and everyone is on great mobile data plans.

When you couple that with high spending power and high consumption power, you have a perfect place to say, "Hey, I have an idea for an online business. Let me try to see if it works." You have decent online adoption rates on one side and strong margins on the other. The ecosystem allows you to start a viable business quite early on, if you've got the right recipe or a good idea to begin with.

It's also relatively easier to set up a business here compared with the rest of the Middle East. Easy in the sense that Wim and I, as non-nationals, were able to walk into the free zone here and set up a company under our name, which is not easy in other parts of the world.

On the other hand, the reality of doing business in Dubai and the UAE is not entirely as easy as it sounds. There is a lot of paperwork involved, and you need a lot of cash outlay up front to start a business. We paid for a full year of office rent, licensing fees, residency visas and health insurance from day one, for example, and all of these expenses make the cost of running the business quite high. So while the margins and the early adoption rates make Dubai very attractive, the cost of building your business is also quite high. I think that there's a lot that can be done to make it easier and less expensive for people to set up businesses here.

Another missing piece in the tech startup in Dubai is the lack of enough local graduates who can code. At present, our graphic designers and developers are remotely based. I would say if this is going to be a market for tech in the future, the biggest thing missing is the talent pool around coders and programmers. It is the biggest challenge in the tech startup ecosystem here.

How effective has the UAE government been in promoting local small and medium-size enterprises, or SMEs?

Regarding the government's role to promote SMEs, I think they do quite a lot here. There are numerous initiatives and awards that they have going on.

I think there's a culture in Dubai and in the UAE driven from the top down to be the hub of innovation and leadership in the region. You can see Arab expats moving to Dubai because they feel like it's becoming the city of opportunity in the region.

It's quite telling that many of the most exceptional startups, whether it's Careem or Fetchr or Souq, that are getting tons of funding right now base themselves here in Dubai. That tells a lot about the UAE ecosystem.

What is one government regulation you would like to see changed to further promote business?

Without sounding too political, I would say that a path should be created for talented people to make the UAE a place they can reside in for the long term. Right now, all these beautiful, talented people who have chosen Dubai as a home to start their careers don't have much security beyond their current job. They might have to leave at any moment. Creating a path for them toward long-term residency in the Gulf could be a great thing. It would also be beneficial to the UAE economy overall.

What role do schools play in prepping the youth to be entrepreneurs?

The most important skill set that schools should teach kids is problem-solving and applying knowledge. The focus should shift away from rote memorization. Success in life nowadays is all about your ability to process knowledge and make decisions based on it. Knowledge, in the age of Wikipedia, is at our fingertips. The real question is what do you do with that knowledge and whether you're able to make the right decisions based on it.

That's a very important skill set for the youth to learn. I was lucky that my schools didn't focus on memorizing stuff, as is traditionally the case in schools in the Middle East. It was a lot more of problem-solving and critical thinking.

Did you ever feel shortchanged for being a woman in a male-dominant tech world?

Honestly, I never felt that I was being shortchanged for being a woman. Whether I was at Fastlink, McKinsey or ServiceMarket, or even here in Dubai, that never happened to me. I don't take it for granted, though. I realize that it's not the same for a lot of women who grew up in more challenging environments. I know a lot of my friends that attended school in Amman weren't allowed to study or work abroad because they were women, but their brothers were. I was lucky like that when it came to career or education; my parents never stopped me; they never said no.

What was the biggest insight you've gained running this business?

The biggest insight, I think, is to never underestimate the power of the internet and of connectivity in general. I personally didn't think people would book certain services online until we launched them, but they did. So never say never. Try it and see. You'll be surprised what customers are willing to do online in the privacy of their own home. Don't just assume that they won't behave a certain way; test it out first.

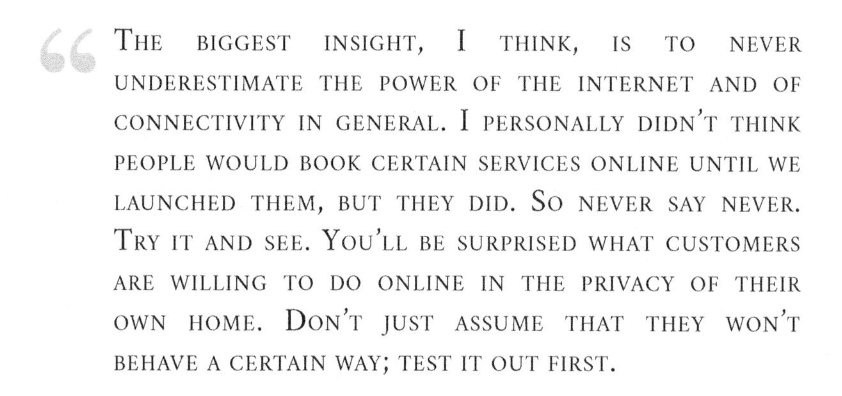

"The biggest insight, I think, is to never underestimate the power of the internet and of connectivity in general. I personally didn't think people would book certain services online until we launched them, but they did. So never say never. Try it and see. You'll be surprised what customers are willing to do online in the privacy of their own home. Don't just assume that they won't behave a certain way; test it out first.

What are you most proud of accomplishing with ServiceMarket so far?

There are many things that I'm proud of. I'm proud that we were able to launch something that was completely new to the UAE. I'm also proud that we chose an industry (home services) that globally, no single online player has "cracked" yet, and that here in the UAE, ServiceMarket is innovating at the same level as home services startups in the U.S., U.K., Europe and Asia.

All in all, I'm most proud of the team we have built. The team at ServiceMarket is my family, and I'm so happy to have put together such a strong, ambitious, creative and committed group of people.

What's your vision of ServiceMarket and the impact you'd like to create?

My vision is that one day, you'll speak into your phone and say, "Siri, book me a cleaner for tomorrow," and Siri will use ServiceMarket to make that happen. I want ServiceMarket to be the one-stop shop for any service you need at home and want the service to be at everyone's fingertips at any time. We are working very hard every day to make that vision a reality—and I hope that if we are successful, we'll have made everyone's life in the UAE a little bit easier and happier.

Looking back, what are your thoughts on the decision to leave a comfortable corporate environment to start ServiceMarket?

The decision to leave my corporate job was the best decision of my life by far. I'm so happy that I took the decision to quit in 2013, even though I didn't have a plan in mind. I wouldn't have imagined that four years later, I would be working with someone I looked up to a lot, having a great time on this journey and building what we've built so far.

ELIE HABIB

Making music accessible anytime, anywhere

Co-Founder of Anghami

WWW.ANGHAMI.COM

Elie Habib is the co-founder of Anghami, the leading music streaming service in the Middle East. In late 2012, seizing the opportunity created by the lack of a proper digital music service, Elie and his partner, Eddy Maroun, launched Anghami (which means "my tunes" in Arabic). Since then, and in less than one year, Anghami has reached more than 60 million users, streamed nearly 28 million licensed Arabic and English tracks and is integrated with seven mobile operators. Anghami successfully raised more than $30 million from venture capitalists and partnered with MBC, the top media group in the region, to raise digital awareness. At Anghami, Elie runs the operations and product development, spending most of his time essentially working between clouds, streams and pixels. Before Anghami, Elie co-founded PowerMeMobile, a mobile messaging gateway provider. Prior to that, he was the CTO of one of the first portals in the Middle East, Naharnet.com. Elie was selected as an Endeavor high-impact entrepreneur in 2013 and a Lebanese Top Entrepreneur in 2012 and 2013.

Can you tell us a bit about your background?

I was born in Lebanon just before the war. Then we had to move once the war started, which affected my schooling quite a bit. I had to adapt to this new environment. One thing that helped me during this difficult time was becoming a scout. It taught me a lot of things, including leadership and working within a group. I learned to make decisions for the betterment of the group, rather than just for my benefit.

When I was eight years old, my father got me my first Sinclair ZX81. It was my first computer. That's when I learned and essentially became addicted to programming. I was constantly writing code growing up. As I got older, I started writing algorithms. The mere idea of being able to create something from scratch was captivating. I was very proud of what I could create by myself, especially at such a young age. I remember developing a software for accounting and stock inventory for my dad's factory. I even sold my first software when I was 18.

When the war stopped, I decided to stay in Lebanon and attend the American University of Beirut. I studied computer science. I became really engrossed in the subject and graduated at the top of my class. Given my high grades, I was offered a lot of jobs. I decided, however, to build software for pharmacies. Prior to that, I had never thought about pharmacies. This field was particularly new to me, but I saw an opportunity. There was no software for pharmacies in Lebanon at the time. So I created a company with two of my friends from university. We called it "ACE."

We specialized in software for pharmacies and eventually expanded to car rentals and restaurants. During 1995-1999, we signed up 300 pharmacies, which was a lot back then. Bear in mind, there was hardly any consumer internet at the time. This was an interesting project initially, but I eventually got bored with it, as I wanted to tackle bigger and more challenging problems. So I decided to move on, though ACE is still around today. However, I learned a lot, especially that you can get into businesses you know nothing about if you're willing to learn and work hard.

When did you first get involved with the internet?

I took an e-commerce software class online. It was interesting. At that point, I didn't know how to code on the internet, only on software. It was a new challenge. So I taught myself and got a freelance job creating a site called GetForLess.com. It was the first e-commerce service in Lebanon where you could browse, buy, pay online and get your purchases delivered. It was quite an interesting project, and all the tech was built just by me. Ever since, I've been in love with the internet.

Shortly thereafter, a team from *An-Nahar* newspaper, which is a leading newspaper in Lebanon, reached out to me to build a portal that was intended to be similar to Yahoo! and would feature news, forums, clubs, shopping, etc. I worked day and night for three months to meet deadline and loved every minute of it. I remember even sleeping in the office at times. I knew I was creating something that was very big, so I poured my heart into it. The passion of creating something that big trumped anything else. It was called Naharnet.

While seeking monetization ideas for Naharnet, I discovered the concept of text messaging or SMS starting from ringtones and logos to massive messaging campaigns. I ended up creating an infrastructure that connects to mobile operators and enables users to send and receive SMS messages. I was proud of creating that, even though that wasn't part of the original scope. We created a company out of that concept—called PowerMeMobile—and scaled a team of over forty-five people working on it to sell the messaging infrastructure to over seventeen mobile operators across the Middle East.

Do you remember how the idea of Anghami first hit you?

My friend Eddy and I were having a conversation one day about skiing. He was telling me how much of a hassle it was to get music on his iPod every time he went skiing. There was no iTunes at the time in Lebanon, so he had to buy the music, put it on his iPod and then copy it. He would have to sit at the computer every time he would want to change the music. He thought that there had to be a better way to do this. That really stuck in my head. Eventually, I told Eddy, "There's a way we can fix this problem." That was how the original concept came about of how we got started working together on Anghami, which is what we decided to call the company, meaning "my tunes" in Arabic.

I then started doing research on how to create the streaming, how to store all the data, how to encode, and all the various aspects of creating this service. I was thinking how to configure such service for the web; meanwhile Eddy was figuring out how we could commercialize this service in the market.

We also knew that mobile operators were interested in adding more value-added services beyond their basic data offering, so we thought they would be potential partners for Anghami. We also thought that we could leverage our experience and contacts with operators, from our experience building the SMS infrastructure, to do deals with operators for Anghami.

WE REALIZED THAT WE HAD TO BE DIFFERENT. WE COULDN'T ASSUME THE SAME MARGINS THAT SPOTIFY WAS DOING. MUSIC STREAMING AT THAT TIME WAS STILL UNHEARD OF IN THE MIDDLE EAST. NOBODY KNEW WHAT MUSIC STREAMING WAS. SO WE THOUGHT MAYBE OUR OPPORTUNITY WAS THE FACT THAT IT WAS STILL NEW, AND WE COULD JUMP ONTO SOMETHING THAT NOT A LOT OF PEOPLE KNEW ABOUT AND BE THE FIRST TO MARKET.

Who was your competition at the time?

When we started analyzing the competition, we came across Spotify. I hadn't heard of them prior, but they seemed to have done something like what we were thinking of. There was also a company called Deezer, but it was a French-only streaming service at the time. There was also Rhapsody in the States, but we hadn't been able to use any of these services or really experience them properly.

We realized that we had to be different. We couldn't assume the same margins that Spotify was doing. Music streaming at that time was still unheard of in the Middle East. Nobody knew what music streaming was. So we thought maybe our opportunity was the fact that it was still new, and we could jump onto something that not a lot of people knew about and be the first to market. At the time, I read a lot about timing, whether you're launching too early or too late, and I was worried about whether we were too early for such a service in the Middle East.

How did you arrive at the right business model for Anghami?

We thought we could try to figure out a better business model than what was out there. That's when we approached Rotana Media Group, the largest Arabic music label in the Arab world. They didn't know much about music streaming back then, let alone were using it to monetize their content. Rotana was especially important for us, being the dominant music player in the region. We wanted to make sure we secured our place in the space by locking in a tight partnership with Rotana, so as to make sure that no one else could come in and take our place. So we did a deal with Rotana whereby they would have license to our platform for three years.

From a business standpoint, this was a great milestone for Anghami. On a personal level, however, this was a very difficult time for Eddy and me. We had just left our older business. Meanwhile, my wife was pregnant with my second baby. I had to put up money for the business from my own pocket. So it was quite overwhelming, but we didn't have a choice. We had to move forward and protect our future business. After Rotana, we went to the other labels. They were much easier to sign. That's when we realized fundraising was critical for our survival.

How was your early experience with VCs?

Initially, I didn't know anything about VCs and had to learn about fundraising on my own. I bought and read this book, *Venture Deals: Be Smarter Than Your Lawyer and Venture Capitalist* by Brad Feld. It was quite helpful. It teaches you what you should expect in a term sheet, which terms you should ask for, which terms you should be careful with, and which terms you should flat-out refuse.

I then started reaching out to VCs on LinkedIn, with very little response back from investors. Then I remember getting a reply that said, "Good luck with what you're doing. There's something called

Spotify. Take care!" I guess most of the replies were very discouraging. A couple of investors dropped out. Eventually, MEVP (Middle East Venture Partners) remained interested and serious about moving forward with us.

We were initially asking for $2.2 million but were able to raise only $1 million. This was very hard for us given our cost structure and growth plans. It did, however, enable us to focus on priorities. That taught us how to do more with less. After six months, we took in another $250,000 from deals we made with mobile operators even before we launched. We wanted to demonstrate we could monetize from day one.

We eventually launched Anghami on November 5, 2011, with Orange, a leading mobile operator in Jordan. It was a great deal for us. We initially launched our app on iOS and then on Android a month later. It was quite challenging to develop those products back then. I think we were the first ones in the region that created a product at such a scale. We didn't outsource any of the buildout, and it was very difficult because we couldn't find the proper talent. I had to learn everything myself first and pass it on to the team. With Orange under our belt, we had a good case study that we could now showcase to other mobile operators.

How did your strategic partnership with MBC happen?

During our launch, we attracted the interest of MBC. They saw that the app had 5 million songs, Arabic and international, on both iOS and Android. They also knew that we managed to build all this with a relatively very small team and very small budget. MBC was impressed with Anghami because we had everything in terms of content, including Rotana. We also had a massive amount of Arabic and international content. When we first met with MBC, we were very small. We had something like 10,000 users per day, but we were very promising in terms of what we had built and how we'd progressed so far.

We realized that MBC could be a big driver for our growth. So we managed to strike a media-for-equity deal, whereby MBC would push us with several million dollars per year for the next three years in marketing ads, in exchange for giving up equity in Anghami. It made a lot of sense, and even though we would end up owning a smaller share in the company, we figured our reduced equity would probably mean a lot more with MBC marketing support. So we went for the partnership. We opened the service to the public on December 30, 2011, and signed the deal with MBC on the same date; that was also the date MBC had started showing our ads. So I could not forget that date. That was another milestone for Anghami.

I remember when MBC first started promoting us, I was on my laptop and there was a TV next to me. When our ads started showing on TV, all our controls, our servers, and everything became red because we had such a spike in usage, more than what our system was intended to support.

We went from 30,000 to 200,000 users in a matter of seconds. We weren't prepared for such sudden growth. We experienced a lot of problems on that day, and we had to learn and adjust fast. We had planned 350,000 users by the end of year one. We had one million users after three months. Then, three million and so on. We blew every expectation that we had very fast.

We also realized at the time we needed more localized content, so we started contacting content owners and content producers to get rights for CDs that were never digitized on Anghami. At the same time, we also made sure to understand what the user wanted and to give them more of what they want. So a person in Jordan is different from a person in Saudi, and the app needed to understand that logic and behave differently. We also needed to adapt to the technology based on internet connectivity and speed per given locality, which also differed from market to market.

We also worked with Dolby, which was great in terms of third-party validation. This helped strengthen our credibility as a brand and enabled Anghami to have Dolby Pulse music sound quality. There was only one other service in the world out of Germany that had this feature. So we were proud of being innovative in that regard.

We worked a lot to make sure that streaming would work well over a 2G network. I remember having a lot of road trips with me, my wife, and the kids, and listening to music from my home up to the mountains. We would stream continuously, without interruption, for the entire time we were there. That was quite an accomplishment. To this date, this feature is still there, allowing users with limited internet connectivity to receive a high-quality audio stream despite local infrastructure limitations.

Another good thing that we did with the addition of mobile operators was structure deals in a way that either they were paying us money or they were giving us marketing exposure. That way we were either growing our revenues or our user base, or both.

We also integrated mobile as a payment method so that the user would be able to upgrade to Anghami Plus, the premium functionality, via their mobile operator. This further helped grow our revenues. To date, 80 percent of our Anghami Plus revenue comes in from our mobile operators because of how we could localize and making sure the content and the user experience, including payment, is the right fit with that market and consumers we were serving.

What kind of challenges did you face early on and how did you deal with them?

We faced many challenges in those early days. I remember we launched Anghami in an office that was very small. We couldn't afford a bigger office. At one point, we had twenty people in fifty-five square meters' space, including the entrance, the kitchen, and the restroom.

We desperately needed to grow our revenues, which depended a lot on advertising. We didn't understand advertising at the time. We initially thought we could sell audio ads because we "owned consumers' ears," so to speak. This proved to be incompatible with the region because there was no one selling audio ads back then. Eventually we figured out advertising, which now represents around 40 percent of our revenue and has become a key component to Anghami's growth.

Even though our investors asked us to grow our active-users segment, we made sure that we always kept working on revenues—hence our focus on advertising and making sure that our revenues were growing as well. We didn't want to risk hitting rock bottom again as has happened before. This entire experience was very educational. It taught us not to rely on whatever metrics, vanity or other, some investors or others tell you and keep our eyes on the prize.

EVEN THOUGH OUR INVESTORS ASKED US TO GROW OUR ACTIVE-USERS SEGMENT, WE MADE SURE THAT WE ALWAYS KEPT WORKING ON REVENUES—HENCE OUR FOCUS ON ADVERTISING AND MAKING SURE THAT OUR REVENUES WERE GROWING AS WELL.

What are some of the most effective marketing methods you found for Anghami?

We've tried many things that failed, that were theoretically supposed to work because they worked in the States or other countries. What we've come to realize is that localization goes far beyond localizing language of the product. It's localizing how the product behaves and how it interacts with users based on their specific local needs and behavior. The way you must market to people in the Middle East is not exactly how you market to people outside; customization by market and market segment is critical.

What we've also been seeing is that our organic traffic significantly beats our paid traffic. The reason organic works best is because when people tell other people about your service, trust gets passed on and they end up trying the recommendation.

Overall, our entire user acquisition strategy relies on data. What we've come to realize is that it's way more effective if we understand what users like and target them as such, instead of, say, sending generic messages to everyone. This takes the guesswork out of the whole thing. When we know that you like, say, a certain artist, we take a targeted marketing approach toward getting your attention. That is the best approach we found toward engaging users and cultivating word-of-mouth.

What we've also learned is that we should focus on offline marketing way more than we had originally anticipated. With so many messages constantly bombarding users online, things get blurry and messages get lost online, whereas in the Middle East, offline messages stand out and can better engage people.

I was in Los Angeles recently and noticed the billboards were mostly those of Amazon, Netflix, and Hulu. It was tremendous to see the focus on selling online content offline. Offline ads strengthen the credibility of online brands in the mind of the consumer, unlike online ads, which are a dime a dozen and don't necessarily communicate you're a good brand or one that people should trust or pay for. So what we've noticed is that when we started placing legit offline advertising, people were starting to love our service more because seeing with their own eyes, outside of their laptop or mobile, adds validation to the service. Granted, they didn't lead to an overnight conversion spike; still, they were essential to strengthening brand equity in the mind of the consumer.

What's your approach to customer service?

For us, customer service encompasses any touch point that the user communicates through Anghami. Since inception, we've added the ability for the user to reach out to us from within the app, and we would reply to them. We have a mailbox for people to complain to, but we also set up customer service around everything social. I'm talking about Facebook, Facebook Messenger, Twitter, Instagram, all of which have also become customer service communication channels.

All these communication channels enabled direct feedback of any given problem in real time, instead of waiting several hours before the customer care replies back. Whenever there is a problem, the customer care team can directly assign it to a product manager, so he can follow up with the problem and fix it.

Users love it because whenever they have a problem, we tell them it's going to be fixed immediately or give them a timeframe as to when it's going to be fixed. If they have an idea or complaint, we also make sure it gets passed to the product development team right away. That real-time engagement with our user base is one of the main reasons why Anghami is currently rated 4.7 stars on Android and 4.6 stars on iOS.

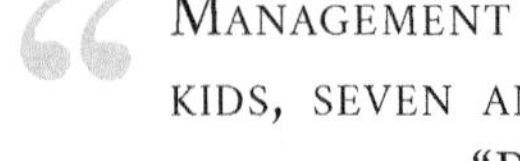

> Management is like parenting in a way. I have two kids, seven and ten years old. I noticed that if I tell them, "Please do this," most of the time they don't do it. On the other hand, if I tell them why I want them to do this, they get it, and they do it.

How would you describe your people management style?

When I want something from my team, I don't tell them, "Please do one, two, and three." I tell them instead, "This is the problem we have. The user is having this problem, and he is not able to understand this feature. So how about we do one, two, and three? Makes sense? Let's test it." The phrase "let's test it" is very important for us, because early on we discovered that we shouldn't trust our guts, that we should test everything first. We have a saying in the office whereby we say, "In God we trust, and the rest we test."

Management is like parenting, in a way. I have two kids, seven and ten years old. I noticed that if I tell them, "Please do this," most of the time they don't do it. On the other hand, if I tell them why I want them to do this, they get it, and they do it. Similarly, I remember one morning at the office, we had some technical problem. So I told one of the engineers to go ahead and fix this and that. I told him exactly what he should fix. Surprisingly, he didn't look at the things I asked him to look at; instead he went to look at where he thought the problem originated from.

The point is that when I told that engineer to go look at A and B, he didn't think that made sense. So he didn't follow my instructions, whereas if I had spent just thirty seconds to give him some background on the problem and explain to him my rationale, he would've fixed the problem within another thirty seconds.

So from that time on, I realized how important it was to always provide the right briefing and explain the "why." Why do you want to do this? This practice has become an integral part of how we do things within the product management team. They never tell an engineer what to fix. They never say, "Just implement A, B, and C." They always explain the context of a given situation and the analytics behind it to further guide an engineer in solving the problem from the right perspective.

What would you like to see in the future for Anghami?

Anghami grew way more than what we thought. A year ago, we crossed 30 million users. Now, we've just crossed 60 million users. It took us four years to get to 30 million users, whereas it took just another year or so to double that number. Clearly, that shows that we're on the right track.

While we believe creating and scaling the platform we have today is a great achievement, we are very aware we need to scale it even further. We also need to reach out to content creators. We think that our next step is to enable more people to create localized music, so that we can foster more Arabic music as a way to further preserve Arabic culture in the region.

We also like to believe that we will be able to change how music is consumed. We're glad to see close to ten million users using Anghami per month, but we think there's a lot more potential. Clearly, to continue to grow, we must think differently. Our future involves creating a different type of content that revolves around music and storytelling, which are very much interconnected. That's how, for example, we originally fall in love with artists, because they have good stories to tell. Lately, music has been devoid of stories. You listen to music, but you don't know the story around the song. We think our job is to become more of storytellers. If everything goes to plan, I think that would be a great legacy for us.

We're also working to create more live content and create more interactions with the artists across the region. That's not exactly tech, but we will keep evolving Anghami till it becomes as localized as possible in the region. We believe that going offline—that is, going out and creating events to engage users, beyond digital channels—is key to growing our user base. It's like we must go offline to hook folks to our online platform. Only time will tell if that's the right strategy.

We really believe connecting people through music, and artists to fans, is our mission. We really hope that Anghami's legacy is impactful. Ultimately, our users and our fans will be the ones voting on this. I'm optimistic about the future of Anghami and the space, though. I'm excited about what's happening in Dubai in terms of tech. I'm also very psyched in terms of what's happening in Saudi with respect to changes within the entertainment sector. The new changes in policies in Saudi and the region, as indicated by government interest to work with Anghami to do concerts, are promising. That really tells us there is a change that's happening, and we are part of that change. We're one of the critical items in the change in terms of entertainment. I really hope that we can fight terrorism, violence, and hatred with music and with the love of life, which is what music really is. I really hope that we will succeed with this mission and be able to leave our mark for the betterment of everyone.

12

OMAR GABR

Debugging applications

Co-Founder and CEO of Instabug

WWW.INSTABUG.COM

Omar Gabr is the co-founder and CEO of Instabug, a software company he co-founded with Moataz Soliman in 2012 that provides bug reporting, crash reporting, in-app feedback, and user surveys for mobile apps. As of July 2017, Instabug has been integrated in more than 800 million devices, including at least 26 of the top 100 apps globally. Instabug is also one of the fastest-growing software as a service (SaaS) companies in the world. He graduated from Cairo University, Faculty of Engineering.

Tell us a bit about your personal background.

I was born August 26, 1990, in Cairo, Egypt, where I lived most of my life in the Mohandessin district in the Giza area. I attended Misr Language School and eventually graduated from Cairo University, Faculty of Engineering, in 2012.

There aren't any engineers in our family, so growing up, I was this kind of curious person in the family who just liked figuring out how things worked. I liked playing with Lego. I liked building stuff and taking them apart. I would break things just to see how they were built from the inside and try to reassemble them again. I was always fascinated by how things were made, rather than the functionality itself. How does a radio work? How does a TV work? I was preoccupied with these kinds of questions from an early age. I had tons of fights with my family about things I opened up, thinking I would easily reassemble them, but of course that wasn't always the case (laughs).

I also had other interests—architecture, maps, you name it, even regular mundane day-to-day products. If it involved any kind of engineering or design behind it, it captivated me. It was as if I wanted to enter the mind of the creator of that machinery or tool and see things from their perspective and understand the behind-the-scenes workings of the world, at a granular level, as if it was some kind of mystery I was unraveling.

So engineering seemed to be the right choice for me. Since I also pretty much all around sucked in everything else (laughs). I really loved algebra, geometry, physics; meanwhile, I didn't like everything else. For some reason, I really hated biology. So you can say engineering was a natural choice, or perhaps my only choice.

I wasn't the kind of person that spent a lot of time studying in school. I preferred to develop a focused framework to learn things fast. You can say I was an efficient learner. Growing up, I also used to play a lot of sports. I was a competitive swimmer, training daily for nearly ten years. So I also didn't have that much time left to dedicate to my studies; all the more reason I had to figure things out fast at school, often last-minute, right before exams.

I met Moataz Soliman, who later became my co-founder at Instabug, in my freshman year at university. We were both studying computer science and communication, where we were learning telecommunications, computer programming, etc. It was always fascinating for me seeing how computers work from the inside, and writing a few lines of code, and seeing that pop on a computer screen. I wasn't that interested in programming, to be honest, but I was very curious and intrigued by the fact that you could build something from scratch from your own laptop.

My grades were kind of OK. Meanwhile, Moataz had the second- or third-highest GPA in the whole university. It was really fascinating meeting Moataz and witnessing a person with such a degree of dedication and drive. We worked together on most of the university projects, whether they were software or hardware. That's when we actually started to develop that kind of relationship that led us to start the company together later on.

Around the same time, I also got fascinated with the global tech scene.

I started reading about unicorns (billion-dollar companies), and I started reading about technology, Silicon Valley, Instagram was just sold to Facebook, startup of the year, and all kinds of tech and startup-related topics and news, all of which got me all the more interested in starting my own tech company.

Take us through Instabug's journey from the very beginning.

During our last semester in college, Moataz and I were just experimenting with iOS, and we started building a basic mobile app. It was a social and geolocation-oriented app. In spite of this being our first time around the track building an app of any kind, we had quite high aspirations for it. We literally thought we would launch and get millions of users the next day (laughs). Then, right before launching it, we decided maybe it would be a good idea to just send it out to a few of our friends and get their feedback. We figured it wouldn't hurt to see what they said regarding design, usability, functionality, and overall potential before we release.

Since our app was global by design, we thought maybe we should also test with a global audience, beyond our small circle of friends. We figured there had to be some kind of website or platform that you could test your beta app on and get user feedback, in exchange for small compensation, say a Starbucks card or an Amazon gift card. Surprisingly, we couldn't find such a website, so we thought that would actually be something interesting to build.

So we decided to pause working on the app and actually started building that platform. The concept was to build a basic website that utilized crowdsourcing for mass testing of beta apps. That way, any developer who was building an app could go to the website and find a community of early adopters who were actually willing to test the app and provide usability feedback.

We decided to focus on building this website for the next few months and ended up applying to Flat6Labs, a leading regional startup accelerator program in Egypt, with that idea. They accepted us, and we got incubated there for a few months developing this concept. This was all fresh out of college in 2012.

We called the product AStarApps and spent a few months working on it before we launched. We then went knocking on every door we could think of all over Cairo, even in Alexandria. We would literally email everyone, go visit companies and say, "Hey, we are a couple of guys that have just built this new tool. Would you give it a spin and let us know your feedback? It is totally for free. We are just here for the feedback."

INTERESTINGLY ENOUGH, THERE WAS ONE PARTICULAR FUNCTIONALITY THAT EVERYONE LIKED. IT HAD TO DO WITH ENABLING TESTERS TO REPORT BUGS OR SEND FEEDBACK EASILY TO THE DEVELOPER OF THE APP, DIRECTLY FROM INSIDE THE APP, INSTEAD OF SENDING EMAIL OR ATTACHING SCREENSHOTS.

We didn't know anything about business or sales at the time. We were just these two inexperienced kids who built something that we thought was valuable, and we were just trying to get out there and get some feedback. Ironically, we were doing manually, the hard way, what this product we built was intended to do efficiently using technology. There was no other way to do it at the time.

We visited more than sixty companies in Egypt that were doing anything related to mobile apps. Things quickly became really confusing and frustrating. Everyone we met had the same feedback: "This product just sucks. It is really bad. It sucks in terms of design. It sucks in terms of functionality. You are combining a few different platforms in one thing, which does not make any sense." Their feedback was as harsh as you can get; they simply hated it.

Interestingly enough, there was one particular functionality that everyone liked. It had to do with enabling testers to report bugs or send feedback easily to the developer of the app, directly from inside the app, instead of sending email or attaching screenshots. As much as everyone loathed everything about this product, everyone thought this functionality was cool.

So then everyone started asking, "If you can give us just this one functionality, maybe we could use the product, but otherwise, forget it." Meanwhile, we were thinking, they don't really understand what we're doing. This is meant to be a whole platform. We can't just break out a single feature and throw away all the other features. They should either take it or leave it. We were now facing a dilemma as to what the next step should be.

I recall one interesting company we went to was like, "You guys look like real nice guys. We don't think that kind of startup life suits you, but the good news is that we have some vacancies. So if you want to join us and shelve this idea, we could actually help you get your careers up and running, and you could just forget about this whole thing." We weren't clear what the right decision was but thought maybe we could just give it another try and spend a few more months on it and see how it goes, then decide from there.

Everyone had the same feedback: "The product is bad; the feedback functionality is good." "The product is bad; the feedback functionality is good," and so on. Eventually, we bought into this feedback and started questioning whether the product as a whole was in fact a good fit, and how do we capitalize on this one feature that everyone liked? We were really lucky in a way to get this feedback early on before wasting more time on the wrong things.

We started thinking a bit differently and trying new things along those lines. We made this really cool video that showed a person holding a phone in their hand and shaking it. The phone then quickly captures a screenshot. They then enter some text and just press send, and their feedback or bug report goes somewhere. We posted this video on Hacker News, which is one of the biggest online communities of developers in the world. The response we got was really interesting. Everyone was saying, "Wow, that's really cool. We are going to try it. How much is it? Who are the people behind it?" What was even more interesting is that the feedback was coming from a diverse group of global developers, not just from Egypt or from any particular country or location. There seemed to be an appeal for this functionality among developers worldwide.

That's when we started thinking, we're onto something big. So we started building a prototype or MVP in 2013, using only the little money that we raised from Flat6Labs. I think we had like $1,000 left in the bank at the time and were desperate for additional funding to get the chance to make something great out of this.

We started talking to investors in Egypt, practically every investor in Egypt. All the investors we met had cold feet. They either didn't get the product or weren't sold on the market opportunity or didn't want to take a chance on some young folks, or all of the above. In short, everyone turned us down. It was really hard. So, with our back against the wall, our only option left was to build the product quickly and see if we could get any kind of traction in terms of usage, and meanwhile spend that $1,000 super-carefully.

That's exactly what we did. We built the prototype quickly, mimicking exactly the functionality we showcased in that one video we made. It was a really simple MVP, where you just shake the phone, enter some text, and send an email to the app or the developer behind the app. That was it!

So we launched in March 2013. We then went back and placed the actual product on the Hacker News site, and people started signing up. We had almost a hundred companies and individual developers sign up for the product just in the first few weeks. It was real interesting to see such uptake early on and all this organic interest from people everywhere, especially for an unfinished, unpolished, and unpromoted product.

In April 2013, we were very lucky to apply to the MIT Business Plan contest in Doha, Qatar. It was a very tough competition that had almost 5,000 companies applying from 21 Arab countries. It covered all kinds of technologies, mobile apps, education, games, software, tools, and all kinds of hardware, coming from the thousands of applicant startups applying.

We went through the entire process. It was a grueling few days, but we were really lucky to win the first-place prize and $50,000 check, which was an infinite runway at that time. We still had the $1,000 in the bank, which we were trying to survive on. Then suddenly, we had fifty times that amount in our hands. So, it was kind of a huge monetary boost that enabled us to implement our plans and not have to hold back. Not to mention, it was great validation that what we were doing was actually promising, as others saw the potential as well. It was very inspiring to say the least and served to motivate us to work even harder.

It was particularly interesting to see senior folks at top technology companies, Google, Facebook, etc., saying that they could really use a product like ours, all the more reason we were now more committed than ever to double-down and make the product even better.

Once we were back in Egypt, we were pushing on all cylinders, racing to building momentum, racing to grow on all fronts. It was quite an exciting phase and very productive to say the least.

A few months later, we applied to attend a big technology event in San Francisco, which was called Mobile Beat 2013. It's a big gathering of mobile developers from around the world. It's an invite-only event, and they choose five companies every year as the most innovative mobile companies to present their product on the stage. Four of the five companies were from the United States. Meanwhile, we were the only company from the rest of the world selected, and no company from Egypt or in Africa had ever been selected in this category. So this was a huge event for us. We were really looking forward to it.

We had everything lined up and worked really hard on our presentation and built all the features we would be showcasing at the event. We were just a week before launching the product at the event. This was July 10, 2013, and a few days before that we had the June 30th mass protests and all this political instability in Egypt. Then everything closed on July 3rd. We came to find out that the American embassy was also closed and there was no way for us to get a visa and fly to the U.S. It was just a sad moment for all of us, because everything was planned, and we felt that this was a once-in-a-lifetime opportunity.

We worked so hard to prepare for this event. We were going to be on stage in one of the biggest mobile events in the world, drawing the best of the best in the industry. We were ready to showcase our product with all the new features we had been tirelessly working on. There was press there, investors there and industry experts. This was the place we needed to be at this moment in time, and we had our invitation and were literally ready to go. It was heartbreaking. It was one of those moments where you feel life is unfair. We did everything right. We worked extremely hard. So why should events in the country outside our control affect the progress and future of the company?

We ended up calling a friend who lived in San Francisco and asked him if he could represent us at the event. We told him, "Hey, we need your help. We need you to get on the stage and present for us in front of all those people." Luckily, he happily accepted and did exactly just that.

He gave the presentation and actually launched the product on our behalf. I guess the lesson here, as an entrepreneur, is to always try to find a work-around, no matter how disappointing a given situation is. It's just part of business and life, as we came to learn.

When did you first make it to Silicon Valley then?

A couple of weeks afterward, things stabilized enough in Egypt that we were able to get our visas. So we traveled to the Valley and ended up staying for almost nine months. It was our first trip there. The main reason we were there was to meet big companies and gain a better understanding of how we could work with them and tailor to their needs. We just wanted to make sure that we had a product-market fit with big companies we would be working with. We knew this was a massive problem we were trying to solve for and needed to ensure we were approaching things the right way from the outset.

While there, even though Silicon Valley is a closed network, we thought it wouldn't be too difficult to set up meetings with all kinds of companies there. We wrote a cold email that basically said, "Hey, we have this new cool product. We just need to meet you and would love to get your feedback." We guessed all the different variations of someone's email, since we had zero contacts there. So, we would send, say, one email with firstname@dropbox.com, another firstnamelastname@dropbox.com, then another firstname.lastname@dropbox.com, and so on. We kept guessing people's emails and sending out all kinds of combinations. It was a bit of a time-consuming process, but we figured some of those emails would get through and land in the inbox of the right person. We did that for around thirty people. We had zero responses, not one. Not even, "Thank you, not interested." So, here we are, two weeks in the Valley, not a single meeting. We're practically doing nothing except guessing and sending emails, then waiting and receiving no replies.

I remember we were meeting one of our advisers at a tech company that he was working at, and right before entering the meeting, there were a few TV screens in the reception showing CNN with a big tagline, "What's happening in Egypt?" Everyone at the office was intrigued by the news and asking us all kinds of questions. It was complicated, so naturally no one had all the answers, so when we told them we were from Egypt, everyone turned around and started asking and listening to us. They were relying on us to shed some light on the situation and give some kind of coherent explanation. Just by saying that we were from Egypt, we got the full attention of people who were similar to the ones that weren't responding to our emails. That's when I thought we'd go back to the people we were trying to meet and piggyback off this sudden interest in events in Egypt. So we went back to all those folks and changed the subject line on the email to, "What's happening in Egypt?" We then sent the same email with a slight revision: "Hey, you are probably watching the news. Egypt is in the news. You probably have no idea what's happening, and we are probably the only two people in San Francisco that are just fresh off the boat and just landed in the city. So if you want to know exactly what is happening in Egypt, we would love to buy you coffee and tell you exactly what is happening. By the way, we have a really cool product that you could just check out. So let us know what you think." The response rate was phenomenally better.

Everyone started responding to these emails, and we ended up meeting everyone. We met with Dropbox, Pinterest, Facebook, Airbnb, SnapChat, Evernote, Square, Vevo, Google, all kinds of big tech companies that you could imagine. We went in there and we talked with them. We presented the product, we got their feedback, and we had really interesting insights about what is actually going on at their end and how we can build something extremely useful to them.

That was another valuable lesson we learned. Just a couple of months back, the events in Egypt were blocking our company's progress. Then we used the same events in Egypt to get our foot in the door with some of the biggest tech companies in the world and move closer to our business objectives. The lesson being, as an entrepreneur, learn to see the positive in a negative situation and try to use it to your advantage. Often, even the same negative situation can be spun around and made to work in your favor. That's one of our biggest mantras we try to instill in our team, which is simply, "Make it happen." Basically, find a way, stay positive, be creative, be patient, whatever, just don't give up. I really think that's why we don't have a micromanage kind of culture at Instabug, because we trust our team to take ownership and figure things out.

Right after we returned, we started raising our first round. We initially raised $300,000 from a few investors, some from Egypt and the Middle East and a few from California. In 2014, we started enhancing the product. We started adding more features. We added support to Android. We built tons of features based on the feedback we received and conversations we had with our users and with the big companies that we talked with. By the end of 2014, we reached the point where we actually had a really good product.

WE WANT TO BREAK THE MYTH THAT THERE'S NO OR CAN BE NO GREAT, WORLD-CLASS TECH STARTUPS COMING OUT OF EGYPT.

How did you secure funds from Silicon Valley investors?

By the end of 2015, in just ten months, we became a profitable company after we introduced a paid-subscription model. Then we applied to Silicon Valley-based Y Combinator (YC), which is one of the top seed accelerators for tech startups globally. They are the most prestigious network in Silicon Valley in terms of the kind of companies that they have under their umbrella. They are also one of the most successful tech investors in the world; they invested in Airbnb, Dropbox, Stripe, and a lot of other wildly successful tech companies. On the other hand, they are a very solid partner in terms of helping guide and support the startups they work with.

We were at YC program in Silicon Valley for three months and were extremely lucky to work closely with Sam Altman, the president of

YC. He was our mentor during the three months we were there. We got to spend a few hours every week with him. We talked about all kinds of things related to our business, including our product, pricing, strategy, team structure, fundraising, user acquisition, etc. That was quite an invaluable, educational experience for us.

Also during our time at YC, we got a chance to meet Accel Partners during our "Demo Day" in April 2016. They later become our lead investor. We met with Rich Wong, who is one of the early and only investors in Atlassian, the company that built Jira and built Bitbucket. He is also an investor in Mopub, Admob, Rovio, and a bunch of other successful companies on Accel's portfolio. Accel is one of the most successful investors in the world. They are one of the first institutions to ever invest in Facebook. They are also one of the biggest investors in Slack and in Dropbox, Supercell, and others. So just having them on board was a huge push for us.

Both YC and Accel were impressed with our product, team, and strategy. We were able to raise $1.7 million from one round with Accel and a bunch of other angels. Since then until now, a year and a half later, we have really focused on growing the product, growing the team, expanding into more verticals, running more experiments, building more marketing tactics within the product, and all kinds of things. So, all in all, things are on track and moving along quite nicely.

What is the main reason why you decided to stay in Egypt versus relocating to Silicon Valley?

We certainly have had many opportunities to establish the company in the Valley. We even had a number of acquisition offers from the Valley that we turned down. We also had other opportunities to relocate to other parts of the world. As attractive and tempting as these opportunities were, we feel we have this kind of responsibility to stay in Egypt and give back to the community that we grew from. Granted, the situation in Egypt at this time is difficult, and a ton of smart people are leaving the country. Still we believe we owe it to ourselves and to Egypt to stick around and set an example by creating this success story that's made in Egypt.

We want to break the myth that there's no or can be no great, world-class tech startups coming out of Egypt. I remember when we were in the Valley and meeting with many companies there, like Lyft, SoundCloud, Snapchat, and others, they were fascinated that there is actually technology coming from Egypt and from the Middle East in general. They didn't really think that there was such a thing going on in Egypt and that there are actually really smart people there.

So we always make it a point to position Instabug as a 100 percent Egyptian company, built by Egyptian talent and proud of it. When Accel invested in us, that was the first investment from Accel partners in Egypt. When YC invested, that was the first investment from YC in Egypt. That's why we didn't move from Egypt and why we are still here with our HQ still in Cairo. That's also why we continue to embrace our Egyptian culture, rather than just run away from it and say we are a Silicon Valley company.

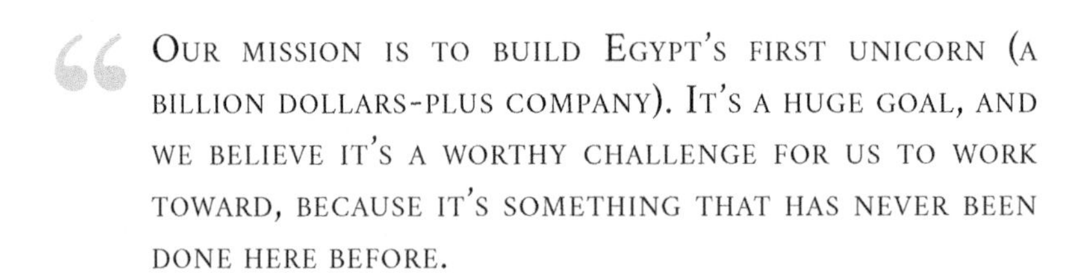

> "Our mission is to build Egypt's first unicorn (a billion dollars-plus company). It's a huge goal, and we believe it's a worthy challenge for us to work toward, because it's something that has never been done here before.

Today, we have mega companies that are using the product, including some of the top companies in the world. We have a solid team that I'm extremely proud of, a team that I learn from every single day. We have wonderful investors. We are well-funded. We are growing on all fronts and continue to live according to our core values, making things happen every day.

Our mission is to build Egypt's first unicorn (a billion dollars-plus company). It's a huge goal, and we believe it's a worthy challenge for us to work toward, because it's something that has never been done here before. It would be a huge win for the Egyptian tech community and startup ecosystem and validate the talent and innovation that we have in the country and region and hopefully inspire more and more people to pursue similar goals.

13

MUHAMMAD CHBIB

Making travel planning and booking easy

Founder and CEO of tajawal and CEO of Almosafer

WWW.TAJAWAL.COM

WWW.ALMOSAFER.COM

Muhammad Chbib serves as the CEO of tajawal and Almosafer, both of which operate under Al Tayyar Travel Group Holding Company. Previously, Muhammad was the founder and CEO of CitraStyle, a global Islamic made-to-measure fashion label. He also served as the CEO of Sukar. He joined Sukar.com in early 2011 and was an instrumental driving factor behind Sukar.com's continued acceleration in growth and stature and its acquisition by Souq.com, an Amazon company. From 2004 to early 2011, he led McKinsey & Company's client service teams on projects for various Fortune 500 companies in the online, financial, technology and telecommunications sectors. He is also an internationally experienced manager with a strong IT consultancy background, having worked with such companies as SAP, Europe's largest software provider. Having held a keen interest in technology, he is an avid reader with interests as diverse as innovative technologies, as well as scuba diving and Bayern Munich football team. A passionate and energetic individual, he speaks fluent Arabic, German, English and French. Muhammad graduated with an MBA-equivalent degree from the Koblenz School of Corporate Management (WHU) in Germany.

Tell us a bit about your personal background.

I was born and raised in Germany. When I turned twelve, I decided to stop taking money from my parents and instead looked at ways and means to be financially independent. I remember having about forty deutsche mark, which I used to purchase a secondhand bike from a classified newspaper ad.

I rode it for about a month and then sold it, I suppose for seventy deutsche mark back then. That's where it all began—I bought two bikes then; one I rode myself, and the second one I sold. So I started trading bikes with the two bikes I would keep buying. Kept one and sold the other for a much higher price, and then after the third or fourth bike that I sold within a month, I started assembling bikes in our backyard, since it offered better margins.

I kept the pace and was doing really well, compared to, say, my friends around my age. To give you a little perspective, the average money my friends would get from their parents in a month would be maximum of fifteen to twenty deutsche mark. Meanwhile, I was racking up 200 deutsche mark on average in profit. So, that's basically how I got what's so-called "the entrepreneurial bug." I possess a full-on active personality trait—always keen on learning and trying new things. What got me really going is my ferocious habit of reading. There was no internet back then, so information was available through TV, newspapers and books. I grabbed every single book near me and read it. I think I was in the seventh or eighth grade when I became the spokesperson of my class; that lasted until graduation.

Shortly after I graduated from school, I came across this article that talked about what one could possibly do after grad school. I recollect the article mentioning a new wave of private business schools that offered an MBA-equivalent degree in Germany, where only the inimitable and the best ones could possibly score a place. I was extremely intrigued and challenged myself to go ahead and apply. Luckily, I ended up passing the tough admission tests and getting accepted. This felt like one significant ignition and an influential space to be in, because when you attend such a program with the brightest minds, it really puts you on a totally different track and a distinctly superior slope in your career.

Growing up, I had always been fortunate to be among the finest students in my class and was recognized as one of the smartest in my school. Then business school happened, and on my first day, I realized that most of the sixty-something students in my class were so much more sharp-witted and smarter than I was. This grounded me in a big way and had me push even harder to compete and excel. One of my fellow students was Oliver Samwer, the founder and CEO of the German e-commerce giant company Rocket Internet. He was super entrepreneurial and, through a host of conversations, got me interested in being an entrepreneur myself. So all that added up to being a crucial turning point in my career.

All in all, I was really fortunate to have been raised in Germany and having the exposure I had early on. Still, being brought up in a Syrian family that's a minority group in a big county, you always have to fight to survive; you always have to be better than the natives to make it. Although I was born in Germany, the mere fact that I was a foreigner and looked different put extra pressure on me to constantly prove myself.

After I graduated from business school, I worked for the SAP consulting arm. A couple of months later, I spoke again with Oliver Samwer. He told me of the online auction house he had created and how he sold the same unit a hundred days later to eBay. Hearing about that was quite an eye-opener. To be perfectly honest, I was primarily motivated by financial success at that point in my life. So hearing about a trade sale of a company that gets you a couple of million dollars in no time was an extremely interesting concept. I decided to resign from SAP to start my own thing. I thought I could also build something similar and have a killer exit too.

I started by writing the business plan. It took me about six months to complete. The next steps included assembling a team, mostly co-founders. I then went on to raise about 8 million deutsche mark (approximately $5 million) in the initial round of financing. We birthed a concept that was a knockoff of an American company called VerticalNet back then. VerticalNet was a leading host of B2B procurement portals. It enjoyed stellar success in the late '90s and early 2000s.

So we launched the vertical B2B marketplace in Europe focusing on the plastic industry. In hindsight, we were too early for the market. We didn't focus much on technology and instead piloted all our concentration on the commercial aspects. We constructed a reverse auction model, in which sellers, not buyers, actually bid for the prices at which they were willing to sell their goods and services. We were in a market that had very few suppliers, which means prices were controlled by the suppliers, so the reverse auction concept didn't really work.

I was twenty-four at the time. I did that for one and a half years, until I realized that this concept was doomed. Around the same time, the first internet bubble was bursting back in early 2001. Investors were getting worried, and funding was increasingly more difficult to find. So we decided to shut down the business and find an exit. We sold the technology to a financial investor around September 11, 2001. We were fortunate to have exited at the right time and cleanly, unlike others who were more affected by this bubble and the downward spiral of global political and economic instability that followed, and went insolvent.

I was the youngest in the company and totally inexperienced in leading people. I went through the whole thing of developing leadership skills without a mentor. I obviously made every possible mistake. One thing I was good at, though, was lining up people behind me. I was always able to excite people, whether it was team members, suppliers, customers, etc. That was one of my strong suits, while everything else, in hindsight, I was just not ready.

Afterward, I decided to do some freelance work with startups. I also worked with some corporates in technical transformation projects, when one of these freelance projects took me to Dubai in 2003. I ran into an ex-fellow student from my business school at Emirates Towers Hotel in Dubai. He said, "Look, I work for McKinsey here in Dubai, doing consulting. Why don't you come and apply for a job?" I was twenty-nine about to turn thirty years old at the time.

Up to this point, I never considered McKinsey or consulting in general as an option for me. I always thought I would not fit the culture, considering I'm too wild for that typical McKinsey profile. However, I figured that I had reached a point in my life where if I didn't actively seek mentorship and relentlessly force myself to fit in a structured organization, I would never have the chance to learn the rules of the game. I would surpass the point where I could prove basically that I could grow within an existing organizational structure. So I took seven interviews and secured a job offer from McKinsey. I then got married and moved to Dubai in 2004 and started working with McKinsey and ended up staying with them for almost seven years in total, with almost two years in between stationed at a client organization in Germany.

At McKinsey, I focused on telcos and high-tech companies. At the end of 2010, I decided to leave the firm and go back to my startup life. Once I took that decision, coincidentally, I immediately got a call from one of the investors in a fashion startup in Dubai called Sukar.-com. They said, "Look, we have a company that we have invested in. It's well funded. Our core investors are Middle Eastern. The company is a clone of Gilt.com." (Gilt is a successful online shopping and lifestyle website based in the U.S.)

It was truly a unique and an unbelievable opportunity that I knew I couldn't pass. You have an industry leader with enough cash, so you don't need to worry about being funded again. Plus, you have enough industry relations and expertise that you can tap into, plus you have great amounts of buying power to operate efficiently.

Sukar.com had been started by someone from my business school, a German-Turkish guy called Saygin Yalcin who is ten years younger than me. He brought it to a level where they felt they needed more seniority in the leadership team to tackle the operation and challenge it. I partnered with the founder and took over as the CEO of that company, grew it basically within one year from $200,000 to $2 million a month in sales, and then we exited to Souq.com. It was not a financially big exit, but the perspective we had back then was that the likelihood of success for a business like this is much bigger if it is part of a big brand like Souq.com.

For me, it was a good story for someone coming from a consulting environment that took over a startup, turned it around, and sold it after just one and a half years. It was my entry point into the startup world in the Middle East. Afterward, I tried my luck with three small startups till the opportunity with tajawal opened up.

How did tajawal enter the picture?

In 2015, I spoke to Al Tayyar Group about setting up their online business, Al Tayyar Group being the largest travel agency in the Middle East. It is listed on the Riyadh Stock Exchange and was already a quite large and thriving company. What I saw looking at the group was that here was a large travel agency, with $2.5 billion annual sales and certainly one of the most successful travel companies in the region, that has yet to capitalize on the internet.

Up to that point, Al Tayyar Group had conducted its business on a traditional basis, offline, without much of an online strategy. I discussed with them the concept of adding a digital arm to their current business, and the more I looked closer, the more I realized that this probably represented a once-in-a-lifetime opportunity of building a unicorn (a company that's valued at a billion dollars or more).

It was truly a unique and an unbelievable opportunity that I knew I couldn't pass. You have an industry leader with enough cash, so you don't need to worry about being funded again. Plus, you have enough industry relations and expertise that you can tap into, plus you have great amounts of buying power to operate efficiently. So all I had to do was assemble a team and build a technology that was superior to the rest of the market and scale that business. It was as much of a no-brainer as it gets, in terms of the sheer potential involved.

For all those reasons, the odds were stacked in our favor. The chances of success are much higher for a startup in the Middle East with a setup like that, on behalf of a large corporate group, than, say, if you had to acquire a financial investment from one of the VCs.

I agreed with the group on launching this business in April 2015, and we embarked on this journey in August 2015. We started with three people, and today we are more than 800 people across four countries, and we've built the company basically from zero in sales in 2015 to annual sales of over $300 million dollars in 2017. It's been quite a ride so far. We're happy with our progress to date, though we realize we are still at the beginning. Our goal is to shape it to be a unicorn, which is quite a unique story to achieve in the MENA region, though we certainly have our work cut out for us.

Take us a bit more on that journey from the decision to take on this project to where you are today.

When I agreed with the Saudi owners to do this project, basically the first challenge was how do I begin; (a) I'm not from the travel industry; (b) I was forty years old right at the time, which means I had enough mileage to understand what I'm good and exceptional at and what I'm not so good at. That understanding was critical for me. Why? Because, as an entrepreneur, it is vitally important that you understand your own personal limitations.

As an entrepreneur, you usually tend to want to own everything; you want to drive everything; you are very reluctant to give away control, and so forth. Over the years, I understood that there are people that are much better than me at doing certain things, so I had to pause, take a hard look and ask myself, "What am I really, truthfully exceptional at?" Sure, I have a strong business degree and self-taught technology by myself. I built my first IBM-compatible computer at the age of twelve. I coded the entire thing myself. I developed databases and sold it to fund my university.

Still, I acknowledged, I'm not an exceptionally great technology guy. I do understand technology from a strategic perspective, in terms of what's coming out next and how can I utilize it in the most effective way, but I'm not a kick-ass technology guy. I'm also not extremely good when it comes to corporate finance or accounting or any of that, and I'm for sure not a typical brand marketer or a performance marketing professional. I have some good ideas here and there, but I wouldn't call myself exceptionally creative to facilitate the way forward. What I realized, though, is that I'm exceptional in finding a bunch of amazing people and making them operate together and building a culture that enables them to give their best and go beyond their limits.

So over the years, I figured what I do best and focused on it purely in all my startups by working toward getting the right people in the right spots. I also built a strong network of people who would want to work with me wherever I go. I think this was crucial in the early days of tajawal and still stands to be important today.

WHAT I REALIZED ... IS THAT I'M EXCEPTIONAL IN FINDING A BUNCH OF AMAZING PEOPLE AND MAKING THEM OPERATE TOGETHER AND BUILDING A CULTURE THAT ENABLES THEM TO GIVE THEIR BEST AND GO BEYOND THEIR LIMITS.

You're also running Almosafer. How did that happen?

When I initially discussed with Al Tayyar Group building an online travel agency for them back in 2015, they had just acquired a Saudi online travel website called Almosafer. Back then, Almosafer had annual sales of around $20 million. In hindsight, Al Tayyar Group had gone ahead with the acquisition for two reasons, the first being, there was an opportunity to acquire a majority stake in a promising and growing Saudi-based startup in the space; the second being, they needed a backup plan in place in case I would fail.

They then saw that within just four months, I built a platform with my team, and we launched and scaled real fast. So they asked me in the beginning of 2016 to take over the Almosafer business and run it as well, on the same IT and marketing stack that I was running tajawal on. So we integrated Almosafer on our technology platform but kept the two brands separate. We now have a two-brand strategy operating under what we call the Al Tayyar Strategic Online Business Unit. We are positioning the two brands to focus 180 degrees on different segments of the market. Collectively, we generated the $300+ million in sales that I mentioned earlier for 2017.

As the founder and CEO of the business, the focus on getting the right team and team-building is my highest priority. I probably invest 80 percent of my time on people-related matters, either recruiting or mentoring, or in simply having lunch with, say, my junior team members in order to get them excited about the company.

What are your most important milestones so far?

The first milestone that you look at in such a business is going live. That was quite exciting, especially since we had launched our technology platform in a span of a mere four months. We also didn't have any background in the travel industry and had to figure out things as we went, making sure things worked, were stable, and had zero downtime.

Second milestone is when you hit a certain round number of bookings, such as 100 bookings for the day and then 1,000 bookings a day, etc. Those are obviously great signs of making progress. Then came for me the most important milestone so far—taking the company from zero to $100,000,000, which not many companies in the region have achieved.

The next milestone that we are looking at now is how do you grow this company from $300 million today to $500 million. So once you hit the $500 million mark, then you need to prepare to become a unicorn. Then the final thing that I have on my radar, which will be a key milestone, is to be profitable.

Any advice related to bootstrapping and fundraising?

Regarding bootstrapping and fundraising, I am a friend of both, but it depends on the situation and also depends on the aspiration. Sometimes bootstrapping makes sense, and sometimes it doesn't. It also comes with a different risk profile, depending on the circumstances you're in. When you're, say, just coming straight out of university, you are probably able to bootstrap. You probably don't have any major commitments financially, and you probably have much more room to sail and learn from your mistakes.

That's much different than, say, if you were forty years old with a family you're supporting, a kid or two or three, whatever. You will have a much different risk profile. In that case, I would say you would need fundraising in order to secure your living if you don't have any backup source of income.

The other thing to factor in is the type of business and industry you're in. What's the likelihood of success of a company that operates in a cash-intensive industry but doesn't have enough cash on hand? Obviously, not very high. Typically, if you want to build something that's really big, it's essential to raise funds very quickly to get you focused on actually building the business. When you don't have funding, a lot of energy actually goes into thinking, "how do I survive," which obviously can be a distraction.

What are your general thoughts on recruiting and culture?

As the founder and CEO of the business, the focus on getting the right team and team-building is my highest priority. I probably invest 80 percent of my time on people-related matters, either recruiting or mentoring, or in simply having lunch with, say, my junior team members in order to get them excited about the company, to better understand their issues and challenges they face, etc. I think this is extremely important. You have to build the culture yourself. No one else is responsible for it but yourself. Sure, others come in the picture and help or even co-build with you, but as the entrepreneur, you must set the tone.

What's your perspective on marketing and branding?

Beyond getting traffic, users, and classic customer acquisition methods, the key to being effective in marketing in the long term, I found, is to build an emotional attachment with your customers. To do so, we focus and invest a lot on branding and building an exciting and emotional brand that resonates with people on a more visceral level. In today's world, people are typically not loyal to any company or product. They only become loyal when they have an emotional attachment to a brand, when they identify with it and what it stands for.

If you take Apple for example, today, Apple doesn't have a lot of differentiation with other brands in the market in terms of technology and pricing, but what they do have is amazing brand loyalty. As a result, they're able to have repeat customers who forget and forgive their mistakes. This is purely because of their genius branding strategy.

The big challenge to a startup would be that the benefit of branding only shows after a year or two. There's a big investment made upfront that does not get recouped for some time. So in order to undertake such an approach, you will need to be very clear about your strategy, and you need alignment with your board and investors. They have to understand that, while you're driving user traffic and engagement, you're building a brand or a position in the mind of the consumer that can become "top of mind" and can sustain customer acquisition without as much continued investment in marketing. Obviously, it goes hand-in-hand with other proven marketing and customer service methods, such as customer lifetime value management, CRM, etc.

It's essential for a founder and CEO of a startup, as well as senior management in general, to actually have hands-on time in customer service.

Any best practices you'd like to share regarding customer service?

I think it's essential for a founder and CEO of a startup, as well as senior management in general, to actually have hands-on time in customer service. Pick up calls, listen to calls, listen to the recordings, understand customer issues, and see how your people are interfacing with your customers. I literally read hundreds of customer support emails and responses by my team every week, which helps me coach my team to go above and beyond customer expectations, with the goal of lifting the quality of the service and increasing customer trust and loyalty.

What has been your biggest source of learning?

It is very intriguing to see how a company like Apple and Amazon are built and how the culture is all designed around users, around the products, and around innovation. I try to learn as much as I can and filter out how the organizational structure is built and what techniques leadership uses in order to foster innovation and customer-centricity.

In my specific industry right now, I also look at the global market leaders, such as Booking.com or Expedia. I like meeting with their senior VPs to understand exactly how they think about changing industry trends, consumer behavior, etc. It gives you a terrific amount of insights into how to structure your organization.

I also benefited a lot from visiting conferences, where I met all kinds of peers, people from industry giants and startups. They helped me question a lot of things that I do internally, and this opens your eyes to think outside of your own scope and comfort zone, and then you can implement these strategies into your organization as well.

What are some of the ways that business leaders can give back?

There are three things business leaders can do to give back, the first being mentorship. If you are an experienced business veteran in a great company, I think it's your responsibility to support other young entrepreneurs by at least giving sound advice. The second thing you can support them with is investment or helping them to attract investments, becoming a board member or adviser for a startup and help them with fundraising. The third thing is to try and develop the local talent pool in the Levant, Saudi Arabia, Bahrain, Oman, etc. This can be done by participating in events to educate students or fresh graduates and by hiring people that have potential in developing that.

What are your future aspirations for your companies?

Our aim is to be the number one brand when it comes to people traveling from the Middle East or within the Middle East. We are trying to focus on the specific local needs of travelers in this part of the world, which are a little bit different in terms of needs you find in Europe and the U.S. So it requires different thinking and approach. That is our primary focus over the next two to three years—to develop a user experience and products that cater to these unique needs.

Another area that we will increasingly look at is global Islamic travel. This is something that goes well beyond the Middle East when we look at the population. We are talking about two billion Muslims around the world, and as of now, there is no single global brand that caters to the specific needs of Muslim travelers.

In terms of regional focus, we will concentrate more on Saudi Arabia as well as expanding across the region. We started in the Gulf and are expanding into other countries in the next two to three years, probably starting with Egypt beginning of next year and then moving to other countries. Depending on how well we handle the situation and the economic outlook, this will definitely be something that we're looking forward to venturing into. Our main aim is to make both brands, tajawal and Almosafer, positive brands that basically stand on their own feet within the next two to three years, tops.

Another thing I am extremely keen on is I want to prove that even in the Middle East, you can create a unicorn, a profitable billion-dollar business, from the ground up within five to seven years only. We're on a very good track so far, but the biggest chunk of hard work is still ahead of us. We're getting there.

SARA ALEMZADEH

Introducing the rent-to-dress model

Co-Founder and Former CEO of Designer-24

WWW.DESIGNER-24.COM

Sara Alemzadeh is the co-founder and former CEO of Designer-24. Designer-24 is a Dubai-based fashion technology company intended to revolutionize the retail industry in the Middle East by providing thousands of designer dresses and luxury accessories for rent at a fraction of the retail price. Before founding Designer-24, Sara was vice president of oil trading at Morgan Stanley. Sara holds a Bachelor of Science degree in Mathematics from Georgetown University and an MBA from Columbia Business School in New York, where she grew up.

I WAS ALWAYS WILLING TO TAKE STEPS BACK TO TAKE STEPS FORWARD. I SAW THE CHALLENGES MY PARENTS FACED. THERE WAS ALWAYS A STRONG FOCUS IN OUR FAMILY ON WORKING HARD AND GIVING EVERYTHING YOUR ALL TO TAKE THINGS TO THE NEXT LEVEL, REGARDLESS OF YOUR SITUATION IN LIFE.

What can you tell us about your background?

I am Iranian and grew up in upstate New York. My parents originally came to the U.S. from Iran for their graduate degrees, and then the Iran/Iraq war started, so we stayed in America.

Growing up as an immigrant in the U.S. with Middle Eastern roots definitely had a large impact on me. It's never easy when your family is first-generation immigrants. This was especially true before the age of connectivity completely transformed what it means to be a global citizen.

I was always willing to take steps back to take steps forward. I saw the challenges my parents faced. There was always a strong focus in our family on working hard and giving everything your all to take things to the next level, regardless of your situation in life. Having said that, I've always felt very blessed as a person. People have different paths in life. You always have to do the best with what you have and move forward.

The concept of having a strong work ethic and drive was ingrained in me since I was a child. My mother set very high expectations always, and my father turned challenges into fun games. He used to bring me with his university students to their competitions. He would give me the same questions they would receive and push me to solve them. I honestly don't remember if I was ever able to figure them out, but the experience really shaped me.

I never thought something was too small or too big in terms of a goal. You do your best to reach your next step. Then you keep going. That's how life is.

I was always extremely active in school, involved in extracurricular activities, and working outside of school so that I could be independent. I started working at a young age—first in retail in my pre-teen years and then as an SAT math teacher. I then received a scholarship to attend Georgetown University to study mathematics.

What was your first job after university?

After I graduated from Georgetown, I moved to New York City and worked on Wall Street for almost nine years at Morgan Stanley. I knew nothing about finance and definitely felt nervous for the interviews. I remember going to the library to prepare. I got a comprehensive finance book and read it from cover to cover, taking notes in a binder I had created. I went to the interview and said, "I can't pretend to be a finance expert, but this is what I've taught myself from books." I think they liked my humility and hustle.

I was very lucky to get a position at Morgan Stanley when I was just 22 in their Fixed Income Sales and Trading program. Every step of my life, I pushed myself to overcome new challenges with the knowledge that the one thing I could control was my effort. That's not to say that I was always successful or confident.

One of my most vivid memories was at my first morning meeting at Morgan Stanley. I stood against the back wall, which was jam-packed with traders, salespeople and research analysts (of which I was now one), speaking a language that sounded completely foreign. I started to overheat, and the faces around the room started to blur. I made my way to the door and fainted right outside the room (laughs).

After the incident, people I didn't recognize would stop by my desk to see if I was OK. My team was incredibly supportive. They didn't prejudge, and it turned into an incident we would laugh about years later. I developed a bond with these colleagues that was far deeper because they saw me through this vulnerable time, and I was inspired to work even harder to prove I was strong enough to be there.

While I was at Morgan Stanley, the company made a decision to start a program sponsoring a group of employees to graduate school at Columbia University. I had about one month to study for the GMAT exam, which was required to attend MBA schools, and fill out school admissions applications. I was already working nonstop, so I just stayed at the office a couple of hours longer every night to prepare for the GMAT and complete the applications.

At the age of 26, I was honored to be in the first group of five selected the year Morgan Stanley launched the program. The one catch was that we had to continue working full-time. It was the height of the financial crisis in 2007, and I was working in a special role with the head of sales and trading management. It was a tough two and a half years, but I would never trade those experiences.

At Columbia, I took a lot of classes in entrepreneurship. I also rounded out my educational gaps when it came to corporate finance and accounting. Exposure just gives you confidence. That's because you don't feel insecure about what you don't know. These classes definitely came in handy years later when I decided to start a company.

We had a wide array of successful people from all industries—tech, real estate, hospitality, trading—you name it, we had it, and being in class together leveled the playing field. I took a lot of classes in options theory, which I was drawn to due to my mathematics background. I emerged from this experience with the desire to take a risk and become an oil options trader, which is not something I would have previously pursued.

I traded oil options for nearly five years at Morgan Stanley. I didn't know what I didn't know. Going through these life experiences is what shapes you. Every time you throw yourself into the fire, you figure it out, and eventually you come out stronger.

I have a core belief that it's not about how smart or privileged you are; it's about your resilience—what you make with what you have. Privilege is a state of mind. Even if it's something seemingly mundane, do it really, really well. That was always a part of my DNA. Also, it is a fallacy to assume from day one that you will know everything. You learn by doing.

Was there a particular experience that influenced you during that time?

Often when you start something new, you're hard on yourself and impatient. You might feel like you're the dumbest person in the room, but that's because you're just beginning. The feeling I had at the first morning meeting at Morgan Stanley was the same feeling I had when I was learning how to use a cash register at a retail store at the age of 15. I would keep asking the sales manager questions, and she said to me, "You need to rely on yourself more. Ask yourself a question first, and if you can't answer it, then ask me." That's exactly what I would do after each sales and trading meeting in the early days at Morgan Stanley. I would always try to figure out what was going on first and foremost by myself. Google was my best friend in those days! (laughs)

Another piece of advice that really shaped me came from my colleague Ken, who I sat next to my first year at Morgan Stanley. He had been with the firm for three or four years and seemed to know everything. He said, "Listen, just put your head down, work really hard and make yourself indispensable. That's the best thing you can do. Make sure that you get the job done extremely well, and everybody will rely on you. In the beginning, it's going to take time, and you're going to struggle, but you have to push through it."

That's exactly what I did. I didn't know how to use Excel, and that was hugely challenging, because everything we did was in Excel. So I would stay very late, every night, and just force myself to learn and get better and better and finish my work, even if it was excruciatingly slow at the beginning. He was right—it all started to sink in, and I became someone my colleagues relied on because I put everything into my work. But this has to be an active choice, and he taught me that. So I learned two important lessons: One, always rely on yourself first and foremost. Two, work hard to make sure others also rely on you.

I HAVE A CORE BELIEF THAT IT'S NOT ABOUT HOW SMART OR PRIVILEGED YOU ARE; IT'S ABOUT YOUR RESILIENCE—WHAT YOU MAKE WITH WHAT YOU HAVE. PRIVILEGE IS A STATE OF MIND. EVEN IF IT'S SOMETHING SEEMINGLY MUNDANE, DO IT REALLY, REALLY WELL. THAT WAS ALWAYS A PART OF MY DNA. ALSO, IT IS A FALLACY TO ASSUME FROM DAY ONE THAT YOU WILL KNOW EVERYTHING. YOU LEARN BY DOING.

How did the idea of Designer-24 come about?

I worked on Wall Street during a boom and bust cycle. The market and corporate environment changed drastically during the near decade I worked for Morgan Stanley. It was an incredible experience that gave me an awesome platform, but I was always drawn to the Middle East and a desire to build something on my own.

I met my co-founder, Ranya Khalil, through her husband. I was his client when I was trading oil. She is British-Lebanese, and we got along well. We both were excited by the prospect of building something innovative in the region. One day over coffee, I shared the idea of designer dress rentals. Weddings and events are a big deal in the Middle East and a very expensive undertaking for most women. We thought a rental business could work really well given the strong demand for dresses in the region, especially if the company was cutting-edge and focused on customer experience.

After doing research on the region, it was very clear that most tech companies started in the UAE. We decided that it would be a good place to base the business for a number of reasons. One, from the perspective of the Dubai "free zone" making life a bit easier to get things set up quickly. Two, the UAE has a large influx of intra-region tourism driven by events. Three, it was clear that there was an ecosystem set up in the UAE for investors and VCs, combined with a decent talent pool environment.

Before our first trip to Dubai, we reached out to different investors and leaders in the ecosystem. We identified Samih Toukan as our primary target investor. We were very impressed by what he had done with Souq as well as Maktoob and the Yahoo! acquisition, which was the first big tech sale in the region. If you can believe it, we reached out to him cold. We sent him a message on Facebook, and he actually responded, which was amazing! This goes to show the power of connectivity in today's environment. It also goes to show that you can never underestimate what could result from your efforts.

We met with Samih on our first trip to Dubai. At that point, we had already started working on the idea and tested many of our hypotheses. We had done numerous surveys and met with designers globally. We pitched the idea of renting their dresses in the Middle East and had spent a lot of time building our brand and getting them on board.

We had also developed a basic website that was an off-the-shelf Magento platform to get something up and running quickly. Initially, we funded everything ourselves.

We met Samih looking for a mentor, as well as an investor to help us take the idea forward and properly launch. We met him in February of 2014. We shared our vision and went through the entire business plan in detail. He loved the idea from the beginning and was very supportive. That was amazing. He introduced us to his business partner Hussam Khoury, and three months later, we had closed the deal with Jabbar and our first outside investment round. We got moving very quickly.

What consumer needs were you trying to fulfill with Designer-24?

Women borrow each other's clothing. It's not something new or something we created. They'll borrow a dress from their friends to wear and give it back. In our mind, we were just rationalizing a behavior that already happens, that's been happening forever, and scaling it.

One of the reasons that we thought the concept would work well in the Middle East is because events are such a dominant part of the culture. I grew up in the U.S., and I can tell you in my four years living in the Middle East, I went to more events in a dress than in my thirty years living in the U.S. That's not an exaggeration, so the demand for dresses is really high in the region.

Also, as a result of going to so many events, women end up with a ton of dresses. That was another piece of the puzzle that really supported the business model. We could recycle that local stock.

So the market supply and demand was definitely there, but also the digital age really bolstered this dynamic. Today women invariably post their favorite looks on social media. She is not just seen by the 100 or so people at the event; her entire digital community sees her, and the image lives on in her digital album forever. In the past, only celebrities had this kind of mass exposure.

What was your strategy for launching?

We discussed different ideas in terms of the underlying assumptions for the business and what we thought the business model should look like.

One was, do we launch with new season stock or act as a platform to recycle stock in the community? Those are two different models, and there are arguments you can make for both.

If you launch with new season stock, it's more capital-intensive to launch and scale. However, you can get to market quickly with good stock. Also we weren't sure how women would react to renting each other's dresses. At least if the dresses came directly from designers, it felt much more anonymous and luxurious.

We decided to launch by securing agreements for new season stock with designers. We convinced about thirty different designers across the globe to launch with us. We felt that made the value proposition very clear to the customer. You can either go buy this dress at a department store today and pay 3,000 dirhams (about $750), or you can rent it from us for 300 dirhams (about $75).

As we moved forward, we started testing the idea of adding stock from the community after we built a brand name, got traction, and took on those early adopters. We started by asking our clients if they wanted to put some stock on the platform to rent. What we realized was that we were actually able to acquire very special pieces through the community and that women were indifferent to whether the dress was new season or not, they just wanted to rent styles they loved that made them feel good.

Today our dresses from the community are rented more than the original dresses we launched with from designers, which is pretty amazing. This goes back to what I was saying originally. You're never going to have all the answers in the beginning. You have to take a step forward, test your assumptions, and build a flexible platform so that you can adapt quickly.

What was the biggest challenge you faced?

The biggest challenge we faced was developing the right marketing strategy. As a startup, it's very difficult to know what and when is the best way to market your product. It really comes down to timing and your product.

I would say that one of the biggest mistakes that an entrepreneur can make is trying to push a product when the product isn't ready. A lot of entrepreneurs prematurely rely on traditional marketing—press, digital ads and social media. We definitely made this mistake early on and allocated too much of our time to creating a buzz. We felt we needed to overcome the taboo of renting, but this was based on our own preconception that it was taboo in the first place. While we got really strong press early on, it didn't convert into the kind of numbers we were expecting.

WHAT WE REALIZED WAS THAT WE WERE DRIVING TRAFFIC TO OUR SITE, BUT OUR PRODUCT WASN'T STRONG ENOUGH TO CONVERT THAT TRAFFIC YET. THAT'S WHEN WE SHIFTED OUR FOCUS TO OUR PRODUCT AND GIVING THE BEST CUSTOMER EXPERIENCE TO THE USERS THAT WE ALREADY HAD.

What we realized was that we were driving traffic to our site, but our product wasn't strong enough to convert that traffic yet. That's when we shifted our focus to our product and giving the best customer experience to the users that we already had. After three to four months of optimizing the site, improving the stock offering and focusing on a top-notch experience for our customers, the product started selling itself.

What advice would you give an entrepreneur?

Be relentless in your commitment to growth—be it in your own personal growth, your success as a manager, the cohesion of your team, your most important business areas of focus, or the growth of those that have put their faith in you as a leader. The only way to grow and move forward is by taking that first step, so don't be intimidated, and take it one step at a time.

What is your advice on recruiting and team-building?

Find people that will work extremely hard. Remember that not everyone is willing to dedicate the time required to make a startup successful. Hard work is a choice, and you will want and need all members of your team to act like the CEO of their area and take on serious responsibilities day in and day out. This was a large challenge I faced early on and something I took for granted after working at Morgan Stanley, where hard work and commitment were the norm. Check with references, especially for senior members that you will need to rely on the most. Startups are grueling, and what differentiates successful ones is the persistence and relentless effort of the team.

Next I would look for people that have different skills than you. It's very important to be honest with yourself about your strengths and weaknesses. Don't try to find a copy of you. You already have you. Try to find people who fill the missing gaps, and make sure those people truly fill those gaps and fill them well, because if they don't, you will end up micro-managing their work, and you cannot scale this way.

In the same vein, all team members should feel that they are really important and have a large part to play. They need to feel inspired to work those long hours and see a path of growth for themselves in the company, because your company is nothing without them. That's the culture I set with my team. We had an open-door policy, and I always wanted all of our employees to feel just as important as the CEO, CTO, or whomever. I always emphasized the future and what I saw in each employee.

Also, don't try to convince people to believe in your mission. You want people to join your team who naturally feel passionate about what you're building. If you find someone who seems like they're really good in one area, but they're not passionate about what you're doing, then there will be some friction eventually. They don't necessarily have to agree with your underlying assumptions, which are always good to challenge. That's where a lot of the innovation comes from, from challenging groupthink and the status quo and finding new and better ways of doing things, but they should be passionate about your mission.

I WOULD LOOK FOR PEOPLE THAT HAVE DIFFERENT SKILLS THAN YOU. IT'S VERY IMPORTANT TO BE HONEST WITH YOURSELF ABOUT YOUR STRENGTHS AND WEAKNESSES. DON'T TRY TO FIND A COPY OF YOU. YOU ALREADY HAVE YOU. TRY TO FIND PEOPLE WHO FILL THE MISSING GAPS, AND MAKE SURE THOSE PEOPLE TRULY FILL THOSE GAPS AND FILL THEM WELL, BECAUSE IF THEY DON'T, YOU WILL END UP MICRO-MANAGING THEIR WORK, AND YOU CANNOT SCALE THIS WAY.

At the end of the day, being an entrepreneur is hard. We work very long hours, and it's not for the pay—it's for building something that will be impactful. We move forward through that passion, that belief in the future and relentless hard work. So I never try to convince someone to join us. If there isn't that kind of chemistry, just like in dating or in any relationship, you can't force it.

What are your thoughts on fundraising and bootstrapping?

Fundraising is one of the biggest challenges for entrepreneurs. Investors like to see traction before investing, so it's a catch-22. They also like to see you have skin in the game. I was able to seed-fund the company myself with Ranya, and I would frequently lend the company money beyond our initial investment while we were fundraising. I think this showed investors how serious I was, but I also recognize I was in a privileged position to do so after having a long career on Wall Street. A lot of entrepreneurs start businesses earlier these days or have different journeys.

When we completed our first investor round, I felt extremely lucky to find Jabbar so quickly. That being said, because the market in the Middle East is much younger than the West, you do smaller rounds to begin with, which means you have to be extremely nimble with every penny you spend.

You realize this whole concept of bootstrapping very quickly and the importance of trying to keep your expenses low, to extend your funds as long as possible and have that runway. You can't spend money without showing growth or traction, so one of the biggest challenges is managing those resources properly, which actually forces you to grow smart and lean.

One of the reasons we tested onboarding stock from the community as suppliers was because it was a great way to increase our product offering without utilizing funds, and it worked really well. Trying to be creative and think of ways you can grow the business and solve for pain points with minimal investments is critical in the early stages, which will ultimately drive scalability in the long run.

What is your approach to marketing and customer service?

The biggest lesson I learned in marketing is that focusing on the customer experience and product is the best form of marketing, especially at the early stages of a startup. Then you can invest in more traditional marketing avenues, once you're at that right stage and you think you're actually going to convert and have a happy customer. For us, our best form of marketing has been word-of-mouth, which again goes back to the product and experience.

In terms of customer service, that also comes down to product and trying to give that top-notch experience. If you're going to spend a dollar on marketing versus a dollar on customer service, I think your money is better spent on customer service, because if you give that customer an exceptional experience, they're going to tell their friends, and they're going to come back.

The most successful marketing campaign we ever did was all about the product and customer experience. We were doing a beta launch of our try-on service, where we send boxes of three different dress styles to women at home to try on before selecting one to rent. We had also recently made the decision to invest in really nice packaging so that the whole rental experience felt luxurious and similar to ordering an expensive dress online.

We decided to market the try-on service by selecting ten women with diverse backgrounds in the UAE to send the boxes to weekly. Our Fashion Director Noor Breish curated the selection for each woman, and we started the campaign a month before the prestigious and quite fashionable Dubai World Cup horse racing event. We made sure the experience was top-notch, from our communication style and packaging to delivery. It was wildly successful. The women loved receiving the boxes every week and would show off the experience and the boxes on their Instagram stories. We had record rentals that month, all from new customers. We hit our capacity limits on Dubai World Cup day, and our team worked around the clock to make sure we fulfilled every order with the same level of care as we had for those ten women.

How do you foster innovation?

I believe innovation comes from the culture you set. If you create an open culture that values each employee regardless of rank or position, you will foster innovation, because your troops dealing with the day-to-day challenges have a ton of insights into your pain points and what you need to solve for. They need to feel valued and appreciated. They need to have the same sense of purpose to drive the company forward as the most senior members, and they need to feel the confidence to speak up. For example, many innovative features we are building around our supplier community have been informed by our operations team.

> YOU NEED TO PHASE INTO LAUNCHES WITH DATA TO SUPPORT YOUR HYPOTHESES BEFORE YOU MAKE LARGE INVESTMENTS OF RESOURCES.

Beyond culture, it's important to have a clear framework when testing product launches and new features. You need KPIs (key performance indicators), metrics and goals. You need to phase into launches with data to support your hypotheses before you make large investments of resources. It's an iterative process, and you have to look at the data and results before you move in a certain direction. We started small when we tested renting women's closets on our platform. We scaled into it without making any large-scale changes to the site. After the metrics clearly supported the launch, we introduced specific features to make onboarding community stock scalable. Everything you work on takes time and resources away from something else. There's an opportunity cost, so you should make a well-informed decision when choosing a direction.

What are your views on work-life balance?

In terms of work-life balance, I have to admit that's something that I've struggled with personally. I think that most entrepreneurs are Type A personalities and are very much into their work, which is both a blessing and a curse. I definitely found that challenging, because your brain never stops working and there is endless work to do. It's especially challenging in the early days, because you have to keep costs low, which means you do everything from strategy, tech, accounting, admin, marketing, operations and fulfillment to fundraising—all while trying to grow the business—but you see, if you believe in what you're building and have that passion, then you enjoy it.

What is your perspective on the startup ecosystem in the UAE?

I've been really impressed with the UAE. I know that it's very easy for people to complain and say, "Oh, this is wrong or that is wrong." But I have to say that I have been so grateful for the support and camaraderie of the VC and startup community.

Samih Toukan and Hussam Khoury built hugely successful companies and made the decision to reinvest in the ecosystem. Today a lot of successful companies in the region started due to their support, and I am proud to count Designer-24 as one of those companies. I was really lucky to find Jabbar early on, because I think a lot of my perspective comes from the support I received through Samih, Hussam, and their network of companies.

When I was ready to launch Designer-24 in a new country, I sat down with Ronaldo Mouchawar, the CEO of Souq, to discuss strategy and the challenges he faced when launching in new countries. I also sat down with Ronaldo when it came time to hiring a CTO. The insights Ronaldo shared were invaluable, and I was extremely grateful for the time he took to mentor me.

I have also found that the ecosystem around the startup community, from press to media, has also been invaluable. The ecosystem as a whole is a developing one, which means many organizations run with an entrepreneurial mindset. I became close friends and a champion of many colleagues in the industry, who inspired me with the way they run their businesses. Lisa Rokny at ITP Media Group is one of those people who I admire for her vision and am grateful for her support throughout the years.

People have asked me if I have felt anything in terms of gender disadvantage. I can honestly say no. If there are any perceptions about the region when it comes to gender, I actually have felt nothing negative with regards to any gender biases in the workplace. I found, if anything, the ecosystem has been very supportive, independent of gender.

It's clear that the region is betting on the fact that the future is in technology. You see a lot of huge investments going into technology companies. You've had the acquisition of Souq by Amazon, which is a huge milestone for the region. A lot of local wealthy families who used to be more invested in traditional businesses are investing more in the technology space and setting up funds to do that, which is really exciting.

On the other hand, it's a question of how fast do you grow and what is the right way to compete globally. Now Amazon has come in and acquired Souq, and others are going to be competing with Souq and Amazon. You have Careem, which started in the region up against Uber. It shows you that the world is looking at the Middle East as an important territory for investing, which is a great thing and shows that things are moving in the right direction.

Also, there are government initiatives to support entrepreneurs in the region, which should continue to support innovation and the development of the ecosystem. For example, in Lebanon, the Central Bank has a fund that supports VCs that invest in Lebanese startups. There is also Saudi Vision 2030, which plans to reduce Saudi dependence on oil by promoting entrepreneurship in all kinds of sectors. All of these initiatives help startups get off the ground.

What are you most proud of achieving at Designer-24 so far?

I would say that I am very proud of the team that we have today. Over the last year and a half, I worked really hard to recruit an all-star team. I definitely made mistakes along the way, but we have now built a senior team that is amazingly effective at managing and driving all the critical areas of our business. We also have a team that is extremely hungry and passionate to grow at all levels.

What's your future plan for Designer-24?

We aspire to lead the way for sustainable fashion and be the global leader in shared economy technology. We are currently in the UAE and Lebanon and soon will be launching in Jordan and KSA. I foresee a world where women can travel without luggage and can book what they want on demand, and at affordable price points.

JON RICHARDS

Providing comparison of insurance services

Co-Founder and CEO of yallacompare

WWW.YALLACOMPARE.COM

Jon Richards is the co-founder and CEO of yallacompare, which he founded in August 2011. Yallacompare is currently the leading finance comparison site in the Middle East. Jon has ten years of digital marketing experience in the U.K. and the UAE, most recently with Propertyfinder in the UAE, where he held the position of online marketing manager. He was born and raised in Wales.

Can you tell us a little bit about your background?

I was born and grew up in a small town called Swansea in south Wales. I was raised by my mom; my dad left when I was two. My grandpa, my aunts and my uncles were a huge part of my life. I always looked up to them. They had successful careers; they had nice houses; they had good families. They taught me morals, respect, and what it means to have good values, so that really formed a big part of my personality.

I also had family that lived in the Middle East, which is how I initially became attracted to Dubai. My auntie married an Emirati gentleman back in the '70s, and they moved to Abu Dhabi, well before it was cool and hip to do so. I used to spend my summer holidays in Ruwais, which is a little oil refinery town near Abu Dhabi. I spent my summers with my uncle, who is an amazing man.

The most important person in my life was Mum. She had to work incredibly hard at two jobs to keep a roof above our head and food on the table. I didn't realize it at the time, but she instilled that work ethic in me. I have the desire to be better and the drive. She was fighting every day for us, and that stuck with me.

I obviously don't have the same pressure she had, though I still fight for what I want and work hard. Also, because of her, I have this mentality that nothing is given to you; everything you get must be earned. She really made a lot of sacrifices for me, and I'm eternally grateful.

Fast-forward to the time I left high school—I decided to postpone college for one year. To be honest, I was a bit of a wild kid. I was partying and enjoying life a bit too much. In that year, instead of attending college, I worked at a web hosting company and processed web domain and hosting orders. I couldn't have possibly known at that point how important domain names were going to be and the impact this online world would have, as it was still so new to the world. This was around 2008, when you could still buy most dot-com domains. I still remember at my job, customers were buying the big brands, like Louis Vuitton for instance, because these big brands hadn't bought their domain names yet.

Even though this was my very first job, I felt like I should run the company after just the first month. It's not because I thought I'm amazing or that I'm special, it was just because I felt like I could see how you could improve things; I could see how you could do things better. I could see how we could build this operation much bigger. I was hard to manage, as I challenged everything we did. Back then, I didn't have the tools or even the know-how to go off and start my own business, but I was starting to see the opportunities the web had to offer. I also started trying to teach myself to code.

After a couple of months, I very quickly realized that coding wasn't for me. I didn't think like an engineer. Through the process of trying to learn to build websites, I also learned SEO. Despite a few failed attempts to get a website or business off the ground, I learned about promoting websites and optimizing websites for Google.

This led to me getting a job in digital at a startup. I started learning even more about SEO and paid-search engines. Then Google AdWords launched, and the world suddenly needed people who knew how to scale websites and acquire customers online.

In the early years of my career, I worked at a few startups, which really gave me a taste of startup culture and how you could mix business and pleasure. Then I moved for a year to a bank in the U.K., which was a great experience, but I quickly realized that corporate life wasn't for me. The idea of working for a corporation, where reporting and thinking about work was more important than actually working, just wasn't right for me. Around the same time, I was on the lookout for something exciting, maybe even outside of Wales and the U.K.

WE HAD AN AWFUL LOT OF CHALLENGES, ACTUALLY, IN THE EARLY DAYS. WE DIDN'T HAVE MUCH MONEY. WE HADN'T RAISED FUNDS YET, SO WE WERE SELF-FUNDING THE BUSINESS OURSELVES. WE DID IT THE HARD WAY. WE HAD TO WORK ON THE BUSINESS BEFORE AND AFTER WORK, LATE IN THE EVENING AND ON WEEKENDS, BASICALLY ANY TIME WE HAD SPARE TIME.

How did you initially end up in Dubai?

I had the opportunity to move to Dubai and join Propertyfinder, the largest property portal in the UAE. Also, since some of my family have lived in Dubai for thirty-plus years, it has always been somewhat like a second home for me. Besides, I was open to a change, and Dubai seemed like a dynamic place, full of opportunities for growth.

I joined Propertyfinder in 2011, when they were about sixteen people —still very small, but they had been around a number of years, and they were on the cusp of doing some amazing things. I built up the marketing team. I was there for three years and really learned an awful lot about how to run a startup, how to grow quickly, how to raise money, and what goes into product and geographical expansion. Helping produce data for investment due diligence gave me great insight into the kind of information investors wanted and the kind of things they look at when evaluating a potential investment.

For me, Propertyfinder was a startup school. I'm sure many of those who worked there in the early days would agree. I have a lot respect for what Propertyfinder has achieved. Michael, their CEO, and the team have done amazing things and grown through the good times and the bad times in the economy. They've gone through it all. So I have a lot of respect for them, and they continue to be one of the premier startups. They are one of the most exciting dot-coms in the region and still have a huge potential for growth.

Perhaps most importantly, it was whilst at Propertyfinder that I met my co-founder, Samer Chehab, who joined Propertyfinder a month after me. Samer and I became friends and would go for lunch every day to discuss startup ideas and eventually form Compareit4me.

What was the inspiration for yallacompare?

While at Propertyfinder, I started what is now yallacompare, which was back then called Compareit4me. To put it simply, Compareit4me was born out of necessity. It was born out of my need to find a bank account, because I just moved to Dubai, and I didn't know any of the local banks. I needed to find out where I could maybe get a car financed and which bank account was going to be the safest, which one would give me the facilities that I needed, like transferring money online. I tried to research, but this kind of information simply didn't exist.

In 2011, most banks in the UAE had a one-page website. They didn't have product information or rates; they hardly had anything. Having just moved from the U.K., where comparison is second nature, it seemed like the obvious opportunity for me to explore. My wife, Carys, was also a big driver in starting Compareit4me, as she worked in one of the U.K.'s leading comparison sites, Confused.com.

Could you describe your business model and how it evolved over time?

In terms of the business model, we started as a comparison of banking products, and the model was lead generation. It has now transitioned to insurance business being the lion's share of our revenue. The transactional nature of our insurance business means we can scale much quicker and drive sales based on targets. So now we are an e-commerce platform, and that change has transformed the business beyond expectations.

Our focus is to save people time and money every single day. In 2017, we sold more than $20 million worth of insurance policies, and we estimate to have saved UAE residents more than $4 million in the process. So our goal is to help people, educate them, and get them better deals. It's to help them get better products, better financial products, better insurance policies that are more suitable for them. I think these things are particularly important in the Middle East. Our goal is to help people make smarter choices when it comes to taking financial products, to make sure they understand the benefits the banking system can offer, but also protect the consumer.

What sort of challenges did you face in the early days?

We had an awful lot of challenges, actually, in the early days. We didn't have much money. We hadn't raised funds yet, so we were self-funding the business ourselves. We did it the hard way. We had to work on the business before and after work, late in the evening and on weekends, basically any time we had spare time.

The ecosystem in the Middle East back then was not anywhere like it is today. Today you have incubators. You have an active early-stage investors' community. In those days, it was much harder. Who do you turn to, and how do you raise money? The answer wasn't so clear. We were lucky enough that after three years of running in bootstrap mode that we were able to get angel funding. That meant that we could quit our jobs and finally get an office, a team and finally start to focus full time on the business.

We initially raised $500,000 to start, and that meant from day one, you don't have time to waste. You're operating on a relatively small budget and need to hit certain targets and milestones and stay afloat till you get to your next cash injection. We then managed to raise our first VC round of funding a year later. We raised $1 million from Wamda Capital, $1 million from STC, and $1 million from DSO. So, $3 million in total.

The validation that you feel as an entrepreneur when investors put money in your startup is awesome; the fact that three of the largest VC investors in the region have picked us is amazing. They also brought a lot to the table outside of the funding, in terms of advice, knowledge, contacts, as well as ambition, goals and challenges. While they bring a certain amount of pressure, they make you accountable and force you to stick to your goals and commitments, and that is invaluable. So, all in all, their involvement has really propelled us forward. To this day, we still receive a lot of support and advice from our investors.

Investors naturally add pressure, because you have someone to report your numbers to. Some don't like it, but the fact that we have to report to a board of investors means that there is always urgency and accountability. We have to hit our numbers. I never want to go to my board and report missed numbers. That's not cool. I don't want to be seen as a failure. So there's definitely that pressure, but it's good pressure. We're happy with our board, and we're happy with our investors. To date, we've gone on to raise more than $10 million. We expect to close another $8-$9 million in 2018.

In terms of growth, what's next for yallacompare?

We've grown the team to around 100 people now and expect to grow even more. We are at the stage where we are looking at product expansion. We're also looking at geographical expansion. I think when you talk about geographical expansion in the Middle East, that's when things get complicated. So businesses like Souq.com are brilliant. What they've done is show that if you set it up right, if you do the right things, you can build a defensible business that expands across the region. Then a big business such as Amazon will come and acquire you.

The average U.K. comparison site might be interested in the scale that the Middle East has to offer, but if they do thirty minutes of research, there is no chance someone from the U.K. comparison team or anywhere in the world would want to come and play in the comparison space here. This isn't copy-paste U.K. There are very unique challenges to operate in this part of the world, especially in the industry we're in.

I know we didn't invent comparison sites, but what we do know is innovation in service. In the U.K., they wouldn't even consider a call center. In Dubai, if you don't have a call center, a customer will not want to work with you. We are still in the part of the world where the person-to-person communication is really important. When we look to the future of our business, we see AI (artificial intelligence) being important, but that's way into the future in the region; that's not today. You can't have a robot talk to consumers in the Middle East at the moment. They want to deal with humans, and that's OK for now.

WHILE COMMITMENT AND DETERMINATION ARE CRITICAL, IT'S ALSO IMPORTANT THAT ENTREPRENEURS DON'T CONFUSE DETERMINATION WITH STUBBORNNESS AND DON'T END UP STICKING WITH A BAD IDEA. INVESTORS INVEST IN PEOPLE, NOT IDEAS, BECAUSE IDEAS AND MARKETS OFTEN CHANGE.

Dubai is nearly the perfect place to start a business. The ecosystem is phenomenal now. You have the support. You have consumers who are ready to consume digital products and services, who want the benefits, who want everything that you're offering. That's awesome, but you need to expand regionally to get the scale international investors require.

With the population of 9 million people or so, for car insurance, for instance, we have a potential market for maybe 1.2 million cars, which are residential cars. Then you go to Saudi and it's ten times bigger, but then the challenges are probably twenty times bigger. So these are the kinds of things that you have to weigh.

I think the challenge for us now, as we move forward, is how do we scale into the other markets? How do we localize the service? We are currently working very closely with an insurance regulator in Saudi. We want to make sure we are going to keep the essence of the service but tailor to specific consumer needs of that market.

What can entrepreneurs learn from your experience?

While commitment and determination are critical, it's also important that entrepreneurs don't confuse determination with stubbornness and don't end up sticking with a bad idea. Investors invest in people, not ideas, because ideas and markets often change. Markets can change. You need to be on your toes and ready to shift strategy or pivot if you need to, till things click.

Being flexible and being ready to listen to what investors have learned and are willing to share, as maybe there's an opportunity there you're overlooking, is important. That approach has probably saved our business, or at least saved us from wasting a lot of time and money going down the wrong path.

What are your thoughts on regional expansion?

If you're in the Middle East, and you're hoping to start a business, you need to be thinking about Saudi. It's tempting to think of Dubai first. After all, Dubai is a great place to start your business. There is great talent in Dubai; there are great opportunities in Dubai; the investors are based here, etc. However, KSA needs to be in your plans early, and you need to start working on the Saudi launch long before you think you'll want to launch. Saudi has to be at the top of the list when it comes to focusing your energy and resources.

One of the mistakes that we made early on is that we didn't consider international expansion. I'm being totally honest with you; when we first launched this business, we thought it would be more like an affiliate business. We thought that maybe we would sit in a coffee shop; we would sit on the beach; the two of us would do work almost like an affiliate website, and we would just double our salary and life would be good.

We initially didn't really consider the potential, but investors came along and were like, "Hang on, this could be much more." "OK, wow, you think we should expand? OK, great!" So it was quite an eye-opener to say the least. When I speak to international investors today, the first thing they typically ask is, "What is your Saudi plan? How is Saudi doing? When are you going to be there?" The reason is because of the scale and the size of opportunity.

If you decide to go after Saudi, you're going to have to make sure your website is not just copy-paste into Arabic with a bit of translation. It better be optimized. We chose our Arabic font with as much passion as we chose our English font. It was incredibly important to us. These are the kinds of things you need to get right to localize.

Another thing we did to further localize to Arabic consumers is change our brand from Compareit4me to yallacompare. Yalla in Arabic means "let's go." It's a call to action; it means go and compare now. Make sure you get the best brand for you. It's catchy and campaignable. Most importantly, it resonates with the Arabic consumer, especially outside the UAE. It's a brand that can go across the region. The reaction to the rebrand has been extremely positive, so we're delighted to see that.

What's your basic advice to entrepreneurs regarding fundraising?

My basic advice for entrepreneurs is get out there as soon as you can and meet as many investors as you can. Introduce yourself and your idea. You want investors to take interest in you and your business early on, even if you're not fundraising at the moment. These guys are going to want to track you. They are going to follow your product; they are going to learn more about you. This all takes time. Much longer in the Middle East than the U.S. or U.K., for instance.

What's your take on marketing for startups?

Make no mistake, having an amazing product or service that no one knows exists is a fast way to fail. If you're not promoting your business, it's not going to grow, unless you're one of the outliers, like Facebook or Instagram, that are almost a once-in-a-lifetime business that don't need digital marketing. For the rest of us, we're going to have to spend some money and build some traction.

Another thing to remember: When you're building a brand, you're not just trying to get customers; you're trying to get the media to buy into you and your mission. One of the first things that we invested in when it comes to human capital was PR. We understood that we couldn't change the industry or the mindset. We couldn't make people all of a sudden think about comparison if they don't today. We couldn't do that with Google and Facebook alone. If people don't search for car insurance, I'm not going to get to them using Google, so PR was and continues to be a huge part of our growth plans.

WHEN YOU'RE BUILDING A BRAND, YOU'RE NOT JUST TRYING TO GET CUSTOMERS; YOU'RE TRYING TO GET THE MEDIA TO BUY INTO YOU AND YOUR MISSION. ONE OF THE FIRST THINGS THAT WE INVESTED IN WHEN IT COMES TO HUMAN CAPITAL WAS PR.

We are also not just trying to build a brand and acquire customers; we're also trying to make sure investors know who we are. We are trying to make sure that recruitment is easier because people have read about us. All these things really help. It means, as a founder, you have to put yourself out there, and I have to talk on panels. It's something I really enjoy doing, though it's a huge drain on time. So you have to be selective and turn down a lot of these things—you can't do everything—but they're so important to do from time to time in terms of networking and getting the word out.

What has been your experience with recruiting?

One of the hardest things to do as a founder is build the senior management team and recruit. We made a million mistakes when hiring for our headquarters staff. We were blindsided when we looked at people's backgrounds. I felt that we didn't vet people enough when we interviewed them. We took for granted that if someone worked for a big brand like Yahoo!, for instance, that the person would be exceptional. That said, we now have an amazing team. We were lucky to hire Jonathan Rawling, who joined as our CFO and has had a huge impact. Additionally, we have added top talent such as our CTO, Hussain Fakhruddin. These guys add value, educated opinions, a new way of thinking, which takes a lot of pressure off Samer and me.

What do you feel is the role of innovation in the context of a startup?

You have to be careful not to get caught up in innovation for innovation's sake. For example, we are only now launching an app. To be honest, I don't expect this to drive a huge volume of sales, but we want to add it to our customer touch points. It's not essential, so we've waited a long time before investing time and energy into it. I see many startups building apps where it really isn't needed; they are so focused on building an app, they don't even know why they are doing it.

What are your thoughts on work-life balance?

Achieving work-life balance is very difficult in the early days of a startup. You do need it, though. You need to avoid burnout. I think one good bit of advice I was given is taking a day to work outside of the office, the idea being that you can get away from the daily grind and stop and think about higher-level stuff and future goals. Whenever I go away, I've found that I'm able to come up with new ideas, new variants on the business. I think of things that I normally wouldn't in the office on a daily basis. So it's been incredibly positive.

One thing I try to do is try to read as much as I can about other startups—how they are running big businesses like Facebook and the challenges they faced and how they overcame.

With Souq.com expanding aggressively and very successfully in Saudi Arabia, how did they do it? How did they overcome the challenges that we are now facing? You know? You can find case studies and all this information; it's out there. If you can't find it, then get out there and get mentors and meet the founders themselves. Don't be afraid to ask for advice or feedback. I find that the community of founders is really generous. When people reach out to me, I am always more than happy to give them advice, because I know how difficult those very early days are. I've always found the same with other entrepreneurs.

IT CAN LOOK COOL AND FUN AND GLAMOROUS TO RUN A STARTUP. THE FACT IS, IT CAN BE INCREDIBLY DIFFICULT, AND YOU'RE THE FIRST ONE IN AND THE LAST ONE OUT. IF YOU'RE NOT, THEN MAYBE THE TEAM AROUND YOU STARTS TO WONDER WHY THEY SHOULD WORK LONG HOURS.

What are the biggest misconceptions you come across about being an entrepreneur?

I ask people, "Why do you want to be a founder? Why do you want to do a startup?" I realize they want to be a founder because they get to choose their destiny. They get to do what they want to do. Maybe they think they can work from wherever they want, and they want to work from a beach. I say, "Forget it!"

Certainly, you can create a lifestyle business where you can take holidays and work from the beach and all that. On the other hand, you can't build a startup that grows 20 percent to 40 percent month to month from the beach, I promise you that. Instead, you're working fifteen to eighteen hours a day in the office, and you're tired.

People need to understand: It can look cool and fun and glamorous to run a startup. The fact is, it can be incredibly difficult, and you're the first one in and the last one out. If you're not, then maybe the team around you starts to wonder why they should work long hours. So you're the standard-bearer, and you're the one that has to set the tone.

As the team grows, you start to do fewer of the smaller tasks, but you're still deep in the detail of almost everything that happens. Maybe you get a bit more freedom as you build your team up. Quite honestly, don't start a startup if you want more free time. Keep your corporate job and get your bonuses and your holidays. There are no thirty-day holidays when you run a startup. I think that is a huge misconception I see with some people.

I also feel a lot of startups think that bringing outside investors and giving up some equity is a negative. They see raising money as you're allowing someone else to have an input into your business. Who cares if you have 100 percent of equity of a tiny business? I think most people would give up 100 percent of their small startup to take 1 percent of Facebook, right? It's value, not percentage; that's what really matters. Not to mention, when you get good investors, they bring ideas, and they bring network. They give to you knowledge and experience that is invaluable, so you're much more likely to reach your full potential.

What role does education play in prepping future entrepreneurs?

I think schools need to really get on with the program and start educating kids to do presentations, create spreadsheets, run a P&L

(profit and loss statement), and all these practical skills they will need from day one on the job. This is simple stuff, yet it isn't taught, and we have a lot of interns and grads at yallacompare. The number of them that can't create spreadsheets and presentations is shocking.

Schools should also be telling their students that there are endless options for them and they can also create their own. They should focus more on creativity. Maybe even teach kids to code in schools, at least learn to build a basic website and basic programming.

What's your personal definition of success?

We are trying to make the simple act of buying insurance easy and as cheap as possible. When we have made insurance comparison ubiquitous across the region, then we will feel like we have succeeded.

On a personal level, I'm trying to secure my family's future. It's important to me that my wife, Carys, and my daughter, Olivia, are financially secure. Luckily, my wife has a very successful career with Mastercard and frankly doesn't need my financial security. Still, as a family, we want to ensure Oliva has everything she needs to become successful and happy when she grows up. Everything I do is ultimately for my wife and daughter. When Olivia sees me on the front cover of a magazine or hears our radio ad, she beams with pride, and I love it. Olivia being proud of her daddy is amazing.

What is your future vision for yallacompare?

In terms of future vision for yallacompare, this business will be the dominant comparison site in the Middle East. We are already the largest. We sell about 70 percent of the insurance products and services that are sold online. So if insurance is sold online today in the Middle East, it happens because of us.

We've still got a long way to go. Our market share is nowhere where we need it to be. We want to be as dominant in Egypt and Saudi as we are in the UAE today. We want to build a comparison site that spans the whole of the region that is genuinely useful to the end customer.

Today on average, our consumers will save $100-160 every time they buy car insurance. We want them to save more. We genuinely want them to really feel the benefit. We're building the foundation to that vision today.

Also, in terms of major successful outcome, or a milestone, if you will, I envision it in terms of achieving some kind of M&A activity or an exit, where you really get the seal of approval. Where an established company looks in on your business and says, "You've built something amazing. I can't replicate this myself. I need to come and acquire you." I think that'll be a huge stamp. It'll be a wonderful feeling. The fact that Souq.com built something so formidable that even one of the largest companies on earth, Amazon.com, had to buy them instead of compete with them is mind-blowing. Ronaldo, their founder and CEO, and company really did a fantastic job. I want to do the same thing in comparison shopping.

All of this is what we're working so hard towards. That's what the next maybe three to five years will bring. There are many challenges; there are new challenges that I'm sure we're going to face tomorrow, and we just have to be as aggressive and as aware and mindful as we've been and keep pushing and being as positive as possible.

16

FOUAD JERYES

Making international shopping easy

Co-Founder and Business Lead of CashBasha

WWW.CASHBASHA.COM

FOUAD JERYES is the co-founder and business lead at Alpha Apps Inc., the creators of CashBasha. Fouad has served as a partner and manager at a number of forward-thinking ventures between the U.S. and the Middle East region, particularly in Jordan.

Alongside his work as director of technology and analytics at Open-Insights, LLC, a data-mining and data strategy firm based out of Bellevue, Washington, Fouad served as "Chief Rascal" at the Arabic content-sharing portal d1g.com and was part of the founding team that started up Jordan's first technology accelerator and incubation program, Oasis 500. Thereafter, he became the manager of the recommendation engine and data team at Blue Kangaroo, a U.S.-based big data firm focused on social shopping solutions with offices in Jordan. Over his career, he has also offered and led technical as well as strategic consulting efforts to top-tier telecom, software and internet giants such as Google, Microsoft, Verizon, and others.

Outside of work, Fouad has been an active participant in building the local tech startup ecosystem. Some of his side projects over the years include Amman Tech Tuesdays (AmmanTT), an open forum for tech entrepreneurs and enthusiasts that has brought together tens of thousands of attendees, and TechTech, an Arabic satellite TV program to highlight tech entrepreneurs and businesses throughout the region. He graduated with a Bachelor of Science in technology and business from the University of Massachusetts, Dartmouth.

Tell us a bit about your upbringing.

I was born October 20, 1985, in Boston, Massachusetts to Amal, my father, who was a talented and accomplished bio-medical engineer with Palestinian roots, and Shireen, a loving full-time mother and educator from Jordan. Catered by my mother, the cultured environment that was our home came filled with music from all sorts of backgrounds and languages. At a young age, I developed a love for music, which was my first passion, but the counter-influence was my father's love for engineering and my admiration of his work as a knowledgeable and dedicated man. My playroom in the house had five networked computers, which I was always tinkering with. Slowly, my curiosity led me to many questions on how things worked, and my father was a wealthy resource that I sponged up.

One day in the early '90s, I remember my father returning home from work with a heavy heart. A victim of the recession at the time, he had informed us that he had lost his job. That's when I realized that my father, whom I had looked up to, was no longer in control of his career or finances. My father ended up staying at home for about two years without a job, but it was a hardship that taught me quite a lot. At such a young age, I realized the weakness inherent in the corporate world, in terms of relying on some other factor to control your destiny.

As a result of this experience, I grew up wanting to be independent and felt a strong sense of obligation to support my family. My parents tried hard to provide for us as much as they could, but there were some definite financial hardships that took a toll on us. Perhaps typical of any family under some strife, I started realizing how my brother and I couldn't have the toys that we wanted and couldn't have that type of life that we thought would be perhaps "normal." I attribute this situation to building a sense of frugality in me to a degree.

We moved back to Jordan in 1993, and by the time I was in fifth grade, I was already well versed with computers and the internet. I still had the desire to dabble in business and trade. With relatively high-speed internet connectivity at the time and technical facilities right at home, my brother and I started a small, semi-fictitious company called FJ Squared or $(FJ)^2$. Both of our initials are FJ, so we thought it would be a cool idea that fit. Way back when CD burners were these clunky and very expensive devices that were far from being in every laptop around, we took advantage of the fact that we could produce a "hot item" for the time. We lined up school friends and family as our customer base started to grow and took intricate steps into making the cover of the actual CDs to be as appealing as possible. The process was consuming back then, as these discs would take four or five hours to burn and tag with labels, but I valued the time and experience. I used to sell them for about 15 JD or Jordanian dinars (about $20) a pop, which was pretty competitive back then as well. Over the course of a summer, I remember making 700 JDs (nearly $1,000), which was a big deal for a kid in fifth grade. It was kind of an eye-opener for me in the sense that I could do my own thing, actually make money on it, and contribute back. So I kept doing that for a few years until the technology caught up in my early years of high school and CD burning became more available. It was a good run that I was proud of, but I still wasn't as enterprising as I aspired to be. I was exposed to what was possible through the men and women around me. Had I not, it might've been likely for me to not know that there was more to gather than this.

Once I got to high school, I noticed that there were other opportunities that I could get into. A lot of students in high school wanted varsity or graduation jackets that were customized for them similar to the ones that are typical in the U.S. So I found a couple of guys that were doing some stitching, embroidering work locally, and I designed a jacket with leather arms and a unique color combination and started selling it in high school. The design and colors caught on with my class of about forty students, but more interestingly, other high schools saw them and liked it as well. I ended up also helping them make their own jackets. So again, my neurons were firing, and my small success there built up my confidence further, making money independently and being in trade.

How was your experience in college?

In 2004, I landed in Boston with not much beyond the cost of the ticket that got me there, and by the end of my freshman year, I had secured a full paid scholarship at the University of Massachusetts,

Dartmouth. I also worked three jobs during college and took an English and business course at the ESL (English as second language) center at the university; I also joined a small business and interned at a local establishment. I made ends meet and then some, but it was my mother's drive in me that kept me disciplined and hungry to excel. I made the most out of my time in college, was active on an extracurricular level, and graduated *summa cum laude* at the very top of my school.

One of the most important work experiences I had then involved a close-up view into the proverbial "American Dream." Part of one of the courses I had in college included working with a family in their basement doing e-commerce websites. They were a very nice couple, a man and his wife, named Dale and Joan. They were doing consulting services to small and medium-size e-commerce websites. This was 2005. It was clear to me that they were just honest people who worked together and loved one another. Their cooperation and humbleness inspired me. It was beautiful in its simplicity, without any grandiose aspirations or demanding responsibilities. At that age, my thinking was that there was no point to be in business if you did not want to grow, build and dominate. I was blind to how work and life needed to remain in balance for a human being to remain content, which eventually took its toll on me later in my career. Although I'd been shopping online for the past few years, they exposed me to the internal workings of e-commerce sites for the first time.

Before graduating in 2008, they presented me with a card. It read, "Fouad, we wish you health, happiness and self-sufficiency." The last bit I regard as the most important piece of advice I have received to date.

What came next after college?

After college, I was burning to start another venture on my own. The idea of getting into digital advertising was intriguing to me, and the market was booming. I designed the product and had the early stages of a prototype ready. I remember coming back during Christmas of

2008 to be with my parents in Jordan over the holidays. I knew of Dr. Usama Fayyad, who was Jordanian and also the ex-chief data officer at Yahoo! in Silicon Valley. He was also a widely regarded expert in the field with incredible accomplishments and a long career working with global tech giants and was someone I looked up to. With much less than six degrees of separation between us, I was able to reach out to him while we were both in Jordan, and he was kind enough to meet with me. When we first sat down, he said, "You know, I have only ten minutes," but that turned into an hour or so pretty quickly. He was interested in learning about my prototype and what I was doing in the digital advertising space and what projects I'd done in the past. He became interested in the venture.

I had no plans to stay in the Middle East after this visit. I wanted to go back to the U.S., because I outright discounted the Arab world to be a "Sahara desert" for technology companies, and I had ambition and a hunger for personal growth. Why would I ever leave America? Well, the economic downturn hit that year, and things looked quite gloomy to raise the funds and achieve the eighteen-month targets of what I had been planning with my product. Considering the circumstances, Usama got in touch again asking if I would like to work with him between Amman and the U.S. at his data-consulting firm until the economy pulled itself together. After a couple of projects, I was assigned as the director of technology and analytics at Open Insights, Usama's company. So there I was, young guy, impressive title, and doing some very interesting work. I was going back and forth between Amman and the U.S. and working with all the brands I dreamed of being in touch with. The greater team on board was also extremely insightful and intelligent, and I learned a lot there.

During my time back and forth between Amman and the U.S., I was incubated inside a small part of a company called d1g.com, which aimed to fortify Arabic content on the internet. At the time, less than 3 percent of the internet was actually Arabic, and there was no real platform out there to host rich media content, and this was pre-YouTube or real blogs in Arabic. It was a very interesting opportunity, so I decided to join. I helped initiate d1g product development and presence in Saudi Arabia and the UAE right from the get-go. I got to understand how different the Arab world was from the western world, as well as how different Arabs amongst themselves were from one country to the next in terms of internet usage. Quickly, I began to realize that there was something special in the "Sahara." There were far too many puzzles to be solved, and nothing had happened yet. The light-bulb moment came in the form of simply seeing the glass half-full, and that the desert may be an opportunity to participate in building an industry in MENA rather than being part of one that is already developed in the west. All of a sudden, there was a sea of opportunity, and I could be rooted right in the middle of it.

How did you get started in e-commerce?

Shortly after d1g, I was part of the founding team of Oasis 500. Initiated by King Abdullah II, it was a bold move to invest in early-stage companies and accelerate them in Amman. One of the companies we invested in was an e-commerce hosting platform that was started by a Syrian that I recruited into the program. He was looking for showcase websites to build his portfolio of sites, and it was obvious to me that a lot of high-fashion e-commerce wasn't catering to the larger portion of the conservative women in the area and that Islamic fashion was on the rise. With a number of small tests and studies, I was intrigued by the opportunity.

I started a website called Hijabik.com, which basically catered to the Islamic fashion industry. We were mainly selling head scarves, and that is a massive industry. The project showed promise right off the bat, and we began seeing interest and orders from the west as well. The interesting bit was that I was a non-Muslim and also had nothing to do with fashion at all but was able to portray a very standard and generally ubiquitous product in a modern way with exceptional customer service. Of course, the regional and international media agencies loved every bit of this odd story. Although I had to forgo spending time on the project eventually to focus on other projects, it was a very important experience because I came in direct contact with the hassles, hurdles and risks that e-commerce merchants were dealing with in our corner of the world.

> It was extremely tough for local customers to make these online purchases, especially from foreign websites. Customers were going through hoops and loops to solve the payments, logistics, customs clearance and customer service issues they faced, and with a large amount being unsuccessful at that.

In 2013, my friend Sinan and I started looking at infrastructure problems in the Arab world, particularly in the untapped and quickly growing area of e-commerce. The obvious observation was that the birth of any transaction is a payment. Any process in the commerce value chain cannot take place unless a payment is made, so in a region where over 70 percent of the population is unbanked or indifferent to banking despite having a regular income, it was a bit of an issue. Still, many people don't trust using credit cards online, even if they did have one to begin with. Thus it was extremely tough for local customers to make these online purchases, especially from foreign websites. Customers were going through hoops and loops to solve the payments, logistics, customs clearance and customer service issues they faced, and with a large amount being unsuccessful at that.

Cash on delivery was no innovation really, as it was the standard method of payment offered to cash customers. It accounted for 80 percent of the market and adversely also around 35 percent of the cash payment failures. Because a mere customer "pledge" with no particular commitment to pay for the item once it arrived was all that was required, merchants were taking up so much risk to get items to customers. "I don't want it," "The order happened by mistake," or the customer simply disappearing were some of the scenarios causing headaches and costing a heavy dime. We thought, "There has to be a better way."

If the customer is serious enough about buying a product, why don't we just flip the equation on its head and do it the other way around? That means, if you're serious about placing an order, you can pay for it locally in cash first, and then the order will be delivered to your doorstep. So essentially, we wanted to do cash before delivery (CBD) to overcome some of the shortcomings of COD. It's kind of what happens with credit cards anyway, but we were catering to the local cash preference.

This became the concept behind a product we called PayHyper, a basic payments API we developed. We built software that created a layer on top of local courier companies and physical locations to create a cash collection network for e-purchases. We realized this would have massive potential, not only for physical goods from e-commerce websites, but also for virtual goods as well, including airplane tickets, hotel bookings, concert tickets, iTunes, etc. At the core, guaranteeing cash payments, especially for cross-border commerce, was going to grow the market even further.

I was able to get our product in front of the CEOs of the larger e-commerce players at the time. They saw the value of what we did, and the benefits it would bring their business, but the initial feedback was extremely counter-intuitive. Our network was asking customers essentially to undo their COD-like behavior and pay upfront. So it seemed there was definitely some kind of reverse learning curve if merchants were to adopt the new approach. At least one larger merchant said they would integrate for a live test, but that would take eight to ten months till their development pipeline would be free. "Bullcrap," we thought. We were a scrappy team of two, and we weren't going to wait around to prove that this would work or not.

We either needed an anchor merchant to get us rolling or we had to think differently.

I take it that's how you got the concept for CashBasha?

Yes, ultimately it was. We knew that the majority of e-commerce being done in MENA was inbound from the foreign sites and not the local ones. Amazon, eBay and other destinations were the trusted brand names with the product variety customers were looking for. Sinan and I thought that there must be a way to map the local mindset and transaction preferences to these sites in a better way. We decided to "eat our own dog food" on the payment side and took PayHyper and re-purposed it to build what we called CashBasha.

Researching the market further, we saw that customers relied on popular package-forwarding services when it came to buying from top online international merchants. While these companies solved the shipping problem, they did not solve the payment problem. Since most of the population in the region does not own a credit card or at least one that is eligible to be used online, as, say, in the case of U.S. merchants still requiring a U.S.-based credit card, they were blocked from shopping on those sites. Additionally, these services typically didn't offer the best customer experience either, because they kept customers in the dark when it came to the full landed cost of the package and completely omitted any local customer service on behalf of the merchant, let alone tailored to the local consumer.

We started thinking about how we could employ our technical experience to channel an almost native experience for customers that was at least ten times better than the existing one. How could we take Amazon.com and create an experience in which they seemed to be as close as possible to the customer and their preferences while offering the best customer service possible? We would allow them to shop for any item and have the full breakdown of the landed price to their doorstep in their local currency and payable in cash through our secure network.

CashBasha offered a very seamless customer experience. It had no prerequisites between customers and their first order. We kept the customer in mind through the value chain and offered customer service levels that were in the same time zone, in the same language and with the best guarantees possible.

Getting to this point was not easy for Sinan and me. After many months of long and hard hours of work on PayHyper with no concrete results, then building CashBasha to generate payment transactions, things were heavy. This was when Sinan suggested we come to a deal, an ultimatum that would determine whether we move forward or completely relinquish the business. The term was to achieve sixty paid orders from customers that we were not in touch with, without any marketing and within the first month of business; otherwise we'd shut down and move on. To our pleasant surprise, it only took two days to achieve those sixty orders, and the market directly indicated that we had something.

We then started looking into automating all the parts of the business and gearing up for scalability. We knew that automation was key in e-commerce and keeping our operation light and lean was equally essential, since we were bootstrapping our growth. Bit by bit, we devised an automated way of getting packages processed more quickly through our shipping partner. We built models for calculating customs more accurately with some machine learning, and we even used Interactive Voice Response (IVR) systems to automate customer telephony interactions rather than employing large customer support teams.

We've done well in the countries that we've operated in and grew quickly to a team of eleven with offices in both Amman and Dubai, UAE. CashBasha is just two and a half years old at this point and has already served hundreds of thousands of packages for Amazon and other major e-commerce sites into the region—I believe, better than anyone else. Early on, we received small seed investments from a strategic investor in the region as well as a Silicon Valley VC.

What toll did this fast-paced lifestyle have on you?

Unanticipatedly, 2013 was a rough year. When you start a company, you know it is going to be difficult, but you really don't know what type of difficulty you are going to face until you are actually smack in the midst of it. Compared with my past, where most of the projects that I worked on were successful in their own regard, my drive, ambition, title, recognition, and income were high, and I hadn't really faced failure yet. Only then, life had begun to wind up a slap and prepare to release it right upside my shaved head. Grass started feeling greener on the other side, the one that I might've left behind.

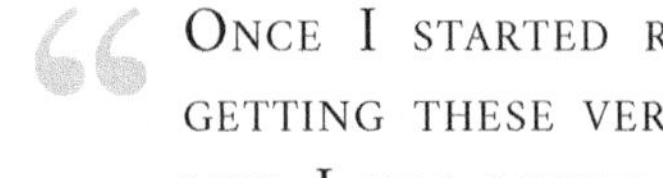

> Once I started reflecting on my life, I started getting these very big feelings of regret. It felt like I was living a life where my priorities were misaligned with my values.

Self-reflection is an important tool, and I suddenly felt that the urge was building inside of me to take a deeper look at what I'd done and was doing. A personal and emotional stress was looming. It was like all of my life, I had known exactly what I wanted to do. I wanted to have my own businesses, put my ideas to work and bring them to reality. I wanted to be in technology. I wanted to do startups. I wanted to be independent. I wanted to grow financially and support my family during the time we had together. I kind of forgot about a lot of the other things in my surroundings, whether they were friends, life experiences, or things that my soul yearned for or wanted. I like travel, music, freedom, just different things. Since it was the only noble thing I had confined myself to, I felt trapped, with my dream as my captor.

To make things worse, seclusion became my company. I was twenty-seven at the time (I am thirty-two now), and it was a very cold chapter in my life. Once I started reflecting on my life, I started feeling these big waves of regrets. It felt like I was living a life where my priorities were misaligned with my values. I recalled working with Dale and Joan in their basement during college and just trying to become the best at my craft and be happy and content with my results. Meanwhile, keeping things in perspective, I completely forgot the importance of that while I was chasing money. My soul was weak, and I was heartbroken.

I was working out of home in the early days of CashBasha when I sank into burnout and depression, literally overnight. I went to bed and woke in a cold sweat of discontent with myself. I didn't want to get out of bed. I didn't want to live. I didn't want to do anything. I didn't want to talk. I couldn't eat. It was as dramatic and pathetic as it could be, quite honestly. It's a point in my life where I realized that the disease of the mind is the most horrid and most undetected of all diseases. It was particularly difficult on my mother, who was very concerned about my well-being and how I was bringing everyone down around me.

Beyond my denial in believing that I could take the reins myself, I eventually ended up seeking medical attention. In the first few minutes, the doctor asked the critical question about any considerations to take my own life, and I was strongly met with an awkward sense of confusion. I felt like I would never consider ending my life, but I somehow understood how it would relieve the agony building inside me and why someone in my position would've. Heavy prescriptions came before me, but I denounced them quickly. I was determined to find my own way before I gave in to the science that might send me on a road to dependency.

This was happening despite having so much to be proud of and grateful for, yet I just couldn't see it. I was deathly fixated only on what was "missing" rather than what I had "found" or was searching for. I then realized that life itself is one big experiment, and even if everything burns to shit and things go sour or bad, still I would come out of this on top, as a more experienced and evolved as far as self-growth is concerned. Society, and perhaps the superficial sector of the world at large, has an obsession with material success that can put you on a competitive path against others, rather than yourself. Although you may win in that environment, if you are true to yourself and your journey, you still lose the game. There is no way around it; that's when I realized that I was edging toward becoming a victim of this thinking.

I also started to understand that growth often comes from vital experiences disguised as pain. So with a big "whoosh," I flushed the pills down the toilet. I was going to take care of myself on my own and no longer rely on a drug, I thought. It was an unbeaten path, and I realized that I would never become the person I once was or what I once had, and I would continue to fail trying to do so. Once I let go of that, things definitely started turning around for me. Famous Chinese philosopher Lao Tzu once said, "When I let go of what I am, I become what I might be." I was to accept that new person for better or worse.

We met Jeff Bezos and the Amazon senior vice president team on November 4, 2016, at our office in Amman. With a nod to how Amazon conducts their meetings, we conducted our session in brief Amazonian style by writing a six-page narrative to describe our proposition. We presented our business model to them and were quite frank in saying, "We know that we are breaking some rules here, but we wouldn't be very good entrepreneurs if we didn't."

What was the turning point, when things clicked?

Over time, my mentality started to shift, and our business began to prosper. Our story started to get exciting, but I really don't know exactly how the upcoming events happened. Some people might say it was divine intervention for these career coincidences to occur, but good karma was upon us, and our work began to pay off. The stars were aligning.

I found out that my uncle's college roommate was actually one of the top people working at Amazon. He was in charge of a number of cornerstone projects over the years and was now head of international logistics and transportation. We connected on a trip of his to Oasis500 in Jordan in 2011, years before we even knew we'd be involved in an e-commerce-related venture. After launching, he heard about us, and we were invited to sit around with him on a personal level, during one of his visits to Jordan in 2015. He was very impressed with what we had done, what we had achieved, and how we were going after very small and difficult countries that were not touched by these large companies like Amazon.

A few calls with their international expansion team later, I ended up getting invited to have a meeting at Amazon headquarters in Seattle, and the stars were aligning even a bit more. In early September of 2016, we received a call that Jeff Bezos, the founder and CEO of Amazon, would be coming into Jordan, and we we would be one of few companies he and his delegation of executives met over their trip to the region.

Most people don't understand that from day one of CashBasha, there has always been this ugly uncertainty in the business that we built, given our dependency on third-party e-commerce sites. As mature entrepreneurs, we recognized these risks but marched on, because the value of tools we could build around the volume this project could generate would be worth the risks. Our hack-ish solutions were smart and neat, but they also gave me nightmares. These thoughts loomed but pushed us toward building our platform and diversifying further.

In October 2016, we won the first-place prize in the largest startup gathering in Istanbul, Turkey. About 25,000 companies applied to be at Startup Istanbul competition, and we won first place. It provided major recognition and some kind of seal of approval. We ended up getting lots of coverage from global outlets like CNN and BBC. It was great in terms of building CashBasha's awareness and credibility. It was another stream of stars aligning before our big meeting.

We met Jeff Bezos and the Amazon senior vice president team on November 4, 2016, at our office in Amman. With a nod to how Amazon conducts their meetings, we conducted our session in brief Amazonian style by writing a six-page narrative to describe our proposition. We presented our business model to them and were quite frank in saying, "We know that we are breaking some rules here, but we wouldn't be very good entrepreneurs if we didn't." Jeff Bezos is notorious for his loud signature outburst laugh, and that statement induced it and filled the room, maybe even the whole building.

LEARN FROM EVERYONE. WHEN I STARTED OUT, I HAD A LOT OF PEOPLE WHO WERE SUPPORTING ME. NOT EVERYONE HAD ALL THE INFORMATION, SO I TRIED TO LEARN FROM OTHERS AS WELL. I ALSO LEARNED FROM TUTORING OTHER PEOPLE. I EVEN LEARNED FROM PEOPLE THAT I DIDN'T EXPECT TO LEARN FROM.

Reading everything there was ever to be read about Amazon and Bezos, we knew they did their own share of hack-ish things to get the ball rolling in their early days, so we weren't ashamed of it. Sinan and I had built an iron stomach after all we'd been through. It was a great moment for us. How many times in life will you get the chance to say something like that in the face of such an accomplished group of people? Let alone a person who, just three days later, became the wealthiest person in the world. Our "little team" was doing something better than they were, and they recognized it. Jeff left the meeting holding our narrative document by his side for the rest of the day.

I look back to the dark chapters in my personal life and then how far we have come along. Being here today, I am not saying that I am completely relieved of the paranoia around our work life and what we're doing, but I believe things can always turn around if you just stick to your guns and keep going.

What's your advice to aspiring entrepreneurs?

My advice to entrepreneurs revolves around four points. The first point being, learn from everyone. When I started out, I had a lot of people who were supporting me. Not everyone had all the information, so I tried to learn from others as well. I also learned from tutoring other people. I even learned from people that I didn't expect to learn from. You naturally gravitate toward people who have more knowledge, age or more accomplishments, but they are not necessarily the people who will give you all the information that you need or give you that spark for a new idea or inspire your next step.

The second one is to follow no one, and this is where I kind of fell for a little bit. I wanted to follow other successful people's footsteps. There is a lot of glamorization in the entrepreneurial ecosystem obviously these days. Some people look at Bill Gates and think, "I need to follow him to be successful." For me, I wanted to follow around successful people in my family and in trade and do what they were doing. Then I realized that everybody has to have their own path, so it's much more noble for you to create your own story and set on your own journey.

The third one would be, look for patterns. There are very clear patterns and trends that happen in business markets. Obviously, the Middle East can be looked at as being a few years behind in some areas, but we're catching on with the internet. Today we see that there is a massive pattern of growth in e-commerce, both globally and in the region. Look for the right patterns as you go along and try to focus on an idea that actually has promise, a good market, and ready and willing investors. It's about looking for patterns and opportunities that are well-timed and being able to ride that wave as much as possible and as long as possible.

The fourth one, I would say: get to work early and work like hell. When I look back, I really believe this motto was essential to my own development. The experiences I gained even from doing small projects, like when I was burning CDs, were very valuable. Learning new things, working on projects, and participating in different learning venues is critical.

You will have to make some sacrifices for your dream. So you have to make sure that is really what you want to do. If it's not, then there's nothing wrong with exiting in search of comfort elsewhere. I truly believe there is only one way to fail, and that is by giving up. I sound like I contradict myself a little bit, but there are some times when it's OK to give up and move on to the next thing. If you are destined to be an entrepreneur, giving up on entrepreneurship might be something you consider a failure. Failing while you're an entrepreneur is just the next step to getting to something that you might succeed at. The way I look at it is that if you want an atypical life, atypical success, atypical learning, and atypical growth, then you surely will have to go through atypical experiences and circumstances to reach that point. Deal with it!

What's your view on hiring and team-building?

We're a small company of eleven people. So there is very little room to go up a corporate ladder. However, what we've always tried to do is to find a particular persona, and that's very clear in the job listings that we put up online. We describe what type of person we would like to join us, not what their technical background is or their experiences are. We are happy to hire for particular positions, but we're not looking to limit hiring to people who only have MBAs, for example, or have X years of experience. I think the relevance of an opportunity depends on a person's relevance to the company first, and then their capability of executing for the need of that position.

Beyond that, we've also been successful by presenting our technology openly to other people—giving technical talks, being present at general events, and having people know that we're approachable and that we're around. We work out of a co-working space in a very high traffic area in Amman, King Hussein Business Park. This is not something we do or like to do by any means, but some of the best hires have been from right next door, and we didn't know about them. So that's how we've built our team so far.

Any advice to aspiring entrepreneurs regarding bootstrapping?

One of the big problems with being able to bootstrap your business is if you're a technology company who is outsourcing your core business or its development, there is something that is definitely wrong with that picture, especially early on in the life of the company. If you lack the technical skill set, you will have to get a co-founder who has the capability of bringing your first product to market without any third-party involvement. Otherwise, you run the risk of a costly operation.

What's your experience trying to achieve work-life balance?

I think I have a lot to say about work-life balance, because we didn't do a very good job there. So speaking of our early experiences, Sinan and I, obviously we were very motivated toward our work and very dedicated to what we wanted to achieve. We pushed very hard on trying to get things out as quickly as possible. When we were twenty-four years old, we thought that putting in these crazy-long hours would be the noble thing to do. We also couldn't imagine being successful without putting in, say, fourteen- and maybe sometimes even sixteen-hour days, crazy times. Our investment, however, wasn't directly proportional to our output, and it took a while to realize it.

I remember that Sinan and I sometimes would try to go to the gym early in the morning at 6:00 a.m. before heading to a crummy little borrowed office that we were using in an older part of Amman. When we would get in, the sun would barely be out; it would be about 7:00 to 8:00 a.m. We would then not get out till 10:00 or 11:00 p.m. at night. We realized that we would be inside all day and not expose ourselves to any sunlight. Not go for a walk, nothing. This really took a huge toll on us and was unhealthy on multiple levels.

Looking back, we let go of time with family, friends, as well as other social aspects. As two rather multifaceted individuals after a greater future for ourselves, our judgment was clouded, but we didn't feel it in the interim. The longer term effects led us into respective depression. We felt detached and secluded by sacrificing so much, yet not attaining the expected level of outcome built in our minds. That is one important thing as well for people who are starting companies; you notice that your mind is working in parallel to your hands and that you are building an expectation or certain image that may not align with reality. You don't start a company to fail, and most people want to achieve a particular level of success, but managing where you go with that effort can deter you from hitting disappointment and burnout.

We both learned that working more efficiently had to become a priority. Dedicating full concentration to that six to eight hours of work and being able to manage a wholesome life outside of work, just as much as managing your day inside work, is vitally important. You may end up going through life realizing that you wasted your youth focusing on something that may or may not work; that is the inherit risk in being an entrepreneur, but preventing yourself from living a full life should never be an option. It's not a noble thing by any standard. What we've realized and part of the reason why I personally fell into a depression is I thought that I was wasting so much time and effort on this dream that might not even give me the fulfillment I was personally looking for. That mix is a recipe for disaster.

Today, we are much more balanced in terms of our lives. I personally am much better at managing my own time. I make sure I hit the gym early in the morning and eat right over the course of the day. I dedicated those eight hours at work to be the only hours I actually dedicate to work. I try to have a life outside of work. I personally have, and everybody probably has, particular dreams that they want to pursue, or particular experiences that they want to attain. For example, I wanted to start a band ever since I was a kid, and I got the chance to do that about two years ago, as an extracurricular activity outside of work. It just so happens that a bunch of people in my work building were also music hobbyists. We wanted to put on a show, and we actually ended up doing a couple of shows after that, and we formed a small band that went around in Amman called Nomads, and it's something I can tick off my bucket list with pride.

> ONE OF THE MAIN THINGS THAT YOU SHOULD DEFINITELY CONSIDER IS JUST REMEMBER NOT TO LET LIFE PASS YOU BY, BECAUSE THERE ARE CERTAIN THINGS IN LIFE THAT I THINK YOU CAN'T PROCRASTINATE ON AND MUST PURSUE EARLY AS WELL AS OFTEN—FOR EXAMPLE, ALWAYS BEING HEALTHY AND TAKING GOOD CARE OF THE VESSEL THAT CARRIES YOU SPIRITUALLY OR PHYSICALLY. THAT'S SOMETHING THAT YOU CAN'T FIX WHEN YOU'RE FIFTY.

One of the main things that you should definitely consider is just remember not to let life pass you by, because there are certain things in life that I think you can't procrastinate on and must pursue early as well as often—for example, always being healthy and taking good care of the vessel that carries you spiritually or physically. That's something that you can't fix when you're fifty.

There are so many lovely things in the world that you want to do that you shouldn't have to wait for a prerequisite to be able to do them. The prerequisite I think in most Arab cultures is that, "Oh, I have to have X dollars in the bank before I can get married/start a business/be happy/travel/be noticed, or I need to have accomplished a particular 'X' before I can do 'Y,' " or whatever. I think that a lot of people put those limitations on themselves and end up wasting a lot of time not pursuing the right things for them, at the right times, with the right partners. These are sad barriers we set.

What resources do you recommend for entrepreneurs?

I've been very fond of Reddit over the years. Not just because it's a fun site, but because there are real communities that are being formed across different interests. Earlier and when I had more time to spend on news sites, I read every single article on TechCrunch, but since that is no longer a good use of my time, I use email lists like those of Inside.com to send me daily updates and headlines over a few topics that I'm excited about.

On an educational level, Udemy.com and other MOOCs (massive open online courses) provided by the leading universities around the world make for an incredible source of information. Tech Talks and TED Talks have also been insightful and inspiring for me.

What do you feel is missing from the startup ecosystem in the region?

I think one of the big things lacking is research and development, which is obviously very much tied to the education system and the government's priorities. Although we consider ourselves here in Jordan, for example, to graduate one of the highest numbers of engineers in the region, many of the skills aren't in unison with modern skills that are in demand today. More so, despite the over-arching agendas of educational institutions that involve a good deal of R&D efforts, they are less funded and thus less pursued by the accomplished scholars of the region or abroad. We continue to ship out rather than import IP developing talent that would subsequently translate into a bustling industry. Looking at the Chinese or Indian models that naturally exported their talent to better opportunities in the west, their governments learned to take advantage of an opportunity to build legislative frameworks to incentivize those minds carrying their nationalities to come back and pursue global opportunities right from home. Of course, we are talking about populations reaching well over a billion, but that doesn't mean that we can't be as effective with millions. We have the money to do it; we just don't believe in ourselves or committing to a long-term vision.

What are your thoughts on the future prospects of the region?

It's extremely exciting to see that the world is looking toward the MENA region, perhaps as one of the last untapped markets, but nonetheless a growing one. Things are still nascent in terms of the internet, even globally, I believe. We do have some acquisitions, with an increasing number coming along the way as well. If you look at the e-commerce market specifically, only a very small fraction of the market is e-commerce compared with the retail market. So there are certainly massive untapped opportunities on that front specifically, and we hope to put our mark on it one way or another.

KHALIL SHADID

Making restaurant reservations a seamless experience

Co-founder and CEO of Reserveout

WWW.RESERVEOUT.COM

KHALIL SHADID is the co-founder and CEO of Reserveout, a web and mobile application for restaurant reservations, allowing diners to quickly search and reserve at restaurants within its network. Prior to founding Reserveout, Khalil worked at Cisco systems for eight years. He graduated from North Carolina State University with a degree in computer and electrical engineering and a minor in economics.

Tell us a bit about your background.

I was born and raised in Jerusalem, Palestine. I attended high school there before going to the U.S. for university. I have been shaped by my upbringing in Palestine quite a bit. I was raised in a part of the world where people had to endure and persevere through various conflicts, in terms of everyday living conditions and ongoing political instability. I went to school in Ramallah, which is sixteen kilometers away from where I lived. It took me more than a couple of hours to go to and return from school each day because I had to go through multiple Israeli checkpoints and roadblocks.

I've always been the type of person that is determined. When I want to do something, I don't give up. Since I was young, I have always been very competitive. I played a lot of sports and was somewhat of a sore loser, I'll be the first to admit, and a lot of these things really came out when I started my own business. These are things you carry with you through life, I guess.

I never intended to be an entrepreneur. I never even thought of it growing up. Both of my parents had great jobs. My mom is a doctor, and my dad ran a non-governmental organization in Palestine. Both were very successful and always instilled in my sisters and me the importance of education and hard work. They taught us how you can change your life and change everything based on your decisions and your work ethic.

The first time I was exposed to entrepreneurship was through my uncle during the time I attended university in the U.S. He lived in New York City and was very senior at PwC (PricewaterhouseCoopers) back then. Then, one day, he decided just to quit his job and start his own business. So I got to see firsthand how hard he was working. He was putting in eighteen to twenty hours a day. He also had just recently married, so I lived through a lot of that with him and saw the roller coasters that he went through. He eventually became highly successful. So that always stuck with me. It also got me thinking, "Why would someone who is doing so well, making a lot of money, leave that to start something that they don't know if it's going to succeed or not?" So that definitely got me to start seeing things in a different light. Until this day, my uncle is one of my biggest mentors and role models. He is someone I always depend on a lot for advice.

I studied computer and electrical engineering at university in North Carolina. While I was still in school, I started working full-time with Cisco systems. Initially, I was in the Research Triangle Park, and then I got moved to New York City, which has always been one of my favorite cities and a place I always wanted to live in. So that worked out beautifully. It was there that I developed my interest in technology and business. I think most of what I know today in business I learned at Cisco. I think it was overall a great place to work.

How did the idea of Reserveout come about?

When I moved to New York, I realized how passionate I am about food and dining out. I enjoyed trying new restaurants and different cuisines. New York offers a tremendous variety of international cuisines and types and variety of foods in general, much more than any city I can think of.

That's actually where the idea of Reserveout was born, in 2010. I was still working for Cisco, living in New York, when I went back to Jordan for my cousin's wedding. I remember I wanted to go to brunch on the morning of her wedding, and to get a reservation at a restaurant was a nightmare. I had to actually call my cousin who was getting married to call a friend of hers to make a booking for me at a restaurant. Then this idea sparked in my head. I thought to myself, "I live in New York, the best city on earth when it comes to restaurants. So why is it so difficult to get a booking in Amman, when I can easily get a reservation at any restaurant I want in New York City with just three clicks on my phone?"

> I thought to myself, "I live in New York, the best city on earth when it comes to restaurants. So why is it so difficult to get a booking in Amman, when I can easily get a reservation at any restaurant I want in New York City with just three clicks on my phone?"

So that's actually what sparked the idea of starting Reserveout. It's not that I wanted to be an entrepreneur. It was the opposite. I was actually very happy at my job. I loved what I did. I loved working for Cisco. I was on a fast track in terms of growth, titles, and everything. I had every reason to stay, but I saw an opportunity that I wanted to pursue and started researching and looking further into it.

In the beginning, I was intrigued by the technology. The more I looked into it and researched what type of technologies restaurants had in Jordan, I questioned how they were managing their reservations and database. What do they look at? What are the tools they have access to? I found that it was very limited. OpenTable, the company I used a lot in New York for booking my own reservations, barely existed in Jordan. They only had about fifty restaurants that were all through international acquisition.

I also learned a lot about how restaurants operated, especially in New York. I was also still assessing the viability of the business and if the Middle East was the right place for it. OpenTable actually had a back end that they used for reservations, not just the interface that I see as the user. The basic concept was to deliver technology to local restaurants for better management of their reservations, to put them online, get them online bookings, and create for them a proper CRM and customer database.

I traveled and talked to a lot of restaurants that year. I used to go back to the Middle East from New York twice a year. That year I went back and forth nine times, and it was mainly to speak to restaurants and assess where I wanted to set up. It was actually not an easy decision, because I grew up in Palestine, had never lived in Jordan, never lived in Lebanon, and never lived in the UAE. I knew that starting this type of business in Palestine would be very difficult, because in order for it to work, it couldn't depend on one country. I would need to scale it across the region and travel out of Palestine, which is very difficult, because you had to cross through Jordan.

So I had to assess that if I'm going to do this, where am I going to do it? How am I going to do it? How am I going to get it funded? There were a million questions going through my mind, but I just had a feeling that this was really what I wanted to do. What was the worst thing that could happen? I start this business; if it doesn't work out in a year or two, I can always go back to business school. So I made the decision that the right thing for me to do was defer my MBA and actually embark on this journey. It took a while to begin, because I was living in New York and trying to start a business in the Middle East.

I finally decided that Jordan was probably the best place for Reserveout to set up. There was lots of good talent when it came to developers, and it was very centrally located, so I could easily travel everywhere in the region. Costs in Jordan were relatively lower than most places. So if I wanted to hire developers or have any type of function, it was cheaper than Dubai, cheaper than Beirut, cheaper than other places, and I had family there. So I made up my mind to set up there. When we started, I had a partner; it was a friend of mine,

Bashar Saleh. He was my roommate in New York. So Bashar and I started Reserveout together.

We both had tech backgrounds. He was a developer and actually working for BlackRock, a financial management service firm. Meanwhile, I was at Cisco on the consulting, marketing side for communications technologies. So we had agreed that we would start the business together and that he would be the CTO and I would run operations and marketing. We put $70,000 together from our savings to start the business.

The first thing we did was start working on the reservation engine, the table management system. Initially, we said, "OK, we have to save money. Why don't we both keep our jobs? We'll start working on this in New York, and once we have a product, we can transition full-time to the new business." Then we realized that it wouldn't work. When you have another job that you are committed to that you actually also enjoy, it is very difficult. Things were moving very slowly.

A year later, we had built some of the technology but were still far from where we wanted to be. We decided that the right thing to do was quit and actually move to Amman and be online, otherwise we were going to waste more time, and it was not going to work. So we picked up and left. Bashar left six months before me, because he was the one actually doing the development and hiring and working with the developers.

I followed six months later, and the rationale behind it was that it would take six months to build a platform. I could do what I needed to do, which was marketing material and sales presentations, etc., remotely while still living in New York, so we could reduce costs, obviously. We wouldn't have to pay me out of the $70,000 that we put together, but we would pay him, since he didn't have an income. Six months later, I left New York and moved to Amman to find that we were nowhere close to being ready to pitch to a client. This didn't matter; we continued to work on the product. At that point, we hired another developer, and I think it took us another year or so before we were ready to go out to market.

How did you develop the initial product?

Although the thought process of starting Reserveout came about in 2010, we actually didn't launch until March 2012. That's when we had our first product ready and we started testing it with restaurants in Amman. We realized that whatever we had built there had a lot of mistakes. We talked to a lot of restaurateurs, and we realized that a lot of things we did, we were thinking as developers, not as restaurateurs. We learned that when we were running the initial beta testing with some restaurants. It took us another six months to go back and re-engineer a lot of it until we had a product that restaurants could actually use.

OpenTable technology doesn't change much; it's not easily customizable; it's a little bit outdated. They basically have a monopoly in the U.S. Meanwhile, very few restaurants had OpenTable in the Middle East. We said, "This is great. We have a clean slate."

We were off to quite a rough start. We thought the technology that we built for the restaurants, the website for the bookings was really straightforward. Later we found out that it wasn't that straightforward. We needed to make a lot of improvements on the UI (user interface) and UX (user experience). Our goal was to build the table management system that restaurants loved using. Based on a lot of the people we talked to, we heard that although everyone used OpenTable, everyone hated them.

OpenTable technology doesn't change much; it's not easily customizable; it's a little bit outdated. They basically have a monopoly in the U.S. Meanwhile, very few restaurants had OpenTable in the Middle East. We said, "This is great. We have a clean slate, and we're going to build technology that grows quickly, adapts and integrates. One that is not tied to a simple hardware. You could run it on anything you want, on a tablet, on a Mac, on a PC." In the meantime, we also got a lot of skepticism and criticism from people telling us, "Why are you reinventing the wheel? OpenTable is already doing this. Why don't you just license OpenTable or a different company for the Middle East?"

Besides OpenTable, there were a lot of companies that built this type of technology. So acquiring the license to the technology of one of those companies seemed like an easier and less risky path to take, as opposed to developing the product from scratch ourselves. We struggled with this decision initially before we decided we didn't want to be at the mercy of a software developer or OpenTable every time we decided we would need a feature specific to the Middle East, like translating into Arabic. We knew we had to localize, and we had to understand how different markets behaved differently and build a product that fit the markets we were after. What works in London and New York doesn't necessarily work in Dubai or Hong Kong, or India, or another place.

We determined that the right thing to do was to build our own platform, and although it was very difficult, very challenging, we understood why there weren't more companies that do this. It really was difficult to build this type of solution, but now, in hindsight, it was probably one of the best decisions we made. That's one of the things that sets Reserveout apart from competition today. Our ability to localize very quickly, to deliver features, to be nimble, to support new platforms when they come out.

We launched our first product in Amman. We had signed up twenty restaurants. We went after the best restaurant groups in Jordan and managed to persuade them to work with us. It was successful, although there was a lot of additional product development that we needed to do. They liked it and migrated fully to it. One thing we didn't anticipate though is, just because we have a restaurant owner buy in on our product, it does not necessarily mean the employees of the restaurant are going to use it.

People don't like change. People think of change as extra work and something they have to learn. Although our system was very simple and intuitive, we ran into a lot of hurdles trying to convince the people at the restaurant to actually use it. We had to spend long hours with them basically forcing them to use the system, instead of writing a reservation on a piece of paper and entering it into the system. It was important that we understood how to make the software simple. We also had to make it in Arabic, because a lot of people in Jordan don't speak English.

Right after we launched, we secured our first round of funding. It was right on time because we were running out of cash, and we had also stopped paying ourselves just to make sure that our teams were paid and happy to continue to work. Then we raised our first round of funding from iMENA Holdings. They were just starting out. So we were the first investment they made, and we raised $1.2 million dollars in two trenches. The first trench was $500,000; the second was $700,000. Once we did that, we started expanding further into Amman.

One strategy that worked was to initially sign up the best restaurants in town. It was easier to get the other restaurants because they looked at what the other guys were doing. They were like, well, if X restaurant chain was on this platform, maybe we should be on this platform as well. If they are using the system, maybe we should be using the system as well. That strategy actually worked in our favor, although to get that restaurant group to sign up with us at the beginning, we had to give it to them for free for six months. So although we did have twenty restaurants, we weren't making any money, not on the reservations, not on the software itself.

In hindsight, this was the right thing to do, getting initial restaurants on board at whatever cost. We learned a lot, honestly, because they were busy restaurants, and it really put our software to the test. We had a lot of glitches at the beginning, but we were very quick in fixing them, and they saw how passionate and committed we were to what we were doing. Although we did have some major issues at times, they were fairly happy with us.

What was your experience with your first geographical expansion?

When we raised funding, we started thinking expansion. There were two cities that we would initially go to, Beirut and Dubai. At the time, we had decided that Beirut would be the first place we would go to. It's only forty-five minutes from Amman. It was easier to get to. We also knew a bunch of people there that connected us to restaurants at the time.

I ended up moving to Beirut and dropping in Amman for one week every month. Once in Beirut, I started going door to door, selling to restaurants, selling our technology and our software. That was the first exposure doing business in Beirut, which was very different from Jordan and Palestine. Doing business with Lebanese is nothing like doing business with Jordanians or Palestinians. There is a learning curve to be done, to "speak their language," behave like them, position your offering the right way. It was actually an eye-opening experience.

Initially, we managed to sign ten restaurants. Then more restaurants started coming on board, but then we hit a wall. The political situation in Beirut was getting worse. People were not going out as much. Restaurants were very skeptical. No one wanted to invest, because we were charging a monthly fee for the software. So a lot of the restaurants said, "OK, we'll use your software, but we don't want to pay for it. We don't know what's going to happen. We might be forced to shut down. We are conserving costs." So we gave them the technology initially for free, but then the free period ended and nothing happened; they still didn't want to pay.

Around the same time, we did an affiliate partnership in Lebanon with Time Out Beirut magazine. We quickly realized that this wasn't going anywhere. If we were to be serious about launching in a city, we had to do it ourselves. We had to invest our own money; we couldn't depend on Time Out Beirut to come and sell the software for us, because it doesn't work like that. Their sales team was used to selling advertising to all kinds of restaurants, but this was something completely different. On paper it made sense, but it was a complete failure.

Eventually, restaurants in Beirut started paying and business was turning the corner a bit, so we decided to now focus on Dubai, which is a bigger market in spite of being farther and more complex. Once again, I picked up my bags and moved to Dubai to start the business there.

Dubai was a different beast altogether, because I didn't know many people there. We had to establish a legal business entity in Dubai, unlike Amman or Beirut, where we didn't have to. You can't go to Dubai without a visa. Fortunately, I have a U.S. passport, so it was easy for me, but not for my partner. Dubai is a big city. We needed to hire a sales team. We needed to hire marketing. We needed to hire support, because day one, when you have a restaurant using your software, something might go wrong. We needed to make sure someone was there to support them.

So Dubai was very challenging right from the outset, but we set up business and started recruiting nevertheless. Initially, I think we looked to recruit from people who were already selling to restaurants —people who worked for Red Bull, people who worked for Coca-Cola. We were also recruiting from group-buying companies, such as Groupon, Cobone, etc. There was also another one that was bought by LivingSocial called GoNabit. So we were hiring salespeople from these types of businesses because their staff was already selling to restaurants.

We also quickly realized that some restaurants in Dubai, especially the ones in hotels, already had reservation booking software. So they didn't necessarily need ours, although we thought we had a better product. Though we kept running into resistance from restaurants and the mentality of, "I'm working with a British company. I'm working with an American company. I'm working with OpenTable. I'm working with Resy, which is an Australian company which has been around for twenty years. So why would I switch to an unproven startup that that's been around for less than a year and just started in Dubai, and no one has used it?"

That was very difficult. Getting any paying restaurants in Dubai was very tough. So, once again, we had to initially give away the license for free. I remember the first restaurant group we ever signed, called The Meat Co. They have great steak houses in Madinat Jumeirah and Dubai Mall and other prime locations. It is a well-known restaurant, and that was really the first client that we signed that people knew. From there, we used that name to get other restaurants interested in working with us.

What's your take on basic steps to building a brand?

It's very important to have very strong branding, very memorable and consistent, always using the same words. Making sure that everyone in the company speaks the same language so if you ask a developer, if you ask the head of marketing, or if you ask a content creator, what is Reserveout? They should all answer the same way, maybe using different words, but the delivery and the messaging about who you are and what defines you should always be consistent.

How did you differentiate your product and service from the established competition?

All the while we were trying to sign up restaurants, we were developing our software, growing it, making sure it was better than OpenTable and better than any of the international players. We had to look at what everyone did, what they didn't do, what we could improve on.

IT'S VERY IMPORTANT TO HAVE VERY STRONG BRANDING, VERY MEMORABLE AND CONSISTENT, ALWAYS USING THE SAME WORDS. MAKING SURE THAT EVERYONE IN THE COMPANY SPEAKS THE SAME LANGUAGE.

If they were doing just reservation and table management, how could we create a more powerful CRM? How could we integrate with the restaurant's point of sale system, so that when you're looking at the guest's profile, you're not just looking at how many times they've been there and what they're allergic to, you also see what they like? You also see how much they spend, what's the average spend per person? What if you can solve a problem for a restaurant by letting them do revenue management? If I'm a restaurant and I had a waiting list of, say, ten people on one table, how can I choose someone that I know will spend above $200, $300, or $400 per person? So these are the things we started thinking of, because we were put in a corner, and restaurants were telling us, "You are new and unproven."

Eventually, we were beginning to get noticed. Restaurants were getting more impressed with our software, our features, and with the interface that we created, and slowly we started signing up more and more restaurants. I started figuring my way around Dubai through lots of trial and error. I also started to figure out what works and what doesn't, until I got to what I call my "dream team" in Dubai, where I had four fantastic salespeople, each of them closing fifty restaurants a month. It was the end of 2015 when I can say the business really started seeing the light at the end of the tunnel.

Around the same time, we started expanding to Doha, Qatar, and Manama, Bahrain, through some of the restaurants we had in Dubai that also had branches in those places. Then we signed our largest client to date, which was Rotana Hotels. We managed to basically sign an exclusive agreement with Rotana, where they would put Reserveout in every restaurant they owned. Over the course of a year, they would add 120 restaurants. We also rolled out another 180 restaurants for Hyatt a year later, between the Middle East and India. We continued to grow and sign large restaurant groups and hotels, including Starwood and Marriott.

This new uptake, especially from hotels, forced us to further develop our offering. We now had to offer staff training and live support, a call center, detailed reporting, and other account management and support tools and services. We even built a module for customer feedback for restaurants to send an SMS or text push notifications to their customers the next day, asking, "How was your meal? What could we have done better?" Restaurants even asked us to push these reviews out to their Google post page and to Trip Advisor. So we were always learning and tweaking the product and offering as we went.

How challenging was fundraising and what did you learn from it?

One of the biggest challenges, and continues to be, in the region is funding. Initially, we raised $1.2 million as I mentioned, then we needed to raise funding again in 2014, and we couldn't find a single VC to fund us. So I had to piecemeal a dozen or so different angels, each one giving me anywhere between $30,000 and $100,000 to raise another $1.3 million dollars around.

I can't tell you how many times when the 25th of the month came and I had only $10,000 in the bank account, and my monthly payroll was $70,000. So I had to manage, get a loan from someone, get an investor to inject money with a convertible note agreement quickly. There were numerous hurdles that I had to jump through to make sure that Reserveout didn't die, but somehow, it always worked out. I never lost hope, and here we are today. We raised an additional $4.1 million from Amman-based Silicon Badia in 2016. We have 4,500 restaurants. We service more than 50,000 people a month, and that number is growing month on month. We do have competitors, but if you combine all our competitors together, they will probably be 20 percent of what we do in terms of volume.

> "Everything you plan, halve the expectations and double the money that you need. So if you think something is going to take you six months, it is probably going to take you a year. If you think you need a million, you probably need two million. If you think you are projecting to make half a million your second year, you are probably going to make $250,000.

Any advice to entrepreneurs regarding balancing timelines, expectations and deliverables?

Great question. My advice to any entrepreneur, and I speak from firsthand experience—everything you plan, halve the expectations and double the money that you need. So if you think something is going to take you six months, it is probably going to take you a year. If you think you need a million, you probably need two million. If you think you are projecting to make half a million your second year, you are probably going to make $250,000.

I put my projections together, then I divide all my projections by half, and I double the money, and then I work backward to see how I can plan somewhere in between. I think this is very important, because what happens is that you budget, you think that you have enough money for eighteen months, but things are taking longer, money is not coming in as quickly, and you are running out of cash, and you must fundraise from a weak position.

You should always fundraise money when you don't need money. You should always be able to walk away from the deal, because that's how entrepreneurs get screwed. That's how you end up in a situation where someone is giving you an evaluation that is not right, but you're about to run out of cash, so you have to take it because it is your only option.

What are your general thoughts on customer service?

I think customer service is one of the most important elements of any business. Customer service is really about putting customers first, making sure that you are very responsive, making sure that you admit fault when it's your fault.

I have a policy: I would never lie to a client if we have an issue, although a lot of other vendors do that. If a customer finds a problem, then they ask me about it, and I find it's a bug or it's something that we did incorrectly, I tell them.

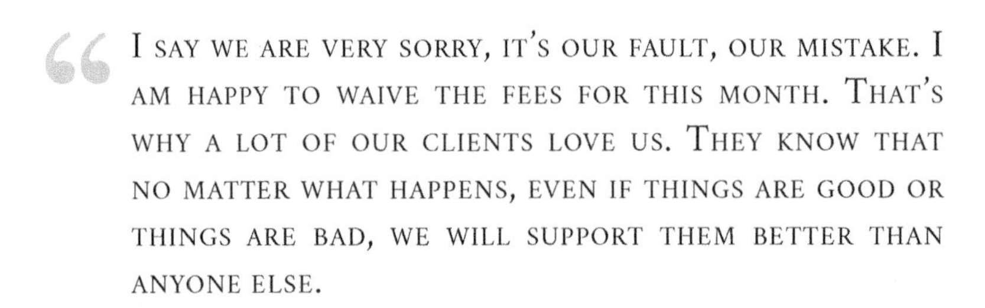

I say we are very sorry, it's our fault, our mistake. I am happy to waive the fees for this month. That's why a lot of our clients love us. They know that no matter what happens, even if things are good or things are bad, we will support them better than anyone else.

When a restaurant is not doing well and they cannot pay us, I make them a payment plan. I want my clients to understand that we are in this together, that this is a partnership, that if I grow, you grow. If you grow, I grow, and if you were going through a rough time, I will help you. If I go through a rough time, I expect you to stand by me as well.

What are some of the ways you're able to gain new insights on your business?

One thing that I always do and find very helpful is I always talk to people about Reserveout, people who are neither entrepreneurs nor investors. Sometimes family, sometimes friends, sometimes people I meet at a dinner table and get their perception of how they see things, because the way I see things and the way someone with different thinking may see something is very different, and I get a lot of insights from doing that. There is no agenda. I am not trying to raise money from this person. I am not trying to hire them. I am not trying to get them to make an introduction somewhere. I'm just trying to put myself in their shoes and understand how they perceive my business.

I also talked to a lot of people from different lines of businesses to see how they do something right—what kind of practices or policies they have adopted and whether it is in accounting, recruiting, whatever it may be, and try to learn from them.

Another thing I do is send my product managers once a month to restaurants, and they spend a whole day there doing nothing, just monitoring, watching how restaurant staff work. We ask ourselves, "Are they using our system efficiently? What can we implement to make their life easier?" I cannot tell you how many ideas and how many new features we come up with just from doing that exercise.

What are your future plans to build off the success you've had with Reserveout so far?

The vision I had for Reserveout when I started was to be the Open-Table of the Middle East, and that vision has since changed tremendously. Now, I am looking to take this global. We already have restaurants in India. We have one deal in Asia and another in Europe. We have a few restaurants in London that use our platform. We are looking now to launch in Egypt, Hong Kong, and Turkey, which are very interesting markets.

There is a lot of talk that innovations cannot come out of this region, and I want to change that. I want to show the world that a reservation management system built out of Jordan, started in the Middle East, can compete globally with OpenTable and with any of these big players outside our home markets.

We've built an amazing technology. Our clients reiterate that when they compare our global competitors' technology and they look at ours, they ask us, "Why aren't you in New York? Why aren't you in London? Why aren't you in other cities?" Now that is becoming very close to my heart, and we have already started the plans of working on that. We actually just started raising a new round of funding. We're doing our series B officially as we speak, and a major part of that funding is going to fund our global expansion. So stay tuned!

18

MAI MEDHAT

Mobilizing events

Co-Founder and CEO of Eventtus

WWW.EVENTTUS.COM

Mai Medhat is the co-founder and CEO of Eventtus, an online platform and mobile app for event planning, networking and ticketing she founded in 2012. It's an all-in-one solution to empower the next generation of event experiences. She has managed to raise $2.65 million of funding for Eventtus so far. Mai is an Endeavor Entrepreneur. She studied computer engineering at Ain Shams University in Cairo and worked in different startups before founding Eventtus.

Tell us a bit about your background and early influences.

I was born and raised in Cairo, Egypt, in a small family. I have one brother. My father is a doctor. He was working in Saudi Arabia for what seemed like forever. So we were always back and forth between Egypt and Saudi Arabia.

I got inspired by my grandfather. We were very close. I always felt we had a special connection. He was a traditional entrepreneur. He owned a printing house. He bought me my first computer when I finished sixth grade, in 1995. I used to play games and browse the internet. I loved it.

Ever since I was a kid, I've always felt I wanted to do something different. I've always wanted to make some kind of impact, to change something in the world for the better. I wanted to feel that I was an active part of society. Though I didn't know at the time exactly how to go about it.

I was a very good student at high school. I was always at the top of my class. I liked studying and learning new things. During the same time, I really got into building websites for celebrities. These were fun projects during my teenage years. I really enjoyed creating those websites and working with computers in general. So I decided to major in engineering in college. I eventually graduated from Ain Shams University with a computer science degree.

We were assigned a graduate project in college. I remember we sat down together as a team and decided we would do something that has some kind of practical application. We didn't want to complete the assignment just for the sake of submitting to the university. We wanted to do something that we could actually implement and go to market with.

We decided we wanted to solve the traffic problem in Egypt. If you've ever been to Cairo, you're aware traffic jams are a massive problem. We wanted to help fix it. We developed a mobile app, like Google Maps to detect traffic. We had algorithms to detect traffic from various cameras in the streets. We even built a machine-learning computer vision system to detect if the street was empty or crowded. Then we made a social component where people could report the traffic status. There were three or four mechanisms to detect traffic.

We received huge support from everyone in the university. We signed up for the Microsoft Imagine Cup competition, which is an annual competition drawing student developers worldwide who are attempting to solve the world's toughest challenges. We ended up winning first place in Egypt and went on to place thirteenth worldwide.

So naturally, we felt we were onto something and wanted to actually take the product to market. We failed miserably because we were quite inexperienced. We hardly knew anything about business. I remember meeting my first VC after graduating from university. I didn't even understand back then why VCs would want to give their money to a group of people or for something that they don't know anything about.

Shortly thereafter, I started to learn and read and watch some videos. I learned about venture capital, management, marketing, sales, and everything else. Then I got a full-time job; so did the rest of my team. We all started working at other companies and forgot about the project.

After university, I attended a lot of events with my friends. That's where I met Nihal, my co-founder at Eventtus, at one of those events. We both shared a passion for technology, so we got along great and eventually started working together.

How did you get the idea for Eventtus?

Nihal and I started talking about how we wanted to work on a special project together. So we started exploring and testing different ideas. We worked on it after hours, and we weren't getting anywhere. If you want to do something, you can't do it while you're working in a full-time job. Entrepreneurship is an all-consuming effort, so it requires a full-time commitment.

Around that time, we heard about the first Startup Weekend event happening in Cairo. I applied for the event, but I didn't get an invitation or a ticket. I decided that I was going to attend anyway. I was interested in learning about what was happening in the startup scene in Egypt and in exploring opportunities. So I went; I actually snuck in.

At the event, I joined a team and worked on a project. We also had in our group Baha Galil, the co-founder of Crowd Analyzer (an internationally recognized social media monitoring platform). We ended up working on two completely different ideas. I was starting to like this startup life. It was challenging but very fulfilling at the same time. I enjoy building things from scratch. I also started enjoying thinking and coming up with answers to all kinds of business challenges. "How can we approach a given problem to solve? How do we structure a project? How to develop everything? What about marketing? What's our business model?" These were all questions you have to constantly be asking as an entrepreneur and make sure you're constantly figuring out answers to as you go.

After that event, Nihal and I started talking about the gaps that were happening during the event. We noticed the event started the weekend of a networking event, and everyone was there to meet other startups, to meet other founders, to meet other mentors and so on. So there wasn't a true platform or an app to help everyone connect with each other. Whenever the organizers wanted to announce something or change something on the schedule, they had to do it manually. They had to use a microphone, or they had to yell. Then we attended another event in Cairo a couple of weeks later after that, and we noticed the same issue.

At the event, I noticed that some of my friends on Twitter were also trying to meet up at this event. I texted them, but I didn't know what they really looked like, so it was very funny, trying to meet someone you only know virtually but have never actually met. We didn't have a platform to connect or share anything that happened at the event. So we started looking into what we could do for events. How could we solve the events' problems?

Then we went to exhibitions in Cairo, and I remember every time I went there, I would come back with a huge bag of flyers and marketing materials from exhibitors. So we sat down and thought, "Why can't we have an app, a platform to connect everyone and stakeholders during the event? It could help people manage events efficiently and help the attendees make the most of their time at these events."

I got very obsessed with the idea, and I was constantly talking about this event app that we wanted to build. Then a couple of weeks after, I decided to quit my job. I felt like I was cheating on my events app (laughs) before even having developed it. So I decided that I would quit my job and I would work on this concept full-time. Then Nihal followed me a week later, and we started working on this full-time together.

How did you go about researching the space and learning about the technology?

The funny part is that I never organized an event in my entire life. So we decided that the first year, we needed to understand the industry. We spent some time visiting as many events as we could and talking to as many event organizers and attendees as much as possible.

Before we started, both Nihal and I were working as a software engineers. She used to develop for Android. I was getting started on iOS development when we spoke about Eventtus. I decided that I had to learn to do it so that we could build the first version of the app.

We did market research, and I started reading and learning about iOS development. I really got into it. One of the most important things for an entrepreneur is you have to be learning things every day. Sometimes you just need to learn and do something. You don't necessarily have to know everything before you start. So we had to learn business strategy and financials on our own. One of the decisions that we made back then was that we wanted to start with our own money. We didn't want to approach investors early on, because we wanted to make sure that this was something valuable and someone out there would be willing to pay for it first.

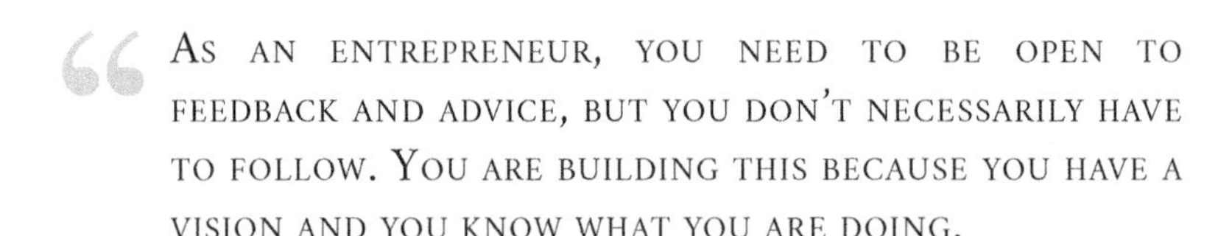

> As an entrepreneur, you need to be open to feedback and advice, but you don't necessarily have to follow. You are building this because you have a vision and you know what you are doing.

How did you process all the advice and feedback you received?

One of the lessons that we learned early on is that, as an entrepreneur, you need to be open to feedback and advice, but you don't necessarily have to follow. You are building this because you have a vision and you know what you are doing. I don't think everyone has the same vision or understanding of the industry. So it's important to keep that focus on your vision, meanwhile filter only feedback that fits with your vision.

I remember how I met our first investor at one of those events. We decided we wanted to launch the app at ArabNet, Cairo. I remember that we had a tiny place in the event. I met a guy from Vodafone. He came to me, and he said, "Hi, how are you doing? Please keep me posted on your progress." A year later, something came out of the blue. It was about Vodafone Ventures and Mohammed Eid. I kept following up with him. Whenever we launched a new feature, or a new website or something, I would text him and then tell him about our updates. So we connected, and he saw the progress that we had made and how we'd matured and evolved as a company. Then he became our first investor in Eventtus. So what I learned was networking is very important. Talking to everyone and hearing feedback from everyone and following up is very important.

What are your thoughts on the role a co-founder plays in a startup?

When choosing a co-founder, a professional partner if you will, it is not necessarily all about the skills they bring to the table. It's also about the personal dynamic as well. It must be someone you can trust. I remember, especially in the first days of Eventtus, and these were the hardest days, Nihal was my support system along with my family.

Whenever you feel down or think, "Why am I doing this?"—as naturally happens from time to time—whenever you keep working and don't see any results, you need someone like that to encourage you, to keep pushing you to your limits, and who has your back whenever something happens.

Sometimes as an entrepreneur, one day you feel like you're on top of the world. You think you're changing the world and you're being recognized in magazines and everywhere in the media. Then the next day you wake up and everything changes. You have all these problems pop up suddenly, and you don't know why you have to put yourself through all this struggle. So as rewarding as it can be, it's not an easy journey, that's for sure. I think that I am very lucky to have Nihal by my side as my co-founder.

> Sometimes as an entrepreneur, one day you feel like you're on top of the world. You think you're changing the world and you're being recognized in magazines and everywhere in the media. Then the next day you wake up and everything changes. You have all these problems pop up suddenly, and you don't know why you have to put yourself through all this struggle. So as rewarding as it can be, it's not an easy journey, that's for sure.

How would you describe your relationship with partners, investors, mentors, and advisers?

I view these relationships as long-term, almost like a marriage. You meet partners and investors every day. You need to find someone who is very supportive, understanding and can add value, more than just money. Investors also bring the value of connections, knowledge, and advice. Finding advisers and mentors is very important as well. I can't highlight that enough. You need to find an adviser that you can rely on, and it goes all the way back to building a support system.

I'm very happy to have Tarik Amin as our investor and adviser. He is very supportive. He gave us a lot of guidance in the last two years, especially with regards to expanding to Dubai and understanding the market there. I believe every entrepreneur needs to look up to someone who has done it before, who understands the startup game, who is involved in the ecosystem, and try to build a relationship with them. It's different from being an investor; it's more like a personal relationship.

How did you develop your technical and business skills and know-how?

The first step was learning about technology and learning different aspects of the technical side of building a startup. As a software engineer, I don't want to say it was easy. Though having a technical background is certainly an advantage, because I developed the first version of the app myself. So I have a good understanding of it.

Whenever we hired someone, I used to interview them myself so that I could go into a technical discussion. They liked it, because we were speaking the same language and we could be on the same page. I think this is very important, but I had to learn everything from scratch. It doesn't matter if you're coming from a technical or business background; as an entrepreneur, you have to wear all kinds of hats and get involved in everything for the company at one point or another, especially in the early stages.

When I started, I remember going to my first sales meeting and failing miserably. I was very nervous on the way to the meeting. I didn't even understand the idea of how I could go to someone and ask them to pay money for something that I built. I didn't get the deal, and it was an awkward and very funny meeting, actually. Then I decided in my mind that I could do it. After the meeting, I had to learn how to do it. I figured, it's my product. It's my company. I know the market. I know the people. I know everything that's related that I need to know. So if I can't sell it, no one will be able to. I realized I had to teach myself sales and business development as well.

I decided to go to as many sales meetings as I could, and in every meeting, I was learning something new and getting better. Now I lead a sixteen-sales-staff team, and we have great clients and customers from all over the world. You have to read, learn, listen to advice, and ask people. Don't be afraid to ask people. No one knows everything. I used to ask my mentors, I used to ask everyone, "How do you do this?" I watched lots of webinars, listened to a lot of podcasts and news from Silicon Valley. I was always trying to learn from other successful startups and figure out what works and what doesn't.

> In 2016, I find myself standing on the stage at Stanford University with Barack Obama and Mark Zuckerberg, founder and CEO of Facebook, talking about startups. So you have to keep working every day to learn new things and grow for yourself and your company. I would've never imagined that one day I would be in that position.

I also remember attending TEDxCairo and meeting Wael Fakhrany, former regional manager for Google in North Africa. His talk was about the discomfort of our comfort zone and how it's important to put yourself in challenging situations that you can learn and grow from. This really stuck in my mind. Now I'm more comfortable with being in the discomfort zone. His talk has really inspired me to go beyond my own perceived limits. I wake up in the morning and I do things every day I never imagined I was capable of doing.

Five years ago, I was working as a software engineer in Cairo, living a normal life with a steady job and social life. So much has happened since, it feels like a thousand years later. In 2016, I find myself standing on the stage at Stanford University with Barack Obama and Mark Zuckerberg, founder and CEO of Facebook, talking about startups. So you have to keep working every day to learn new things and grow for yourself and your company. I would've never imagined that one day I would be in that position. Not any of this would have been possible without taking those little uncomfortable steps every day that get you moving forward and ultimately closer to your dreams.

What were some of the first steps you took to develop the culture at Eventtus?

One of the most important things that I really focus on at Eventtus is the culture. I am so lucky, because every day I hear the team say how much they love working at Eventtus. They love the team, culture, and environment. We have people apply to work with us because they heard that the culture and the team are great.

We always try to give our team a sense of ownership. We wanted people who can rely on each other and feel a sense of value in their purpose. Whenever we have an event or a big client, we pick developers to attend the event and be on-site for support. We have a transparent and flat organization. We share everything and have monthly meetings to discuss what's going on.

How important is achieving product-market fit from the very beginning?

I think finding product-market fit is one of the most important things for a startup. Every startup is different based on the market and the idea. For example, in Eventtus, we knew from day one we wanted to build something local. That's what we had in mind initially.

Then when we did our market research, we realized that our solution could be made global. So we started thinking about getting the app exposed to as many people as possible, to as many events as possible. That's when we decided to spend a year traveling around the world attending events. We went to the U.S., went to Dubai, went to Kenya. We went everywhere trying to understand the different kinds of international events so we could build a global product that could be used for events anywhere.

At the same time, we kept on building for our local market, so we approached the local events and attended them. We tried to see if they could actually pay for it, but having this global mindset, it got us exposed to a lot of challenges related to events on an international level. It actually helped us grow out of the local market. Now we serve events everywhere. We have events in the U.S., London, Dubai, Beirut, etc., while still operating the business out of Cairo.

I have met a lot of startups who want to build something global and then they don't think of their local markets. Then they struggle with promoting and selling their products. It would be easier if they looked locally and decided to build something very customized for the local market, and build on top of or in parallel with a global market. We managed to balance between local needs and global needs. Now we have localized product, local presence and an international expansion plan to as many cities as we can. I think this is something startups need to plan for, balancing between local and global focus.

WE HAVE THIS HABIT OF ACTUALLY GOING TO EVENTS THAT REPRESENT US AND STAYING AT THE END OF THE ROOM TO SEE WHENEVER PEOPLE ARE USING THE PHONE IF THEY'RE USING THE APP. IF THEY ARE, WE WANT TO KNOW HOW THEY USE IT, THEIR BEHAVIOR AND IF THEY ARE TAKING NOTES OR OPENING ONE OF THE FEATURES AND SO ON.

What is your product development process?

With every event we do, we learn something new, and then we gather feedback from attendees and organizers. We go to events and observe how people are using the app. We have this habit of actually going to events that represent us and staying at the end of the room to see whenever people are using the phone if they're using the app. If they are, we want to know how they use it, their behavior and if they are taking notes or opening one of the features and so on.

We have a massive backlog of all the features we want to build. We actually have a product roadmap for the next three years. Then the trickiest part is to try to drive, while adding the right features at the right time. We need to make sure that it's not too early or too late and always be ahead of the competition.

We actually spend a lot of time on research and building user experience through interviews and feedback; we're big on that. We establish our own timeline and make sure not to over-engineer things. We really try to add value for the event organizers, and whenever we do a feature, we try to make sure that it's adding value to the user experience. At the same time, we try to build a world-class platform that is more user-friendly and more useful than that of our competitors, who are mainly from the U.S. and Europe.

What did your initial marketing consist of?

In the beginning, we started off with event organizers. We focused on tech startup-related conferences and events, because it's in the community. We counted on getting valuable feedback that we could incorporate into improving the app. We started with this segment. We also used social media as well. We approached event organizers through Twitter and Facebook, and we used our network.

One day when I was in Dubai, I reached out to a friend, and I got the phone number of the founder of STEP. I called him and I told him, "Hey, this is Mai from Eventtus. I'm in town for a couple of days." He replied, "I'd loved to meet and learn more about what you do and discuss the potential of our cooperation." He had heard about Eventtus through social media and other events that we have done. He was open to meet, and then we signed a contract with them. They are now one of our biggest clients. We have worked with them for a few years now.

This relationship has helped us expand out of the region. We worked with them with startup-related events in the region. Then we went to another vertical as well, and we did the same. We approached a few people, and then the network effect kicked in; we got so many referrals to other event organizers. The events industry is somewhat of a close-knit community, and everyone knows everyone. So referral is a huge thing for us.

We treat every client as if they are our biggest client, and we try to give them all the support and attention they need to ensure repeat business. We also use the usual marketing activities, like social media, Google AdWords, digital marketing and content marketing. We invest in our blog and other content marketing as well.

What are your views on work-life balance for an entrepreneur?

Oh my God! I don't think I'm the right person to talk about this (laughs). It's very hard to have a work-life balance, especially for an early-stage entrepreneur. Having said that, there need to be things you do outside work that help keep you mentally sane, healthy, energetic and positive.

Especially with what I'm doing now—we now have a team in Dubai and Beirut—I literally live on a plane. I go to events everywhere. It's not a stable life at all, but I consider myself fortunate to have it. What I try to do, however, whenever I have time, is spend quality time with my family and friends and really engage with them.

I also have to accept the idea that I might have to miss occasions like, say, my best friend's birthday. It really helps to have family and friends who understand and support you. They know that I'm not pretending to be working, that I am actually working. They understand this is my life and that I have a company to run, with all the responsibilities that come with that.

Two years ago, we used to work 24/7. We didn't take any days off. We didn't take vacations or anything. Then Nihal and I decided that we have to take at least Friday off. We don't necessarily do it every week, but at least we try to do it. We try to focus during the weekday and work very hard, then take at least a day off every week.

Every now and then, we take a couple of days off. I remember we were very lucky last month to be able to take an entire week off, both of us at the same time, and the business and everything was still working. The clients were happy, and nothing went wrong. That means we built a responsible team who can manage things while we are away.

Any good learning resources you recommend to entrepreneurs?

I think *The Hard Thing About Hard Things* is a great book for entrepreneurs. *Predictable Revenue* is another great book for a non-salesperson or non-finance person to understand how to build a sales team. I also like to read articles on TechCrunch and Mashable. I've been following TechCrunch Disrupt for many years. I find it to be an invaluable resource. I remember, for example, I saw the presentation and pitch of Trello, a great company that I came to admire, and it's a product that we use. I saw how they evolved and got acquired. It's an amazing story.

Since you are "the queen of events," I have to ask—any local startup-related events you recommend?

I don't know about "queen" (laughs). On a regional level, STEP conference and RiseUp Summit are the two biggest entrepreneurship events in the region. ArabNet, as well, especially ArabNet Dubai. Each one of them has a different flavor, though. They each bring investors and speakers from outside. ArabNet is more of a corporate event. If you need connections with corporate and government, it's a great event to attend.

Another good one is Mix N' Mentor. It was personally beneficial to me in my own development as an entrepreneur. I use Mix N' Mentor as a platform to understand a different market like Mix N' Mentor Oman, Beirut, or Dubai. So it was a great platform to mix with other entrepreneurs in that market and get a sense and insights about that market.

What is the biggest misconception about starting a business?

There is a myth that if you start a business and it succeeds, you'll be a millionaire and will no longer have a boss, and you can just kick back at a resort while everyone sweats it back at the office (laughs). I'm exaggerating, but that's the notion, when the reality is the exact opposite. As an entrepreneur, you have to work extremely hard, every day. There is no way around it. As your company grows, you have to work even more so. In the beginning, I thought that whenever I hired a salesperson, I wouldn't work on sales anymore. Then I found out that there are now ten more things that I needed to do. So it's not that easy. Having said that, it's OK to fail. It's OK to mess up sometimes. We need to accept failure. This mindset is unfortunately not all too common in our culture, when in fact it is an intrinsic part of the entrepreneurial journey.

What's your future expansion plan for Eventtus?

We're growing our sales and technical team. We're expanding regionally. We're focusing on the Gulf countries next year. Then we'll start looking into expanding outside of the region afterward, starting with Turkey and by the following year, China. We are also assessing starting to work with corporations for their internal events. So, a lot of exciting opportunities out there and we're just scratching the surface.

19

AMIR BARSOUM

Revamping personal healthcare services

Co-Founder and CEO of Vezeeta

WWW.VEZEETA.COM

AMIR BARSOUM is the co-founder and CEO of Vezeeta.com, the first digital healthcare booking platform in MENA, launched in late 2012. Vezeeta is an innovative platform in the healthcare industry that's focused on solving numerous challenges related to healthcare services in the region, including lack of accessibility and medical data availability. Prior to Vezeeta, Amir was a management consultant at McKinsey & Company, where he served several healthcare and FMCG (fast-moving consumer goods) entities in both the public and private sectors in Europe and MENA. He then led the strategy of MENA markets for AstraZeneca pharmaceuticals. Amir is also an Endeavor Entrepreneur and sits on the board of directors of Endeavor Egypt and is a board member of Entrepreneurs' Organization. He holds an MBA from the American University of Cairo, Bachelor of Pharmacy from Ain Shams University and an Executive Education Certificate from Harvard Business School in scaling startups.

Tell us a bit about your background and any early business experiences.

I was born in Cairo, Egypt, to a family of entrepreneurs. My dad owns a decent-size chain of pharmacies that he built from scratch with no family or outside support whatsoever. My dad has always been a great inspiration and a major influence on my upbringing. I was raised to think that, whatever I would do in life, I would end up being an entrepreneur.

My initial thinking in high school was that I would be a pharmacist and run the family business, taking it to the next level. Hence, I went on to study pharmacology but later decided that I would rather build something of my own. My dad was very supportive and was certainly a big mentor in my life. He initially supported me to start a parapharmaceuticals distribution company. In the beginning, the company did not do so well, so we decided to shift focus to importing product and manufacturing products for pharmaceuticals like cosmetics. Eventually the company picked up before my dad and I decided to sell to Iraqi investors.

I then started applying for jobs while finishing my MBA at AUC (the American University of Cairo). I got two job offers then, one offer from a multinational FMCG in Dubai and another from McKinsey's Cairo office, literally in the same day, in the same hour. I decided to go for McKinsey, where I would mainly work in the healthcare, pharma and FMCG sector.

My wife then had a baby, and I decided, maybe it's time to have a job that is less hectic and less demanding. So I left McKinsey and got a job as head of strategy for the Middle East and North Africa region for AstraZeneca, a U.K.-based pharma company. The role involved some travel to Dubai and Brussels, Belgium, with a focus on the region as a whole, where I was responsible for overseeing portfolio management, market expansion, M&A, and many other functions related to strategic position in such a large corporation. As time passed, it became clear to me that I would prefer to do something that was not so corporate. I even considered going back to consultancy and maybe even get in private equity investments, or start my own business and become an entrepreneur, which was my original dream.

Around the same time, in 2011, I met my co-founder, Ahmed Badr, through a connection with Ziad Mokhtar. Ziad was a friend of mine from McKinsey. He had left McKinsey to run one of the most well-known venture capitalist funds in Egypt, called the Technology Development Fund. He told me he had a friend who was looking for a partner to build something around a SaaS solution. When I met Badr, he was mainly focusing on providing accounting solutions to SMEs. I told him, "You know what? I really see value using this technology in healthcare."

It was an interesting technology, though my understanding about technology at the time was zilch. I knew absolutely nothing. It was like a new language for me (laughs). Nevertheless, I decided I would somehow get myself educated. So I read a lot. It took me a good six months of reading and studying to wrap my head around the technology and figure how we could use it. Badr and I then came up with the idea of building electronic medical records for doctors. We pitched the idea to Ziad and managed to raise seed capital from his Technology Development Fund in mid-2012, and from here we were off to start this new company.

We started off by building a medical records solution. We developed the product and went to market to try to sell. We initially thought we had landed a gold mine. Every ten doctors we tried selling the product to, eight signed. We felt that this was really going to be huge. Three months later, we realized that nobody was using it. I would say this was one of the biggest setbacks that I've ever encountered. We had put so much into this and had very high expectations and failed miserably.

Ironically, when I was at AstraZeneca, I remember going to my boss to tell him I was resigning. I told him, "I'm building a software company that would sell software to doctors." He asked, "How are you going to make money?" I answered, "Doctors are going to pay a subscription fee." His response was, "I have never heard of a more stupid business idea than this. But if you change your mind and you would like to come back, you have a place here." In retrospect, I think it was quite generous of him.

How did you get the idea of Vezeeta?

In the face of this disaster, we went back to the drawing board and the product-market fit discussion. We asked ourselves, "Do we need to pivot, and if so, how? Is there any hope? What can we do?" It was a tough and challenging period, since we didn't have clear answers. We decided to introduce a practice calendar management system, which also didn't work as well as we initially thought. That's when we decided to launch the booking platform and re-branded the whole company to Vezeeta. Vezeeta took off very well right off the bat; we were finally onto something.

The initial concept of Vezeeta was based on the premise that healthcare really lags behind when it comes to technology adoption. Every service you retain has, practically speaking, gotten much more advanced in using technology over the years; meanwhile, healthcare has not. One small example: Medical prescriptions are still manually handwritten notes today. Meanwhile, legal contracts are not. So certainly the healthcare service industry is yet to catch up on technology. I'm not referring to medical technology, which continues to advance; I'm referring to the services surrounding the healthcare professional and healthcare service providers, the glue that holds everything together. It's yet to evolve and remains broken in two major ways.

One is lack of accessibility. There is no way to access healthcare without information. Traditionally, the only way to know where to find a good doctor is to ask a friend, who has had firsthand experiences. The question then is, what do you do when you have to look for a specialist or another type of healthcare provider to address a specific disease or inquire about a personal or private issue, say, a psychological-related condition? It becomes quite tricky.

Two is lack of medical data. Medical data gives the healthcare provider information that helps them decide on your medical condition. Lack of availability of medical data is a huge problem in this industry. You go to the doctor, he makes his diagnosis and he sends you to get your lab tests, but you forget to bring your lab tests or misplace them. Somehow, he doesn't get your lab test results when he needs them, and there's no easy way for him to access this data any time while he is assessing your condition.

These are the two main hurdles in the way of great healthcare service in the region. These are challenges that you find in Egypt, Morocco, Jordan and even Dubai. So we thought if we came up with technology solutions that engaged the decision makers, the gatekeepers of the industry, who are the doctors, then we will actually convince every other single player in the industry to adopt this technology, one at a time. Our ultimate goal is to create a complete ecosystem that provides affordable solutions that overcome the challenges of accessibility and medical data availability. That's the whole concept behind Vezeeta, and that's where we started.

In fact, much of the success behind Vezeeta today comes from its unique ability to address real, major problems faced by patients when trying to access doctors in the region. Choosing the right doctor is a tough decision, and patients can spend significant time and effort researching in order to get the best medical service. Also, the wide variance between the quality and cost of doctors is another problem. However, the major challenge is the actual booking process. Patients can spend up to five hours on the phone just trying to get an appointment.

We have managed to overcome all these pains by offering verified reviews on our platform for all subscribed doctors, highlighting their price points and expected waiting times, to ease choice and empower patients.

After we got started, we built our first software and went to doctors. Digging deeper, we realized that doctors are busy and don't have the human capacity to support the process of filling out medical records. We realized that medical records would come later, as they require more integration with the different players. Instead, we decided to focus on the first part of the problem, which is lack of accessibility.

That's when we introduced Vezeeta.com as the first online healthcare booking platform in the region. Almost every doctor we pitched the service to, telling them that they would need to pay a subscription fee to get access to the platform, was skeptical. Most of the doctors didn't believe this would work. We were acquiring doctors at a very slow rate, thirty doctors one month, forty doctors the next month. We sensed something was definitely wrong but couldn't figure out how to fix it. We knew we really needed to shift strategy or some kind of adjustment to get things growing in a more promising pace.

How did your strategy evolve over time?

Around the same time, Aspen Institute selected a dozen or so startups from the region for a trip to Silicon Valley to meet and learn from different big tech companies there. We were one of those selected. So I was fortunate to go on this amazing trip in February 2017. I remember having a meeting with a senior executive at Uber, who during our meeting asked half-jokingly, "So, what do you want from me?" I told him briefly about our business model. He responded, "The monthly subscription fees model doesn't work. You should go to a transaction model. I have another meeting at eleven. Good luck!" and left the room. It then hit me right then and there. I thought to myself, "Wow! That's a very interesting idea." So I came back to Egypt, and the first thing I said was, "Guys, how about we stop billing doctors on monthly subscription fees. Let's just see if we charge on a transaction basis if anything would happen." In the first month we introduced this model, we acquired 500 doctors, up from just 34 the month before. Keeping in mind that our software didn't support this new model whatsoever, so we had to manually calculate the transactions at the end of each month, doctor by doctor, on an Excel sheet. It was chaos, but we got more organized and updated our software to accommodate this new model. Nevertheless, it was a major breakthrough for us. The following month, we acquired 300 doctors, and we've kept growing steadily since then. I think this was a major breakthrough and really the starting point of Vezeeta as we know it today.

We kept on building Vezeeta under this new model. We also dropped the whole idea about providing SaaS and thinking of the service as web-based, and anything unrelated, so we could focus on what's working and really growing our platform.

We really started to grow, adding more doctors, more specialists, and more areas. Patients also started to roll in quite nicely. Then we reached a point where we said, "You know what, let's do a very serious capital raise of $6.5 million." I recall some of our early investors from Jordan coming in before we implemented the transaction model and said, "We don't see a good business model, but we see a very good team. So we will invest because of our faith in the team, but we really need to figure together how we can change the value composition of the company." After the initial round and our pivot to the transaction model, investors were quite impressed, and all decided to participate in that round, and we were able to close the $6.5 million.

I think another big breakthrough we had was when we introduced patients' reviews of their doctors and healthcare providers. Basically, the patient would write, "Doctor was good. He gave me the right amount of time and listened and was very knowledgeable and professional." Or the patient would say, "Doctor had me waiting for a long time at the clinic and seemed in a hurry and when he finally showed up quickly wrote me a prescription without really listening to all my symptoms."

Then one day, I got a call from a very senior doctor who said, "I am a well-respected doctor who has signed up on Vezeeta, and I'm going to close down my accounts on your platform if you don't get rid of this review system." I went to meet him to try to address his concern. I explained to him how we're just unveiling word-of-mouth in a much easier and faster way, which ultimately benefits good doctors. I also told him that, "If you remove this one negative review, nobody will believe the other good ones. So why don't we leave it and see what will happen in terms of flow of the patients." Despite the negative reviews, the reviews actually helped him get much better exposure, and he started viewing the reviews as a great tool. Ironically, this doctor is today one of our biggest advocates and a strong believer in Vezeeta.

Did you ever think about quitting Vezeeta?

Funny you ask—I would say I think about quitting once a week on average (laughs). It is very tough running a startup, as there is a continuous fight between growth and sustainability. It can squeeze you. Growth needs investment, and sustainability needs cost-efficiency. So it's certainly a tough balancing act. Not to mention, you hit those rock-bottom points from time to time. I particularly recall how challenging our second round of financing in 2014 was with Silicon Badia in Jordan. There were delays in getting the financing term sheet, and at the same time we still had to get approvals from the investment committee. The challenge was we were running quite low on cash. So that was a close call.

I WOULD SAY I THINK ABOUT QUITTING ONCE A WEEK ON AVERAGE (LAUGHS). IT IS VERY TOUGH RUNNING A STARTUP, AS THERE IS A CONTINUOUS FIGHT BETWEEN GROWTH AND SUSTAINABILITY. IT CAN SQUEEZE YOU. GROWTH NEEDS INVESTMENT, AND SUSTAINABILITY NEEDS COST-EFFICIENCY. SO IT'S CERTAINLY A TOUGH BALANCING ACT.

Can you give an example of a misstep and what you learned from it?

Taking money early on generally increases your likelihood of making mistakes. When we started Vezeeta in 2012 by building medical records through the provision of EMR (electronic medical records) to doctors, many doctors quickly abandoned our platform. At the time, we believed that it was purely a commercial issue, when the real issue was that the doctors did not have the incentive to integrate digital patient records in their daily practices. In hindsight, we didn't have product-market fit. Raising funds early and having money on hand can be a bit tricky and needs to be managed carefully and frugally.

What are examples of lessons at Vezeeta you wish you had learned earlier?

There are two that come to mind, and both are related to team-building and who you bring and keep on board. The first lesson is to hire folks that make up for your shortcomings and offset your natural pitfalls. Badr and I were never marketing guys, and we understood that and tried to recruit someone who could fill in this gap. Bringing on board Fawzy Abu Seif as CMO (chief marketing officer) and partner in 2015 to take the lead on the marketing function truly changed Vezeeta. I remember thinking this guy was crazy when he initially suggested re-branding our logo only a month or so after joining the company. Back then, it was orange and red. A couple of months later, he decided to launch a huge ATL (above the line) campaign, targeting a massive market segment at a very hefty investment size. I also remained skeptical. Despite the many deliberations and doubts on the impact of this campaign, we went ahead with it, and it was truly a turning point for the company. Hiring the right expertise and knowledge along with the understanding of what you clearly lack is key to success, and without that expertise we would not have made it.

The second lesson is to fire faster. Lack of fit with company culture and low-quality caliber of employees tend to harm the company directly and indirectly. You end up seeing great talent leave because of the continuity of bad performance brought on by the "bad apples." Great talent wants to work with great people. Recognizing and taking actions does not predominantly make you a bad employer.

What is your advice to entrepreneurs in regards to fundraising?

My first advice to entrepreneurs regarding fundraising is to simply take as much money as you can. Money is scarce in this part of the world. Even for a company like ours that is raising pretty well, money is extremely scarce and difficult to get.

My second advice is you need to understand that if you want to build a big organization, you will need to raise big tickets. So make sure that you are set on a relevant vision that has the right size of investment supporting it.

My third advice is to always remember fundraising doesn't start and doesn't stop; it is 40-50 percent of any CEO's job. The value of fundraising is not only about making money or getting money to the company, but also reviewing and revisiting your strategy and how you position and articulate your story. I really believe, as an entrepreneur, some of your biggest lessons happen while you're fundraising.

> MY FIRST ADVICE TO ENTREPRENEURS REGARDING FUNDRAISING IS TO SIMPLY TAKE AS MUCH MONEY AS YOU CAN. MONEY IS SCARCE IN THIS PART OF THE WORLD. EVEN FOR A COMPANY LIKE OURS THAT IS RAISING PRETTY WELL, MONEY IS EXTREMELY SCARCE AND DIFFICULT TO GET.

What's the difference you found between working in a startup versus corporate environment?

Working for a startup is literally beyond hectic. No corporate job can ever compare to working in a startup. You practically have two kinds of days in a startup: a day where you are facing very serious, life-threatening challenges and you need to put in massive effort to overcome this hurdle; another kind of day where you are growing at an enormous rate and you don't have enough resources, including managers and staff, to keep up. That's why I always say, "This is not a nine to five job, and we only recruit people who believe in our mission and who are willing to put in massive effort and long working hours, because they are driven by our mission."

What are you most proud of achieving in Vezeeta so far?

Building this company from scratch is our biggest accomplishment.

Granted, we're just in the very beginning of the road. Still, I'm very proud of how far we've come. Today, we are without a doubt the only company in this region that has managed to make doctors and healthcare providers use their software. It's literally a life-changing experience for these providers. We spend 70 percent of our budget making sure we continue building value to our providers.

What are your aspirations for Vezeeta?

There are two very important objectives we're trying to achieve with Vezeeta in 2018. One, we're after building a very serious regional footprint. We've expanded into smaller markets, but now we're going into the bigger markets, like Saudi and the Gulf.

Another major goal for 2018 is integrating with other non-clinic providers, such as diagnostics. In short, 2018 is about solving the healthcare accessibility problem in the region. Afterward, we will start focusing on the medical records problem. Providing wide access requires us to significantly expand our healthcare providers network. We will need to acquire doctors in private clinics and in public clinics. We will need to acquire outpatient hospitals and diagnostic centers. We need to do that on a regional basis as we expand into new markets and geographies, meanwhile, continuing to provide greater healthcare accessibility to our patients, whether they are insured patients or out-of-pocket patients. Time to get to work!

20

ABDULAZIZ AL LOUGHANI

Redefining food ordering and delivery

Co-Founder and former Managing Partner of Talabat.com
Managing Partner at Faith Capital

WWW.TALABAT.COM

Abdulaziz Al Loughani is a co-founder and former managing partner of Talabat.com, the premier food-ordering delivery service in the Arab world, which was acquired by the Germany-based e-commerce powerhouse Rocket Internet for $170 million in 2015. He is currently co-founder and managing partner at Faith Capital, a venture capital practice that is focused on the GCC. Previously, Abdulaziz was the founding executive vice chairman of the Kuwait National Fund for SMEs Development, an independent public institution responsible for developing the entrepreneurial ecosystem in Kuwait (2013-2017). Prior to that, he was a director at Global Capital Management, the alternative investments arm of Global Investment House, and was responsible for establishing a venture capital practice at Global.

Abdulaziz has served as a member of the board on a number of companies within the MENA region in the banking, healthcare, manufacturing, consumer finance, food and beverage, and real estate sectors. He is also an active angel investor, mainly in technology startups. He is also a member of the World Economic Forum Global Shapers Community, Kuwait chapter. He holds a bachelor's degree, a double major in information systems and e-commerce from the University of Toledo, and an MBA from London Business School.

Give us a little bit of background about yourself.

I was born and mainly raised in Kuwait. I was also fortunate to be raised very early on outside of Kuwait, in the U.S., some parts of Europe, as well as Asia. Even though I was only a child, I think it prepared me subconsciously to engage with different kinds of people from different cultures, with different perspectives. It also got me learning different languages early on. The experience was eye-opening in terms of getting to see firsthand the struggles people go through around the world, versus only being exposed to the comfortable living conditions we have here in Kuwait.

I continued my education once I was back in Kuwait, in middle and high school. I was actually terrible in school except for two key subjects, math and Arabic. I was particularly good in math. I even took an AP calculus class when I was still very young.

After high school, I attended university in D.C. to study for my undergrad. At the time, I didn't have any focus or career goals, but I definitely knew that I was very passionate about math and information systems. Growing up in Kuwait, I was very impacted by Sakhar, which back in the '80s was the IBM of the Arab world. Sakhar, which was actually founded and managed by the father of a friend of mine, ignited my interest in computers and technology early on. So I double majored in information systems and e-commerce. Around the same time, I also became interested in finance and did very well in finance classes in college.

After college I came back to Kuwait and worked in private equity. I figured I'd do that till I decided what I wanted to do next in life. After six months, I decided to start an online pharmacy platform with my business partner. I did that for a little while before the Talabat opportunity come knocking.

How did Talabat enter the picture?

Around the same time, a bunch of my friends from what we call locally the "Duwania," which is our hangout place, were starting an online food delivery service called Talabat. Talabat in Arabic means orders. The idea was to offer a faster and more convenient way of ordering food than traditionally had been the case. I was very intrigued by the model and immediately recognized its sizable market and saw the massive potential it had. So I decided to close the pharmacy platform and join as co-founder in Talabat, along with some members of my current team and head operations.

The concept of Talabat was really based on serving the needs of food ordering, which back then in Kuwait was quite a well-developed industry. There was already a huge market for food and dining. At the time, Kuwait had a population of 3 million and had countless outlets of local food franchises. There was a huge market for food, though traditional food ordering through analog and voice was just miserable in terms of consumer experience. The idea was initially inspired from Otlob in Egypt, which was a pioneer in online food ordering and delivery in the Arab world. We had a lot of respect for what Otlob had accomplished at the time but felt that we could do a lot better ourselves with Talabat.

We started working on the product. This was back in 2005. There weren't so many resources, references, or examples in general to look at. The literature simply didn't exist. There were hardly any resources or people around us to tap into to learn about building a digital product or a tech startup. There were no shared best practices anywhere from similar companies that we could use. We had to come up with our own methods, learning by trial and error, and often by getting knocked down. We were on our own.

Given that we were pioneers in the space in Kuwait, it gave us a tremendous head start opportunity, because no one was really venturing into the space at the time. We were the only game in town. However, if you look at the infrastructure that was available in Kuwait at the time, internet penetration was only around 30 percent. Internet access was quite expensive and ran mainly on dial-up, which was very slow and primitive. These were certainly challenges we were up against, though my fellow co-founders and I actually perceived them as opportunities. We knew that sooner or later, internet would become faster and cheaper and more widely used. So we saw a window to build something now and grow as internet access and speed increased. That's the bet we made, which proved over time to be spot-on.

We initially started with a web-based platform. We focused a lot more in the beginning on the functionality of the website, not as much on the design. While the design was simple and user-friendly, we were more focused on building the right kind of features for different browsers and making sure that they were all functioning quite well.

Early on, we spent a lot of time developing and refining the product, constantly simplifying the online food ordering process, and further tailoring to customers' needs, in preparation for going live. We had two kinds of customers, since we were essentially a two-sided platform. We had the supply side, which mainly dealt with restaurants. We also had the demand side, which were the end customers.

Initially, we focused on acquiring restaurants and building up our supply side, taking advantage of the extensive personal network access we had back then. As early adopters, we were primarily sustained by our personal friendships, or out of their sympathy, may I say (laughs). Later on, getting the kind of bigger restaurant chains proved to be a big challenge, in terms of consuming lots of time and effort. We eventually decided to compromise on money. So in order to onboard those restaurants faster, we offered the service for free to a lot of restaurants, especially the bigger chains. As soon as we had a few of those larger chains, that's when we launched.

Fortunately, we also had open access to customers back then, in the sense that Google Ads didn't have as many restrictions as it has today. We were allowed to really push out through ads and tagging multiple industries, multiple verticals, without any real limitations. For example, if a big World Cup match was on or a popular artist performance was playing, and you were searching online for that event, you would see a Talabat ad simultaneously. Today this is almost impossible to actually have.

We also briefly experimented with traditional offline marketing during that time before quickly realizing that wasn't the best channel to market our product. So we doubled-down on digital marketing. Our primary focus at the time was on how can we get more eyeballs, get more transactions, more orders to the restaurants? Luckily, we had a product that we monetized from the very beginning, so we could reinvest revenues we generated back in marketing, further acquiring more customers, and so on. It was a winning formula.

Meanwhile, digital infrastructure in Kuwait and regionally was evolving as we had expected, proving to work to our advantage. As the government and telecom operators really started investing in the infrastructure, the quality, speed, and price of internet services significantly improved. From traditional dial-up to DSL to fiber-cabling across all of Kuwait, and telecom operators investing in optimizing current services and adding new services, the price of access went down. As it kept going down, demand for internet shot up. All of which only helped fuel Talabat's growth. Whether you call it market conditions or luck, I think that was an important factor to our continued success.

As we started to grow, we kept learning and getting better and better. We started learning more about consumer behavior. We started learning more about heat maps. We started learning more about the campaigns, how to really optimize the cost for bidding on certain keywords. We started learning about SEO and continued to refine our thinking and execution.

The product itself went through quite an evolution, as we saw it developing similarly in other parts of the world. We started by routing orders via a fax machine, for example, and then slowly moved into a software that we started installing on computers and laptops of the restaurants we worked with. Later on, we introduced an SMS-based system to complement the web-based platform. Then there was the smartphone introduction, initially on Nokia and followed by Blackberry, which made it a lot smoother for restaurants to manage their orders.

For the first few years, we were all alone; there wasn't any competition. Despite that, we never got complacent thinking we had a clear first-mover advantage; instead we always made sure to stay on top of our game. Over time, we realized that competition had suddenly begun creeping up, which actually made us work ten times harder. We realized it wasn't just coming from small startups; it also came from large, well-funded players. All the more reason we stuck to our guns and continued to push even harder to stay ahead. Luckily, we had created a world-class product and assembled a stellar team, so the bar was quite high for any competitor to try to match us.

How did Talabat's expansion in the region come about?

In 2008, I recall reading on the web the announcement of Yahoo!'s acquisition of Maktoob.com. This was such a seminal point in the history of the tech ecosystem in the region, a remarkable milestone at the time. It really started broadening our thinking from the local 3 million population we had in Kuwait mindset we shared, to suddenly shifting our thinking more regional, to the 300 million Arab population, stretching from Morocco to the UAE. We especially started looking at the 50 million population in the GCC as our potential market and benchmarked ourselves against that.

That's also when we decided to branch out to Saudi Arabia, being a similar culture, we thought. It's also right across from Kuwait. We figured, if we're able to do it in Kuwait, we will be able to do it in Saudi. We initially started our expansion project in Saudi through local partners we identified. We decided to go and launch with a franchise model. In 2008, we entered into a franchise agreement with a local Saudi company to set up and manage our Saudi operation. We were quite excited working with a local company, with local presence and local market knowledge. As it turned out, we faced lot of challenges with our Saudi franchisee partner. In spite of the fact that they were paying a healthy franchise fee, we ran into all kinds of issues with quality control, operational efficiency, and managing certain functions centrally from Kuwait. You can say that our judgment was clouded by the generous offer we received. We later came to realize we had made the wrong decision regarding franchisee partner selection when things didn't pan out well.

Beyond execution and mindset challenges we had with the partner, we also came to realize the opportunity cost of the company's valuation if we didn't get Saudi working and what further challenges might arise at the time of exit as a result. In short, we ended up reaching a settlement with them. It was certainly a misstep on our part that we had to learn from the hard way. Lesson here is that company culture is very hard to clone and franchise, especially remotely—all the more reason to be particularly selective when it comes to finding the right franchisee partner.

Saudi was also quite a cultural shock and a big challenge, to say the least. We brag in our part of the world that the region is a 350 million population market with a massive economy, that it's a homogeneous market, with the same culture, same language, and same consumer behavior. The reality is that this is not entirely true, as we learned the hard way with our expansion to Saudi, which was very different from Kuwait, to our surprise. In fact, the region is a quite fragmented economy; it's not really integrated by any means. Even within each country, we operate in very different working environments and culture. For example, doing business in Riyadh is very different from doing business in Jeddah or doing business in Sharqiyah (the eastern province of Saudi).

We started realizing that properly setting up Saudi operation was going to require a lot of money. So we decided we need to fundraise, to either sell part of Talabat or fundraise to fund Saudi expansion—Saudi, of course, along with Egypt, being the largest market in the region and a key foothold. We figured we needed around $3 million-$4 million. Back then, there were hardly any incubators, accelerators, or angel investors in the region. Not many early-stage funds were available in general. Definitely no one was writing $3 million-$4 million tickets back then. The reality was revenue was our best source of funding, so we were stuck with that obviously to the determinant of our growth potential until my current partner at Faith Capital, Mohammed Jaffar, acquired Talabat and significantly funded the business over the next couple of years.

He later became the CEO, and I continued in a non-executive capacity.

How did the exit to Rocket ultimately happen?

When competition became quite fierce regionally and we saw that consolidation was happening, we started to look into exit options to a much larger, more well-funded player that could take what we had built to the next level. My partner Mohammed was instrumental to the exit to the German e-commerce powerhouse Rocket Internet in 2015 for $170 million.

USE THE RIGHT GROWTH METRICS WHEN YOU'RE SCALING, BECAUSE PERCENTAGE OF GROWTH EARLY ON IS NOT REFLECTIVE OF ACTUAL SCALE. IF YOU'RE GROWING FROM ONE ORDER PER DAY TO TWO ORDERS PER DAY, AND YOU THINK YOU'VE GROWN BY 100 PERCENT, YOU'RE WRONG.

I think because we were market leaders in all countries we operated in, our books were clean, because we had invested in the right people and had documented standard operating procedures, the right infrastructure, and had the best product, from user experience to customer care, you name it. We became a very compelling opportunity for Rocket Internet. Back then, I can promise you that Talabat was a ten times better product than any other food platform in the whole world. So these were the primary reasons why Rocket ended up acquiring Talabat at two times average multiple with comparables in terms of valuations, and as they were making acquisitions also in this part of the world.

I actually just visited Delivery Hero, Rocket Internet's highly successful food delivery flagship company, operating in forty countries and just recently IPO'd (was initially public offered or listed on stock exchange). As you walk into their office, you see Talabat's logo, right in the middle of reception, and you feel really proud.

Any quick tips you have for entrepreneurs from your experience?

I have a few granular tips, if you will, that I would like to share from our experience, and what I've seen often gets overlooked by entrepreneurs—in addition, of course, to the traditional advice of working hard, always learning, and never giving up on your vision.

> UNDERSTANDING HOW YOUR STARTUP FITS INTO THE BROADER MARKET IS KEY TO BUILDING A SIGNIFICANT EDGE OVER YOUR COMPETITION. YOU NEED TO KNOW YOUR COMPETITION VERY WELL AND DEFINE WHAT SETS YOU APART IN THE MIND OF THE CONSUMER, IN TERMS OF BRAND, POSITIONING, OFFERING, SERVICE, PRICE, AND SO FORTH, SO YOU CAN OUTSMART YOUR COMPETITION.

Use the right growth metrics when you're scaling, because percentage of growth early on is not reflective of actual scale. If you're growing from one order per day to two orders per day, and you think you've grown by 100 percent, you're wrong. This percentage is not indicative of your growth, nor is that figure indicative of future growth in the long run. You also need to understand your unit economics, which is key to understanding what your business model could look like when it scales. It also gives you good understanding of how much incremental growth directly affects your bottom line as you move forward.

Understanding how your startup fits into the broader market is key to building a significant edge over your competition. You need to know your competition very well and define what sets you apart in the mind of the consumer, in terms of brand, positioning, offering, service, price, and so forth, so you can outsmart your competition.

Explore adding more products and services to satisfy additional related customers' needs that you surface as your business grows. The ultimate goal should be to offer multiple products or services aligned under one vision. You stick to just one offering for too long, and you risk losing market share. You always have to evolve and expand your offering to better service your customer.

Be a community leader. We firmly believed in Talabat being a proactive contributor in the community. When my partner, Mohammed Jaffar, took over the business at Talabat in 2010, one important initiative he introduced was that 1 percent of our revenue would go for doing good in the community. This 1 percent came in many forms, not just contributions or charity in the community, but also technology and technical support we provide for the community.

Provide the right working environment. I think that's another thing we did very well at Talabat. We were able to create a meritorious culture, where the ideas with the best merits always came out on top, as opposed to traditionally corporate culture in the region, where seniority often triumphs.

Don't take legal shortcuts, because they will end up biting you in the back later on, as their effect will multiply as business grows. Ultimately, they will either cause problems, increase your business risk profile, or harm your valuation when investors come in the picture. Unfortunately, we had to learn this the hard way.

What are your thoughts on the startup ecosystem in Kuwait and the region?

Incubators, accelerators and investors are much more looming today in the Arab world than say ten, even five, years ago. Today, any Arab who has a good idea and the right resources, or skills to develop this idea into a product, has multiple venues to use as their nurturing home, in contrast to the small apartment we started with Talabat twelve years ago.

In 2012, I remember we were fundraising at Talabat, and I went to the Kuwaiti government and pitched them to establish a venture capital fund. I highlighted all the important entrepreneurial ecosystem building blocks and the need for such an entity. I was able to get government buy-in to develop such a vehicle to help build the startup ecosystem in Kuwait. In 2014, it became the National Fund for SMEs Development, which is really the equivalent of the SBA (Small Business Administration) in the States. It is an SME agency, but it is focused on licensing permits, funding, learned access, business development, training, incubation for entrepreneurs, for SMEs, for all kinds of sectors. I ended up becoming the executive vice chairman of the National Fund for SMEs Development, a $7 billion capitalized SME-focused agency.

Don't take legal shortcuts, because they will end up biting you in the back later on, as their effect will multiply as business grows. Ultimately, they will either cause problems, increase your business risk profile, or harm your valuation when investors come in the picture.

We ended up spending the first year and a half in that effort laying the groundwork in terms of infrastructure of policies, procedures, red tape bureaucracy that we would have to overcome. Fast-forward to 2017: Just for that year, we've actually funded 240-plus startups in Kuwait in different industries and sectors. We've trained also 1,800 entrepreneurs, and it's really something that I'm proud of here in Kuwait.

So certainly there is a positive change being made. On the other hand, 90 percent of our workforce in Kuwait is state-employed; meanwhile, unemployment is a ticking bomb, not just in Kuwait, but facing the rest of the region as well. The region averages at around 70 percent of the working population to be state-employed, and more than 60 percent of youth still aspire to be working with government. The alarming part is that around 60 percent of the Arab population is below the age of 30. So certainly there is a massive challenge on hand today.

What are your views on the role of government to promote SMEs?

This subject is dear to my heart, so I spend a lot of time researching and working on it, and I have lots of thoughts. For one, I think the role of governments in the Arab world when it comes to business is to act as a regulator, rather than an operator, which is the current role many governments in the region are taking. So governments' role to promote SMEs has to happen in collaboration with the private sector.

As Josh Lerner describes in his excellent book, *Boulevard of Broken Dreams,* where he addresses why even advanced economies fail, or have failed, in building entrepreneurial ecosystems: The main reason is that their governments actually take on a more active role, therefore extending the bureaucracy of governments into the entrepreneurial world. Instead, governments should just get out of the way and provide more space for entrepreneurs to work, meanwhile creating the proper kind of legal framework that supports a more venture-friendly environment.

Granted, there are plenty of SMEs developmental programs, but what's really missing on a regional level in the Arab world is a more established venture capital asset class. The asset management industry in the MENA region manages approximately $73 billion of fiduciary money. Of that $73 billion, less than a billion dollars is actually invested in venture capital as an asset class. Now despite that, a lot of private money is being poured directly in technology and in startups in the region, but the asset class is significantly underfunded.

In the first half of 2017, close to a billion dollars has been invested in startups regionally. There is a positive trend in private investment in the asset class, but a lot of it is coming directly for startups rather than in a more organized and structured asset management/venture capital asset class. So governments and sovereign funds really need to look at this asset class commercially, rather than only depend on the developmental money that is being poured into SMEs and not producing significant jobs.

Banking regulations and central banks also have to update their regulatory frameworks and become more inclusive of the entrepreneurship community and traditional SMEs than they are currently. I think the best example I can highlight is really what the Lebanese Central Bank has done through Circular 331, where it has unlocked around $500 million worth of investment reinvested in the venture capital asset class.

What does the role of education play in developing entrepreneurs?

Education in our part of the world is very textbook-focused, and we need to graduate more applied learning than only textbook-smart people. I think that the entrepreneurial mindset needs to be learned early on through extracurricular engagement of professors at colleges.

We need to embrace the notion of learning to create one's future, rather than learning to get a job. That's an underlying shift in mindset that needs to happen in both the educators and the students. I also think that exposing the youth to success stories like Talabat, and even bigger ones, will resonate and inspire a lot of aspiring entrepreneurs in this part of the world. It resonates because they're locally grown examples and created by folks with similar backgrounds, often from humble beginnings, who managed to build great things.

What have you been working on after Talabat's exit?

Since Talabat's exit in 2015, myself and my partner, Mohammed, basically started investing in entrepreneurs and tech startups. I'm currently invested in around six startups and involved in a lot of entrepreneurial initiatives in the region. In 2017, we started Faith Capital, which is a venture capital practice focused on the seed stage, especially around tech startups in the Gulf. So, all in all, my interests have now evolved to help growing the startup ecosystem here in Kuwait and, inshallah (God willing), throughout the region.

21

NIAMA EL BASSUNIE

Facilitating cross-border B2B trade in Africa

CEO and Co-Founder at WaystoCap

WWW.WAYSTOCAP.COM

NIAMA EL BASSUNIE is the co-founder and CEO of Casablanca, Morocco-based WaystoCap, the first African-focused B2B merchandise marketplace. Previously, she worked in PwC in London's markets evaluation and energy markets team. She earned a double master's degree from The London School of Economics in international relations (M.A.) and in decision sciences (M.S.). She also holds a double first B.A. in economics and politics from the University of Sheffield in the U.K. and is a chartered financial analyst (CFA).

Tell us a bit about your personal background.

I was born and raised in Casablanca, Morocco. I went to the Casablanca American School (CAS), which is an international school. Our class was at least 50 percent international students, so from an early age I developed a global perspective, which affected my worldview.

Growing up in Morocco, a major influence was seeing my parents build a business from scratch, grow it, and make it a success. My mother was my role model; she raised a family while also being an active entrepreneur. That really impacted my personal ambitions. I always knew from an early age that I wanted to do something of my own. I never joined the family business because I wanted to have a firsthand experience of starting something on my own: building it, growing it, and developing it.

I was at CAS in Morocco until I went to the U.K. in 2002, after high school. I went to the University of Sheffield, where I studied economics and politics. I then went to the London School of Economics, where I did a double master's, international relations and decision sciences. Afterwards, I joined PwC (PricewaterhouseCoopers) as a graduate on their Markets Evaluation and Energy Markets team, in London. I am also a chartered financial analyst.

One of my first assignments took me to Cape Town in South Africa, where I spent close to six months working with one of the largest energy companies on the continent. Meanwhile, I was also looking for something to do on my own that would be more hands-on.

A friend in London was starting a business and was looking to source used cooking oil (UCO). He was planning to use UCO as fuel for a green taxi company he was putting together. He knew I had experience in energy projects, so he came to me and asked if I could help source the fuel.

I proceeded to research the opportunity in North Africa, having an existing network; although my friend's business didn't take off in the end, I used this network for my purposes and proceeded to find buyers elsewhere in the EU. Not long after, the Arab Spring took place, and a lot of factories closed in Egypt, including my supplier's. Despite a turbulent start, I decided to continue trading on the side while I was still with PwC.

I began trading with no specific strategy or vision. It was really about capitalizing on opportunities, so it involved all kinds of products in many markets. In 2011, an opportunity had opened to source cement from Turkey to Guinea. So I decided to go to Conakry for four days to look into it. That trip changed my life, and I ended up staying eight months. It was during that period when I saw the huge opportunities that exist on the continent.

How did WaystoCap enter the picture?

During that time, I also met my two co-founders of WaystoCap. We did some consulting work together for Moroccan companies looking to expand into west Africa. Then we decided to set up a trading firm, an import and export business. This was back in 2014. We didn't have a vision of creating an online marketplace then. We just focused on Moroccan suppliers selling into West Africa. We actually only started with canned sardines, which is one of the main products that Morocco is known for in the region. That's when we encountered firsthand, as traders, all kinds of challenges. These were numerous pain points that buyers and suppliers in the region are constantly trying to resolve, anything from verification of counterparties, to making sure the payments are secure, to actually finding prices that are competitive. There was a huge list of pain points that both suppliers and buyers were experiencing, and even more so with the buyers.

We were up against those challenges from the very first transaction. That's when we got the idea of starting an online marketplace for B2B merchandise for Africa. That's how that original vision started forming. We would find a buyer for canned sardines, and then they would ask for spaghetti, then they would ask for palm oil, then they would be asking for other products. So, we were like, "Let's just create a marketplace that would actually address the ongoing challenge of matching buyers and suppliers." We initially thought of ourselves as this kind of matchmaker. Then we realized our role was much bigger than that.

We realized we needed to build an ecosystem that would include different services, that would truly facilitate trade. So beyond matchmaking, we had to figure everything involved in the trading process, from verification to helping with the operational aspects of the transaction in terms of logistics, to financing, to payment and so on. This is also when we realized that we really needed to use technology and we needed more resources, both human and financial, to fully embrace this opportunity. So we decided to fundraise.

We initially tried to fundraise in Morocco, but the ecosystem wasn't really ready for a tech startup like ours, in terms of our risk profile. This was evident by the mentality of the investors we met with. So we decided to look abroad. We applied to San Francisco-based Y Combinator (YC), a leading American seed accelerator, and got in, in early 2017. We flew there and spent four months in San Francisco and had a great fundraising experience. We were fortunate to find YC. They really believed in what we were doing, were excited by the vision, and most importantly were aligned with our timeframe. They completely understood that what we were trying to do was a long-term play. Trying to change an industry and the way cross-border trade is done is not something that can happen overnight. So they were extremely aligned with how we wanted to do things. We ended up raising $3 million from Y Combinator eight months ago and came back to Morocco and continued marching forward.

We came back in April and have been expanding since then. We've grown the team. We started up another office in Cotonou. We set up an entity in London. Meanwhile, we continue to refine the product and expand our local presence. It has been a really exciting journey for us so far, the last two years of setup and this year of expansion.

Can you please elaborate on the consumer problems WaystoCap is trying to solve?

The main problem we are trying to resolve is facilitating trade for African businesses so they can buy and sell securely. So essentially, we're trying to create a trusted platform where companies in Africa can buy or sell products easily.

When we started trading ourselves, like I said, we faced all kinds of issues in terms of importing and exporting from untrustworthy suppliers, to expensive financial instruments, to lack of insurance options, and that's when we realized there was an opportunity for us.

For example, sometimes you would be trying to find buyers and you would have someone who is calling you every day, he calls you at 11 p.m., 12 a.m., all kinds of hours, and at the end, nothing happens after a couple of weeks, and you think to yourself, "Oh my God, I've been just wasting my time." The same thing happens with suppliers. You try to find suppliers that are verified. You don't even know where to start your search. Do I just Google something like "palm oil suppliers"?

It was very frustrating in that sense. How do we find verified suppliers? How do we find verified buyers? Then you get buyers who can't finance because of expensive rates of local banks for traders. So on one hand, you have all these challenges in the industry that you're trying to solve. On the other hand, you're trying to do so in a digital way, whereas a lot of established traders and traditional trading in general remain offline. We had to ask ourselves, "How do we bridge this gap? How do we bring this cross-border trade into the digital era, that is actually going to create more trust for all of the counterparties in the ecosystem?" That's what we have been focused on. So we're focused on what can we do to reflect how traders already do business, but figuring a way to do it more efficiently and more securely and in a much more transparent way.

How does WaystoCap work?

WaystoCap is focused on inbound and outbound and intra-Africa trade—trade flow from and to Africa and within Africa. We focused initially on west Africa and on food products, especially those that have high purchasing frequency, so things like canned food, pasta, rice, oil, and sugar. We now have started expanding into other industries, so we really follow where our buyers take us in terms of their purchasing needs. Then we started focusing on construction material products and consumer products and specific in-demand items like baby diapers and cleaning products.

In terms of profile of suppliers, we have a good mix of medium- and large-size suppliers who are looking to get into African markets, who are looking for new expansion and growth opportunities. On the buyers' side, we tailor to small and medium-size companies, where our platform is nicely adaptive to such SMEs and their needs. They don't typically have a procurement office or procurement division or an importing officer. That's where we come in the picture and help out. Obviously, they need to have had imported before, otherwise they would not be able to bring in the merchandise.

We charge a referral commission on every transaction, so that way our interests are aligned with both our buyers and suppliers. We're standardizing our commission based on product item rather than product category, to accommodate for all kinds of products and situations.

What were some of the challenges you've encountered, and how did you overcome them?

In terms of challenges, there have always been challenges and still are, because we are going after a big problem. I think the key to work through those challenges is to always keep perspective in terms of what our users want and how we can best satisfy those needs.

So we're constantly thinking, "We need to create this 100 percent ultimate platform, but it also needs to reflect what our users want, how do our buyers communicate, how do they want to communicate, what kind of platform do they want?" These and other questions we're constantly asking ourselves to solve, for challenges we face on a daily basis.

Trying to fundraise in Morocco was also quite frustrating. At times, we were dealing with investors who were extremely demanding. Other times, you found investors who wanted to take a big share of the company for a small investment. For me, the key lesson from all of this is that, as an entrepreneur, you always have to look elsewhere when you don't find something that's actually aligned to what you want, whatever that is—whether that's investors, advisers, or networks. You always have to think global and keep going after what you want. That's why we went to the U.S. seeking to fundraise there, which worked out quite well with YC. We would've wasted more time in Morocco and likely not found the right kind of investor or the right deal structure, had we not made that decision to look outside Morocco.

You always think that, "Oh, once I reach this point, then things will get easier," but it does not get easier. Somehow as you progress, as you expand, as you grow, you begin to face new challenges. Actually, every phase of the business has its own unique challenges. That's also what makes the journey so exciting. So the key is to really get better at making decisions and breaking down problems into manageable components that you can take apart and work through.

What's also been exciting for us is just seeing how things progress when we started ramping up and growing. To see a lot of things that we put down on paper, in terms of vision and what we wanted to achieve, actually take place is very satisfying for us.

Talk to us about specific problems you faced developing a cross-border trade marketplace.

The challenges we face are unique, more complex, and international in nature. You cannot just send something two blocks down the street and get your customer to return, as is the case with a local B2C e-commerce service. In our case, if the container's left the port, it's left the port.

There are also other sets of challenges you face that don't necessarily exist in more developed markets. We intend to create a paradigm shift in that regard, by building a trading platform that actually bridges that gap. Our goal is to offer security to our suppliers, but still making it as cheap as possible for our buyers.

We have to come in to secure both parties in terms of risks. So we're starting to bring in new services, such as insurance, that allow us to secure both counterparties during the trading operation. Another thing we're doing is building to qualify and verify counterparties, so we're able to further qualify and verify parties. In doing so, we are able to build more trust within our platform. Meanwhile, everything else, from logistics to other tools and other areas, we will optimize for later, once we've solved for the main pain points.

What's your perspective on finding and working with a partner?

There are probably different schools of thought when it comes to partnerships. From my experience, it's been so important for me to be friends with my co-founders well before we started working together. They are the same friends I could hang out with, I could have a good time with, and I could get along with. The chemistry was always there from the beginning, so it was just a matter of making sure that we also have an aligned vision and similar ambitions, which is critical. If you have founders' disagreements on vision and on ambition, it's not going to work, no matter how much they liked each other on a personal and friendship level. You need to be fighting together on the same vision. Also, if you have, say, someone who has a lot of ambition and someone who does not, then it will be difficult to work together, so they have to match on ambition and commitment as well.

IT'S BEEN SO IMPORTANT FOR ME TO BE FRIENDS WITH MY CO-FOUNDERS WELL BEFORE WE STARTED WORKING TOGETHER. THEY ARE THE SAME FRIENDS I COULD HANG OUT WITH, I COULD HAVE A GOOD TIME WITH, AND I COULD GET ALONG WITH. THE CHEMISTRY WAS ALWAYS THERE FROM THE BEGINNING, SO IT WAS JUST A MATTER OF MAKING SURE THAT WE ALSO HAVE AN ALIGNED VISION AND SIMILAR AMBITIONS, WHICH IS CRITICAL.

The other reason I found being friends with my co-founders was important was because startups are a bit like a roller-coaster ride in terms of emotions. There are highs; there are lows; there is excitement; there is frustration; there are breakthroughs; there are setbacks —you name it. So when you have co-founders or partners that you can rely on, that you can depend on when you are going through a low, they will help bring you up and vice versa.

You also have to have defined roles and responsibilities and the right organization structure for your company. You need to also make sure you are not overlapping functions within the company, especially since things naturally become more complicated as the company grows. For example, in our case, I deal with the strategy, vision, hiring and lot of processes in the company. Meanwhile, our COO has been dealing with our trading operation, setting up local offices, as well as sales and BD (business development). We also have our CTO, who oversees the platform and product development and all the technology that goes with it. Then we have our head of platform and growth, who is focused on everything involving marketing, growth, and merging traditional trading practices with more efficient and scalable solutions.

So having different roles and different responsibilities is critical for us, and so is making sure that there is good communication between all of us and we're all on the same page at all times. It's easy on a day-to-day basis for everyone to get away in their work and lose track of each other. So it's important to have set times to make sure that, at least on a weekly basis, we all just sit down to discuss where everyone is, what problems we are facing, and make sure we're all aligned.

WE TYPICALLY FOUND THE BEST TEAM MEMBERS WHEN WE KNEW EXACTLY WHAT KIND OF PERSON WE WERE LOOKING FOR. THE MORE SPECIFIC YOU CAN BE ABOUT THE PROFILE YOU NEED FOR A GIVEN POSITION, THE MORE EFFECTIVE YOU WILL BE IN RECRUITING.

What are some of the best practices you found around recruiting and team-building?

We typically found the best team members when we knew exactly what kind of person we were looking for. The more specific you can be about the profile you need for a given position, the more effective you will be in recruiting. I also believe an entrepreneur should not shy away from trying to convince people to join their startup. Granted, when you go to someone and ask them to join your startup, you are really asking them to change their life and whatever they are doing right now, which is a big ask. So the key insight in my experience has been to make sure that you explain your vision well and have a good story to tell that captures the essence of your business and what you're trying to achieve. You have to sell the dream, so to speak.

You also have to be transparent about what kind of work and effort is required, because you don't want to be misaligned with whomever you are hiring. This is especially important in the early phase of the company, where you're still building the core team. So everyone must be aligned, because the idea is that this core team would eventually be the future managers of the company as the company grows and expands. The same advice applies to partners as well.

We also try to create a fun working environment. We organize a lot of team and social activities, for example, because it's important for the team to bond together. After all, they probably spend more time here than they do with their families at home, so if they feel this is home, too, in a way, then there is a lot more motivation, dedication, and commitment. This all allows the company to run better and smoother.

Lastly, you should be recruiting on a continuous basis. You've got to proactively keep the recruiting pipeline full. So then you're not like, "Oh my God, someone just left, and I need to hire someone right now," and risk having to rush last-minute or make those decisions haphazardly.

What's your advice to entrepreneurs regarding fundraising and engaging investors?

I think it definitely depends on the type of business you are in and what sort of startup you want to build. You also must realize fundraising doesn't necessarily equal business success; it's only a means to an end. I think a lot of entrepreneurs make the mistake of viewing it as a destination, rather than a building block of a successful company.

We bootstrapped for a couple of years, which I think was extremely beneficial. It helped us ensure the foundation of the business was set up as efficiently as possible. It also allowed us to validate some basic assumptions we had and get early traction way before we started approaching investors. Of course, you still don't have 100 percent ideas for everything you are going to do, but at least you have a working model and proof of concept. By then, you certainly have a much more refined vision of what needs to get done and how to go about it and how much it will cost.

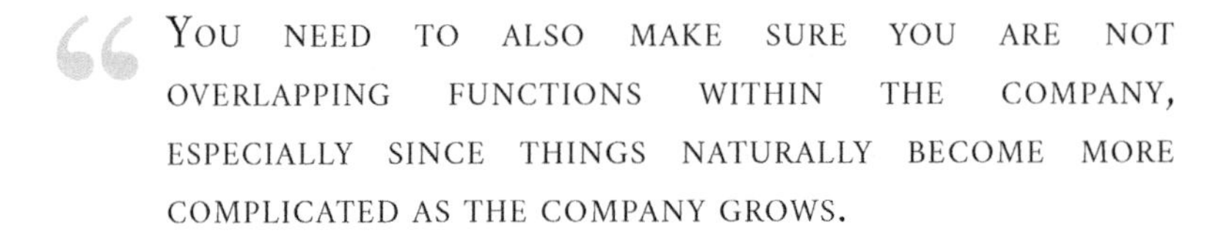

> YOU NEED TO ALSO MAKE SURE YOU ARE NOT OVERLAPPING FUNCTIONS WITHIN THE COMPANY, ESPECIALLY SINCE THINGS NATURALLY BECOME MORE COMPLICATED AS THE COMPANY GROWS.

One thing I did initially was I built a detailed spreadsheet of which investors we wanted to target and why. This allowed me to be selective on who to approach, whether because they invested in similar companies or in similar geographies, or because their approach is long-term and seems to align well with ours. Then I always try to find a mutual personal connection with an investor and get an intro, someone who basically recommends us to meet the investor. This always works better than cold emails, which typically don't work. Whenever I ask for intros, I always say why I want that intro, why that investor is relevant. That's very important. Obviously, if you don't have an intro, you have to keep trying in different ways to engage with that investor directly or indirectly till you get a meeting.

I think preparation is key when you're meeting investors. For example, if an investor asks you a question about what you are doing, how you are going to do something, or your numbers, or what you have done, and you are unsure or you are unclear, it does not reflect very well, and it undermines the investor's confidence in your business and in your ability to manage. You need to know your numbers. You need to understand why you are doing what you are doing. You need to have a crisp vision and have articulated it very well in your investor pitch deck and supporting material.

What is your general advice to entrepreneurs regarding customer service?

If you want to attract customers, especially if you're trying to bring something new, you have to educate your customers. Then you have to be responsive, and you have to be an effective communicator. Most importantly, you have to really listen to customers' feedback and relate that feedback to the product team and desk team so you can eventually incorporate it into your product. So customer service is key. I cannot overstate.

How do you cultivate open communication and collaboration among your team?

One thing we found that works is for our entire team to all be on the same floor. I think that kind of open environment makes it easier to have access and communicate with other team members. I also think it's very important to let every team member voice their opinions, especially because a lot of ideas actually come from team members that deal with customers on a day-to-day basis and ones who are constantly looking for potential solutions.

The other thing is you have to make sure some of those ideas do actually get implemented, because it's very motivating to cultivate that culture when people propose ideas and the ideas make sense in that plan, to actually go ahead and implement them. You just have to make sure those ideas strike a balance between being creative and innovative and at the same time being fast to actually deploy, to test and to iterate. The key is just having that openness and flexibility.

What's your perspective on the startup ecosystem in Morocco?

Morocco's startup ecosystem is just getting started. We lack success stories that can encourage entrepreneurs to see building startups as a viable career choice. I believe this will change in the coming years as greater support is being provided by both government and corporate initiatives. Having said that, there has never been a better time to be involved in a startup in Morocco.

There are a few missing gaps that can help increase the probability of success for startups in the areas of fundraising, mentorship, and legal frameworks. On the fundraising front, we need more early-stage funds and regional VCs and angel investors participating in the ecosystem, not just private equity firms that look at the occasional startup opportunity. We also need a lot more angel investors with the right mindset, not ones who ask you what collateral you will provide in exchange for their investment. So there is a lot of work to do in terms of changing the mentality regarding risk and startup investments.

As far as mentorship is concerned, we need more mentors that truly understand startup concerns and are able to give advice. Often for advisers to really contribute, they need to have a vested interest. So actually allowing advisers to start getting advisory shares, which legally is very complicated in Morocco, will be a step in the right direction.

Finally, the legal framework is too complex and does not protect international investors' interests. This is why, for a Moroccan startup to attract startup funding, it either has to create an international entity or struggles to convince serious international investors to act locally. The legal framework also does not really offer the possibility of investing using sophisticated financial instruments, warrants, or convertible securities and notes. The ability to attract top talent with employee option pools is also not currently possible within Moroccan company law.

What are you most proud of achieving so far?

I think I'm personally most proud of seeing the impact we actually have on the SMEs that we are dealing with and seeing them grow on our platform. That's because we allowed this company to focus on its core business and expand its markets in Africa.

I'm most proud of the evolution I've seen in our team as people have joined us and become real contributors to our vision. We've also had the good fortune of being a well-known startup in Morocco, and it's great to see the entire ecosystem benefit from our startup. It's actually allowing both suppliers and buyers to move the supply chain more frictionlessly.

What's your vision for WaystoCap?

In three to four years, I would expect this platform to be addressing more SMEs' issues as they work cross-border in Africa, meanwhile offering additional services via third-party partnerships. We plan on continuing to build a product that solves the real needs our market faces. Ultimately, we are trying to facilitate cross-border trade, thus there are parts of that we are building ourselves and other parts that we will be depending on partners to provide. Our aim is to also be able to make our clients more comfortable and trusting with using a digital platform, meanwhile continue to bring cross-border trade in Africa into the digital era. This will be a twenty-year project!

22

ZAIN ALABDIN TAWFIQ

Making personal and professional feedback easy

Co-Founder and CEO of Sarahah

WWW.SARAHAH.COM

ZAIN ALABDIN TAWFIQ is the co-founder and CEO of Sarahah, which he launched in late 2016. Sarahah is a social networking service for providing anonymous feedback. It is currently one of the leading consumer apps globally, having acquired over 300 million registered users worldwide. Previously, he worked for Saudi Aramco. He graduated with a bachelor's degree in computer science from King Fahd University.

Tell us a bit about your background.

I was born in 1987 in Dhahran, Saudi Arabia. I was raised and lived my entire life here. I always say that it's really a special place for me, so much so that I have never left for more than three consecutive months. I traveled a lot, but every time I felt like moving, something took me back to Dhahran.

I am Saudi, and both my parents are Saudi. They always cared about me, my success and well-being. Even at an early age, they used to buy me computers and anything technology-related. They were always a great support to me and continue to be so till today and are really proud of what I've achieved so far.

Growing up, school was particularly educational for me. My parents were really big on my education, so they enrolled me in the top private school in our country. I was fortunate to attend a private school where they focus on practical subjects like public speaking and learning to speak English. My dad also complemented my school's efforts by teaching me English after hours from home. I was also very lucky to have access to the internet at a young age, well before most of the rest of the country. It actually became available in the area where I lived very early, even well before AltaVista and Yahoo!

I used my dad's laptop since I was very young. I remember monitoring how tech companies like Microsoft, Google, and Yahoo! compete with each other. I learned programming when I was thirteen years old. I created my first website in high school. It was about how stuff works, giving scientific explanations of how different things function. It was called Xainoo. That was my mom's nickname for me. I was also fortunate to have a great teacher in school who used to talk with me a lot about the internet. That also got me very interested in the topic. Around the same time, I also became interested in electronics and hardware.

> "I used to be a very fragile person. Now, I'm no longer as stressed by everyday life situations, as I used to be before the illness. Whenever I'm faced with a problem or crisis in business or in life, I'm better able to face it.

After high school, I applied and got accepted at McGill University in Montreal, Canada. I moved to Canada to pursue my studies in computer science. Everything was going great, and I was looking forward to going abroad and attending university, when I started to get all kinds of weird feelings. I didn't feel well at all. I got checked and was diagnosed with a brain tumor. They told me I was actually born with it, which explained a lot of events that happened earlier in my life. Nevertheless, I was quite shocked.

I became critically ill at that point. I had to come back to Saudi after only two months of going to Canada. I needed to be close to my family during this very difficult treatment period. I ended up having brain surgery. After the surgery, I took a break and decided to stay in Saudi Arabia and attend King Fahd University in Dhahran. I thought that my illness was over and it was time to ace my degree in Saudi as I was already a top student, but it took me a full nine years just to finish my bachelor's, as I had epilepsy due to the earlier surgery, which required me to have two more brain surgeries and a surgery to put titanium in my skull.

So what impact did being ill have on you in terms of your outlook on life?

I used to be a very fragile person. Now, I'm no longer as stressed by everyday life situations, as I used to be before the illness. Whenever I'm faced with a problem or crisis in business or in life, I'm better able to face it. I became so much stronger that people question how I don't react to situations that they feel are disastrous. I would say, "Calm down... let's think calmly." That made me make better decisions, not in spite, but because of the illness. After my illness, I made it clear to myself that I'm on a journey to make a positive impact in my country and in the world.

How did Sarahah come into the picture?

I tried many things and kept developing all kinds of websites, always with the goal of building a mass user base and reaching the world. I had a website about stocks. I had a website about educational videos. I had a website about social media analysis. I was always on the lookout for the next big opportunity or breakthrough, and when it didn't pan out for whatever reason, I would just shut down and move on.

I kept searching for the one killer idea, and though I never lost hope I would find it, I was increasingly becoming more frustrated that I wasn't able to come up with a single great idea. I wasted a lot of time thinking and researching for this one magical idea with nothing to show for it, though I realize now I had learned a lot in the process.

After graduating from King Fahd University, I joined an Indian IT company called WIPRO before going to Saudi Aramco. I wanted to work there, as I was actually born and raised in Saudi Aramco campus, so I really valued their work environment. My boss at the time was Mr. Saleh Al-Ghamdi. He was fifty-plus years old and a grandfather. He was a great boss and a big believer in individual empowerment. He was someone I really respected and looked up to.

Mr. Saleh used to conduct meetings regularly and ask me, "Zain, how do you think we're doing? What can we improve on?" That used to catch me by surprise. I would ask myself, "Mr. Selah is a senior consultant in the company, and I am just a new hire, so why would someone with his experience, with this age gap, ask for my feedback?" While I appreciated the sentiment of my boss valuing my opinion enough to ask for it, as well the intention behind it to learn and improve, I felt something was missing.

See, in the Arab world, age gap commands great respect, so much so that I cannot call him by his first name. I have to say Mr. Saleh. I also cannot be real candid with him and give him constructive feedback or critique in any way, even if he's directly asking for it. I remember thinking that one day, if I ever took his position, I would solve this problem by making it easier for employees to give candid feedback to their older and more senior bosses.

As I started thinking more about this, I initially thought that a suggestion box of some kind would solve this problem. Then I asked myself, "Why a suggestion box when I can automate?" At the time, I didn't want to continue working as a financial analyst. I really wanted to be in programming, as I always loved IT. So I felt that maybe this was my chance to prove myself internally at the company and ultimately get transferred to the programming department. So I decided to create a website that would solve this lack of candid feedback issue in the company. That was how the concept of Sarahah came about.

Before I started this website, I created a survey with just two questions: "Are you interested in hearing the honest feedback from your direct reports at work?" and "Are you interested in hearing the honest opinion of your friends about you as a person?" I also asked my friends and people I knew the same two questions. The results I received were really promising, with the vast majority being eager to receive feedback.

I decided right there and then to work on this, after working hours. I started going to this café as soon as I finished work at 4 or 5 p.m. and stayed late into the night, working on this new website. I didn't spend much time in planning, to be honest. I just started programming. I decided to call it "Sarahah," which means honesty in Arabic. I chose the name because I really love the Arabic language and appreciate Arabic poetry. I also believe that someone should be proud of his identity being an Arab, so I resisted numerous requests to change the name. Some people I talked with were like, "One day, your website may reach the West. What are they going to say—Sarahah, ha, ha, whatever? Why don't you just pick an English name that everyone is familiar with and can easily pronounce?"

TWITTER'S ECOSYSTEM MANAGER GAVE ME THIS ADVICE. HE SAID, "I TOLD A FRENCH PERSON IF YOU WANT TO REACH THE U.S., START IN FRANCE." I REMEMBERED THIS ADVICE, AND I THOUGHT, I AM SAUDI AND I WANT TO REACH THE U.S., SO I MUST START IN SAUDI. THE RATIONALE BEING THAT YOU SHOULD REACH MASS SCALE IN YOUR COUNTRY BEFORE EXPANDING, AND ONE WAY OF ENGAGING THAT INITIAL LOCAL SEGMENT IS TO COMMUNICATE WITH IT IN ITS OWN MOTHER TONGUE LANGUAGE.

In the beginning, I made the website as simple as it gets. It was just one page. My goal was to create a platform where users can provide and receive anonymous feedback. Then my sister came to me one day and said, "Do you remember Honesty Box?" I Googled and came to find Honesty Box was a plug-in on Facebook and apparently had the devil icon as its logo. It basically set the stage for negative feedback, and I thought, I am going to do the complete opposite. So I had this message, "Leave an honest feedback message :-)" It was meant to create a friendly environment and encourage constructive feedback and overall positivity.

When I created Sarahah, I recalled advice I received a while back. I once had a website about social media analysis, and I got to speak over Skype with Twitter's ecosystem manager at that time. He gave me this advice. He said, "I told a French person if you want to reach the U.S., start in France." I remembered this advice, and I thought, I am Saudi and I want to reach the U.S., so I must start in Saudi. The rationale being that you should reach mass scale in your country before expanding, and one way of engaging that initial local segment is to communicate with it in its own mother tongue language.

In the first month, only seventy accounts were registered or so, in spite of the fact that I had sent it to a lot of my friends on WhatsApp and shared it on my Facebook and Twitter accounts. I really tried to get the word out about Sarahah, but it just wasn't picking up. Around the same time, I started learning about a marketing methodology about finding the right person or "connector" to convey your message, which made a lot of sense.

So I approached my colleague at work, Najla. Najla is unique in that she is very connected to a lot of social circles. I told her, "I really feel you can spread Sarahah's message well to your network," because she just seemed to know everyone. She told another employee in our department, who comes from a very large family spread all over the region. She ended up posting Sarahah's link on her family's WhatsApp group. Then, as a result of her reaching out, a famous SnapChatter talked about Sarahah, and many people started to use Sarahah, and suddenly it started trending in the Gulf region. It even quickly became one of the most famous local hashtags on Twitter that companies used to advertise for their products.

In February 2017, shortly after I released the website, Sarahah received thirty million unique visitors just from the region, while the website was Arabic only. I recall the real growth spurt happened when it hit Egypt, being a large population country with more than 90 million people. The growth was so significant that it ended up crashing Microsoft North Europe cluster. I have an email from Microsoft basically saying, "You crashed our cluster. Please reconstruct your website to meet our requirements." This brought a big opportunity. Microsoft offered me $120K in credits, rapidly deployed a fix to their servers, and became a strong partner for Sarahah. Our partnership enabled Sarahah to grow really fast. We were offered hosting by many big IT companies, but the support we receive from Microsoft outweighs the value of discounts we would get elsewhere.

At that point, I realized I could no longer operate as a one-man show. I knew I really needed help if I was going to do this thing right. So I approached my friend in college, Hani Al-Zahrani, to ask for his help. We had a computer science lab together in college. We always felt we would make a great team and that one day we would start an IT company together. He worked with me pro bono. He would come after work to the café and stay with me late in the night, giving me advice and helping me with whatever I needed. So eventually, I thought, it's time for our partnership to become official, and I offered him an opportunity to join Sarahah. He accepted, so it was exciting to finally partner together on our own project, as we'd always wished we would do one day.

It was time to release the mobile app and the English version of the platform. This proved to be one of the best decisions for Sarahah. The timing was right, as the initial critical mass was built with the Arabic interface, so adding English took things to a whole new level. In July 2017, Sarahah became the top free app in more than thirty countries, including the U.S., U.K., and France. In the U.S., Sarahah remained the top app for the month of August, 2017 topping Facebook, YouTube, Instagram, and WhatsApp. In fact, Sarahah actually reached 100 million registered users faster than top global social networks like Facebook and LinkedIn. In less than ten months from launch, we had already reached 100 million accounts!

We currently have more than 300 million registered accounts globally. Since then, we have gotten a ton of coverage globally from media who became interested in the Sarahah phenomena. I had interviews with Arabic, American, Colombian, Indian, and African media outlets, and others. As our user base grew, so did interest from international investors in Sarahah. We received inquiries from large VCs in the U.S., U.K., Germany, China, Malaysia, and many other places. We even managed to pique the interest of top Silicon Valley VCs like Sequoia Capital and Kleiner Perkins, whom we've met recently.

FUNNY ENOUGH, I INITIALLY HAD SET A PRELIMINARY GOAL TO REACH 1,000 REGISTERED USERS FOR A STARTER. WHILE OF COURSE I HAD BIGGER ASPIRATIONS FOR SARAHAH, I WAS SATISFIED IF IT REACHED THAT NUMBER IN THE FIRST FEW MONTHS. ... THEN, SUDDENLY, THE NUMBERS STARTED INCREASING DRAMATICALLY EVERY DAY. THE COUNT STARTED THOUSANDS, THEN TENS OF THOUSANDS, THEN HUNDREDS OF THOUSANDS, THEN MILLIONS ONCE WE TRENDED IN THE U.S. APPLE STORE. IT JUST EXPLODED. IT WAS SOMEWHAT SURREAL.

Funny enough, I initially had set a preliminary goal to reach 1,000 registered users for a starter. While of course I had bigger aspirations for Sarahah, I was satisfied if it reached that number in the first few months. So as the numbers were climbing closer to 1,000 registered users, I thanked Najla for her help hitting my target. She answered, "Let's hope you get one million users," and I was like "OK, OK, maybe one day, but I'm really happy with what we've reached so far." Then, suddenly, the numbers started increasing dramatically every day. The count started thousands, then tens of thousands, then hundreds of thousands, then millions once we trended in the U.S. Apple store. It just exploded. It was somewhat surreal.

What was also surprising was the level of user engagement, which was relatively high. Granted, there is something about Sarahah's platform that you wouldn't compare to other social networks like Facebook and Twitter, in terms of everyday usage. It was still impressive by any measure you look at. We're constantly working on increasing app stickiness and everyday usage, and user engagement, and hoping to improve as well.

Can you think of a big business challenge you faced and lesson learned?

When we became popular in the Arab World, we were attacked by hackers. I remember that day I was out with my mom when I found out the bad news. Unfortunately, we weren't set up securely at the time. We were actually quite vulnerable, but we were lucky to be hosted on a strong platform like Azure. So I quickly contacted Microsoft, who came to our rescue. The hosting is quite expensive, but it had an amazing security level and overall protection capabilities against hackers and malignant programs. They were also very supportive and taught me a technique that helped protect against future attacks.

Fortunately, the situation got under control, and the damage was minimal if any. We took early measures, but we started to take many additional measures to ensure protection of our system, especially our user data. This was a great lesson in proactively planning for both upside and downside, by thinking of all the different possible scenarios and outcomes and making sure you're well-prepared for them in advance, as opposed to being reactive after the fact.

Can you talk a little bit about the skepticism and controversies around Sarahah?

When Sarahah made it to the top of the charts, people were questioning how the app was able to reach to the top position. Even Apple was in in disbelief! Luckily, being hosted on a credible platform that allows you to verify our behavior and making sure that we always respected laws and regulations assured all entities that all of Sarahah's growth was legit.

WE TOOK EARLY MEASURES, BUT WE STARTED TO TAKE MANY ADDITIONAL MEASURES TO ENSURE PROTECTION OF OUR SYSTEM, ESPECIALLY OUR USER DATA. THIS WAS A GREAT LESSON IN PROACTIVELY PLANNING FOR BOTH UPSIDE AND DOWNSIDE.

We also tend to be attacked a lot through the media, saying that Sarahah can be used for bullying. From the first day, I wanted Sarahah to be a constructive platform, and we continue to take measures to ensure that, but as with other social networks, it can be used and misused. You can find people who use Facebook to bully. Same is true for Twitter. Even before social networks, before web 2.0, people used to bully using emails. There was a recent magazine article which came out that was very fair to Sarahah, when the bullying issue went all over the media in the States. It stated, "Don't blame the creators of this platform, rather blame the misusers."

Having said that, we're certainly doing our homework to be proactive and prevent as much of that as possible, as protecting our users is always on top of our list. So we started using more advanced filtering and reporting systems to ensure that. Another important development we did was that we created what we called "Sarahah index." It's basically a measure or score of how constructive the user behavior is. For example, if I send you a Sarahah feedback and you receive a reply with a smiley face, then your Sarahah index is going to increase. We will sense that your message was constructive, but if someone responds to your feedback with a sad face or reports your messages or blocks you, your Sarahah index is going to go down, since, more likely, your feedback was not useful or constructive; maybe it was too harsh or too negative. As your index score goes down, we will limit the features you can use. If your index sinks real low, we know that you are misusing the service and we will block your account or remove it altogether.

What other user applications or behavior have you stumbled upon?

We now have companies like Netflix, which has a Sarahah account; so does Careem (a leading ride-hailing service in the Middle East). Houston Press has one, too; Sony PIX; Prince Mohammad Bin Salman College; and others. So, more and more, companies are finding it useful to have a Sarahah account to listen to their customers.

Another interesting use is this one NGO (non-governmental organization) in India, a foundation called Aware. It uses Sarahah to receive anonymous sexual assault questions. People who get assaulted are often shy to ask questions in person or reveal their identity, so they use Sarahah to do so privately. We also have *Life Hacker Magazine;* their health editor uses Sarahah to receive anonymous health questions. We have university professors and politicians using Sarahah. We even have a congressional candidate using it. He posted his Sarahah account and asked his supporters to get on Sarahah to input their concerns, and he addresses them live on YouTube.

One interesting thing we've noticed a bit recently also is that people working in the media tend to love Sarahah and create personal accounts. I mean, every country that we enter and trend, we see a lot of people from the media who use Sarahah. We also have musicians, we have gold medalists, you name it, so our challenge now is to make Sarahah useful for all kinds of market segments.

In terms of product development and marketing, what do you attribute Sarahah's growth to?

I think the simplicity of the product is key to Sarahah's growth. Lots of companies and developers tend to add a lot of features and make their product complicated. I was a bit guilty of that in the past whenever I developed websites. Then I started noticing how much users cared about the simplicity of the experience. So I always advise entrepreneurs and developers to build something super-simple that achieves the goal or intended effect you're after, then implement some techniques, like sharing on social media. If the product is simple and intuitive, and you're solving a real need, the product will market itself.

I THINK THE SIMPLICITY OF THE PRODUCT IS KEY TO SARAHAH'S GROWTH. LOTS OF COMPANIES AND DEVELOPERS TEND TO ADD A LOT OF FEATURES AND MAKE THEIR PRODUCT COMPLICATED.

The other advice I give in that regard is if you don't need to have ads, don't. I am against paying other companies to advertise you. I'm also against paying famous people or "influencers" to retweet or talk about you. I believe if you have a good product and implement a few effective social media sharing techniques, you wouldn't need to spend anything to acquire users, at least for most projects. I'm sure there are exceptions here and there. We're proud of the fact that our marketing cost to date is zero dollars. We have not spent a single dollar on user acquisition. Since we're self-funded so far and had no access to outside capital, that worked out nicely.

A lot of entrepreneurs would say, "I applied all of this advice, but I'm not getting anything in return." Allow me here to tell you that there is no sure formula or guarantee that this will always work. You must do your homework and try a lot of things and keep what works; there is no shortcut around that. I feel we have done that in Sarahah, and I thank God for the success we had as a result.

What would you like to see change in the Arab world to help promote the startup ecosystem?

One of the things that I really would like to see change would be a more hands-on approach in the universities, with a lot more workshops and more focus on IT projects. In the meantime, have less emphasis on lectures. I always felt that I benefited a lot more from working in the lab or on practical kinds of projects at university, as opposed to just listening to basic theory and taking notes.

The other thing I would like to see change is greater exposure to accomplished entrepreneurs, to folks with track records, not just in terms of providing advice and inspiration, but who are willing to provide hands-on support and learn-by-example type. I'm referring to one-on-one mentorship sessions, where you can pick up the phone and consult with a successful entrepreneur who's been there, done that, etc. I think that would be extremely beneficial.

Having said that, there's a lot of support from government to startups, at least in Saudi Arabia, as was the case with Sarahah. We actually received a lot of support from the government. I was even offered a job by the government, in their digital transformation program of Saudi Vision 2030, so that I can help other Saudi startups and government incubators. They also incubated Sarahah and gave us plenty of free services with no equity arrangement whatsoever, including office space, PR, legal, and HR support. So they supported us and continue to support us today. We're very thankful for that.

What are you most proud of achieving so far?

Whenever I go to events, or even over private messages I get on Twitter or other social networks, people tell me, "Zain, thank you, we are really proud of you. People of Saudi Arabia and the Arab world are really proud of you, that you were able to take a Saudi application on top of other top apps like WhatsApp and Facebook from the States. We didn't know that this was even possible, to take a Saudi app and make it global." While that's very touching indeed, a bigger pride and honor is to make my parents proud for their continuous efforts over many years to ensure I get the opportunity to excel. I'm just happy to make them proud and feel that their efforts have paid off.

What's your future vision for Sarahah?

I have three aspirations. My first aspiration is I want Sarahah to become the global feedback solution of choice for both individuals and organizations. We want "sarahah" to become a commonly used word globally, to mean giving honest, candid, and constructive feedback. I want to hear someone saying, "Let me tell you my sarahah about this." I want to use Sarahah to make a positive impact in the world, positively affecting hundreds of millions, if not billions, of people.

I also see a massive opportunity to provide Sarahah as a corporate solution for intra-organizational feedback. I think this can really transform the workplace and the way people learn on the job. As we're learning, this also represents a big opportunity for us to monetize our platform, along with other sources of revenues we started tapping into, such as ad sales. In fact, Microsoft signed up with us a big sponsorship package back in May and now is offering to co-sell our service to corporations. So there are tremendous opportunities out there on the B2B front that we're just beginning to scratch the surface for. I also want Sarahah to be used to make sure the customer's voice is heard so that organizations change for the better by listening to their customers. So that's my second aspiration.

My third aspiration, as I once told *The Wall street Journal,* is for Sarahah to be a catalyst for the Saudi tech startup ecosystem and somehow help Saudi Arabia transform into a tech hub similar to Silicon Valley. To know that Sarahah didn't just help our individual users and corporate clients, but also was able to provide clues and inspiration to other local entrepreneurs who would go on to build world-class products and reach the world, that would be very fulfilling to me.

23

PHILIP BAHOSHY

Connecting entrepreneurs with local investors

Founder and CEO of MAGNiTT

WWW.MAGNITT.COM

Philip Bahoshy is the founder and CEO of MAGNiTT, the largest investment data platform for the MENA startup ecosystem, investors, entrepreneurs and corporations. Raised in the U.K. with Iraqi origins, Philip obtained an MBA from INSEAD in 2013 and a B.S. in economics from the London School of Economics. During his time in Dubai, Philip worked at Oliver Wyman in the financial services practice for three years, followed by nearly three years at Barclays Wealth, working as chief of staff to the CEO, advising on strategic initiatives. Philip has lived in the UAE for more than ten years and is passionate about developing the MENA startup ecosystem.

Tell us a bit about your background and the environment you grew up in.

I'm originally Iraqi. Both my parents were from Baghdad. I was brought up in London, where I did all of my education at Sussex House, then at St. Paul's, and then went to the London School of Economics (LSE), where I studied economics.

During a fascinating period in the eighties and nineties in the U.K., London was beginning to take off. I was getting an extremely international and cosmopolitan experience. My education from a young age was instrumental in shaping my thinking for years to come. All the schools were extremely competitive, which provided me the confidence and desire to continue to excel.

St. Paul's was renowned as being the most international school in the U.K. Its founder, John Colet, opened St Paul's School in 1509 to educate boys from all nations and countries, regardless of race, creed or social background. This international environment was essential in helping me learn the skills to interact with people from different ethnic backgrounds at a very young age.

LSE is also an extremely international school. I recall my first visit to the campus during an open day. I recall being in the elevator, where I felt like I was in Babel. Six conversations were taking place in six different languages. I found it fascinating. I thrived in such an international environment, where you're exposed to folks with different origins, cultures, and perspectives. I just loved it. It also encouraged me to pick up a few languages. I ended up learning French, Italian, and Spanish.

I was fortunate to have grown up in such a multicultural environment, as it certainly has shaped me quite a bit and helped me develop the ability to interact with different types of people and cultures. I think eventually it set me up to have a global mindset and to venture out of London to the Middle East.

LSE was also renowned as being a breeding ground for banks back in the day. Meanwhile, I was more interested in the understanding of the operations of companies and the world of management consultancy.

After LSE, I successfully joined Mercer Oliver Wyman in their London office, which was a specialist management consultancy firm and financial service. I also believe that put me in very good stead, because the learning experience of doing consulting, I find, is great prep for becoming an entrepreneur. How to tell a story through presentations, how to create effective financial models, how to interact with senior management and how to build a rapport with team members in high-octane project environments were all qualities that I relate to now as a founder.

What was your first encounter with the Middle East?

In January of 2008, I was asked to do a project in Kuwait. As an Iraqi, I was fascinated to go and travel to Kuwait. I figured things had calmed down on the political front since the war; besides, I wouldn't bring too much attention to being Iraqi anyway. So I decided to go for it. I ended up spending a full year in Kuwait. A massive positive benefit of being a consultant is that you get to spend weekends traveling. This was when I discovered and became enamored by the region.

Having the opportunity to travel within the region was quite an eye-opener. I obviously already had some affinity for Arab culture given my background; nevertheless, I had never visited or lived in the Middle East prior to that. In fact, on my first trip to Kuwait, I actually didn't know where the UAE was on the digital map on the screen in front of me. Little did I know it was to become home for the next ten years. I also realized a huge opportunity for me to add value with my education and ability to blend with the cultural aspects of being Arab. Projects in the region were like creating art canvases from scratch, while projects back in the U.K. were like oiling a well-crafted machine.

In January of 2009, I decided to make the plunge and move to Dubai with Oliver Wyman to continue that journey of discovery. This took me to projects in Qatar, Abu Dhabi, Bahrain and Saudi Arabia.

This led me to the next chapter in my career, where I worked at Barclays. It was a great opportunity. They wanted someone to advise the head of the private bank on strategy for the Middle East. I spent three years doing chief of staff strategy roles. This again provided invaluable experience for my startup life, where I moved from an out-of-house consulting role focused on strategy and storytelling to in-house support, with a focus on implementation. I went from having a role where I was advising clients, but not necessarily being involved with the implementation, to being fully responsible for the implementation and not necessarily being interested in consulting presentations. The role was much more hands-on and about actually getting things done. Here I met a mentor to me who was the CEO of the private bank. He continued to guide and shape me with feedback and support. He was instrumental in highlighting the importance of having a strong vision and the importance of articulating well, while creating a work environment where people worked individually and collectively for a common purpose.

After three years of doing that, it was time for me to try and work out what I was going to do next. I jumped on the idea of doing my MBA, which I did at INSEAD. I spent six months in Fontainebleau in France and six months in Singapore. Besides the great education I received, INSEAD gave me an opportunity to travel and get exposure to Asia, the U.S., and Europe. To this day, I remember a quote from our first day at INSEAD, where the dean highlighted based on an INSEAD research piece that "the most common trait of successful CEOs of Fortune 500 companies are individuals who have lived in or worked in three countries for a period longer than six months during their lifetime. The skills learned to adapt change are essential to the growth of the person's character."

After INSEAD, I joined our family's business, which I did for a year. However, I became disgruntled and frustrated and sought to pursue my own career opportunities and create my own path and destiny. I felt I was not utilizing the skills that I had acquired over many years and I had more potential to tap into.

How did your desire to do something different on your own originate?

Around the same time, I had a conversation with a good MBA friend of mine, Eduardo Cervone, over a weekend where we were celebrating another a friend's wedding in Spain. I opened up about my frustration and told him, "I'd love to try and do something on my own and want to break into the startup space." He said something that hit a chord with me and has stuck to me to this day. He said, "Philip, you're twenty-nine years old. You're in a position where you're not locked in a job. You really don't have anything that's holding you back. You're in a perfect position to take that risk. If you don't do it now, you never will!"

Upon my return from the wedding, what he said rang in my ears, and I couldn't get it out of my head. I woke up the next day and sat myself at a desk and, effectively, wrote the entire 1.0 version of the MAGNiTT business plan in two days. Music in ears with no distractions, I used all my MBA experience and consulting experience knowledge and wrote a fifteen-page outline of my vision and plan for a platform that would "Tinder-ize" the process of connecting MBA entrepreneurs to MBA alumni. I put everything from what I learned in my MBA on paper.

> "He said, "Philip, you're twenty-nine years old. You're in a position where you're not locked in a job. You really don't have anything that's holding you back. You're in a perfect position to take that risk. If you don't do it now, you never will!"

The original idea for MAGNiTT was based on the concept of, "How can you connect MBA entrepreneurs to the alumni network from the university that could support them with their businesses?" At INSEAD, we did something called "blue ocean" strategy, where we reviewed a popular site for dating. The logic behind this site was that they have Ph.D. scientists create algorithmic, scientific formulas and questionnaires. That meant that, as a member, if you completed fifteen pages of a questionnaire, the platform would connect you with your perfect match. It offered the most scientific, backed-by-evidence system to ensure success in your dating life.

It was considered "blue ocean" because it was this revolutionary approach to dating, and it had this huge success rate. What I found absolutely fascinating was that, while everybody was sitting in this class listening to this, 50 percent of the men in the room were using Tinder. Tinder was this new and explosively growing dating app at the time. It allowed people to connect without providing any guarantee of success. It is based on this "swipe right," "swipe left" selection interface, which formed the basis of the discovery and matching of dating candidates. Tinder gives you a very simple platform that connects two people together and provides you the channel to communicate. Then whatever happens afterward is not their responsibility, and it is completely free.

I sat there, having gone through all of the entrepreneurship classes at INSEAD and done the Startup Bootcamp. It got me thinking, "Well, why do you always have to do business plans and business presentations and term sheets and Excel spreadsheets, when, ultimately, if a few people like the idea, you just open a communication channel between them? Then let them communicate and see how they can develop a relationship, without having to have all of this detail.

So MAGNiTT started as the equivalent of Tinder for MBA startups. I originally focused on MBAs because one of the things we'd learned at INSEAD was to focus on a niche and build from there. The thinking is that the network effect is more likely to take place when you effectively solve a pain point for a defined market segment, than to try to solve everyone's problems all at once. That made sense to me, so that's exactly the approach I took.

What were some of the challenges you faced when launching MAGNiTT?

One of the biggest challenges that I faced was trying to build a community, which although niche in its nature with MBAs, was a global product and audience. While this product appealed to every university entrepreneurship department I spoke with, whether it was Harvard, Columbia, Stanford, etc., they all wanted the product and not the community.

They essentially wanted the community to be self-sufficient, and since I wasn't a tech person, I wasn't quite comfortable building out a product. So that became a real dilemma. I had to ask myself, "How am I going to grow this, if I'm not going to get the traction? I could start with INSEAD, but where do I take it next?"

Around the same time, I was showcasing the MAGNiTT initial MBA platform at the STEP conference for startups that spring in Dubai, in March 2015, when folks started asking, "Why is it just for MBAs?" "Why are you making the platform exclusive?" I was like, "No, I'm not exclusive. It's just I found a niche. I believe that you need to start with a niche and build it out." But the answer didn't seem to resonate with anybody there. That's when I started thinking hard about the model, and eventually, a couple of months later, in the summer of 2015, we removed the MBA restrictions and made the platform a connection platform focused on Dubai and the Middle East instead of this global platform.

At what point did you rethink the product and go about changing the user experience?

While I liked the idea of "Tinder-ing" the process, and it certainly is a popular format, people are just used to seeing tabulated formats of information when it came to startups and investment decision-making. When it came down to trying to gather data, it was quite clear the reason why people were using the site as a double-sided market, with entrepreneurs on one side and investors, mentors, advisers, and others. So we said, "Well, let's just create the largest community platform, connecting early-state entrepreneurs with stakeholders in the ecosystem, and build out the platform accordingly." So we started building out.

Initially it was difficult to convince both sides to share their information. Where was the value? We realized the importance of creating calls to action on the platform that stimulated founders to share their information. We tried to bring a call to action to give people the ability to pitch to VCs and for people to connect to angel groups. We then decided to collaborate with many of the conferences. We wanted to give them free tickets or a free booth; we thought of bringing on service providers to try and curate legal advisers, to bring on different people to the platform that these startups weren't typically able to connect with.

What we realized was the more value we created for those startups, the more they were ready to share their information. So we began to see this object of usage on the site where the entrepreneurs were basically trying to connect with the different institutions that they hadn't otherwise heard of or didn't have access to. They were also able to share information between themselves without the information being disseminated to the wider public.

I think that there's this prejudice to the Middle Eastern mentality of, if I'm not introduced, then it's not of interest to me. In other regions, people welcome the opportunity to share introductions, where in the region people held their contacts very dear. So we kept asking, "Well, how can we kind of break down those barriers?" Which is to educate people in this space of what's going on. How do we give entrepreneurs visibility? So that became a key area of focus and a big part of MAGNiTT's mission, which is, how do we give those smaller entrepreneurs and startups a voice to be able to find and connect with the right stakeholders, whether they are investors, mentors, advisers, professional service providers, etc.

As MAGNiTT continues to develop, what other challenges have you faced, and how did you manage to move forward in spite of them?

As MAGNiTT continued to develop and while I have had my own share of struggles—whether it was UI, UX, funding the business, developing strategy, etc.—finding a co-founder and the right talent, or at least the right affordable talent, required to scale the business became increasingly more difficult.

I realized at the end of 2015 that you cannot build a startup alone. While I was unable to hire, I had to find innovative solutions for help. That's when I became more heavily reliant on interns. Interns proved to be an amazing resource. There is a huge proportion of fresh graduates who are looking for jobs. Many are from outside of the UAE looking to move to Dubai or who are coming back. They are very educated and hungry but are often unable to get graduate positions.

Many of them were looking for a brief solid experience more than great pay, per se, at this point in their careers.

> THE OTHER PART OF THE HUSTLE IS TO KEEP KNOCKING ON DOORS AND LEARN TO DO IT TACTFULLY AND INTELLIGENTLY. WHEREBY HERE, IF SOMEONE HASN'T HEARD OF YOU, THEY WILL LIKELY NOT REPLY TO YOUR EMAIL. MAYBE THEY DON'T NECESSARILY WANT TO MEET YOU. IN BOTH CASES, YOU JUST NEED TO FIND ANOTHER REASON OR "HOOK" TO ENGAGE THEM.

I happily and freely continue to recruit interns to join us. Interns come with their own challenge of having to continue to re-train them, and you're only going to have them for, say, four months. So you take what you find, which is only part of being resourceful and "startup hustling," which every entrepreneur needs to do, especially in early days.

I also created a board of advisers, which I find is an under-utilized resource for the region. In fact, in the absence of having a co-founder, I used my board of advisers as a pseudo-co-founder. Two areas that are a challenge when starting a company solo are, one, not having someone to share the world load with, and two, not having someone to debate ideas and strategy with. My board of advisers at my early stage were able to support me with both of these. I brought on experts for their time in exchange for equity who helped shape the MAGNiTT proposition further.

The other part of the hustle is to keep knocking on doors and learn to do it tactfully and intelligently. Whereby here, if someone hasn't heard of you, they will likely not reply to your email. Maybe they don't necessarily want to meet you. In both cases, you just need to find another reason or "hook" to engage them. If you are at a conference, you'd want to introduce yourself. If you have a mutual connection, then you'd want to try that channel. You may also want to research and filter what they're focused on at the moment and try to find some kind of tie-in with what you're offering them.

I remember, there was one gentleman I encountered who said, "You're probably the most persistent person I've ever spoken with, but I guess that's why you're succeeding in what you're doing." I asked, "Have I annoyed you?" He said, "Well, you managed to do it politely, but you still managed to do it persistently." That's particularly important, especially when you're starting out and relatively unknown and haven't developed your network yet. Obviously, as you build more credibility and reputation and expand your connections, things get a bit easier and more efficient. But it's something that you have to earn the hard way; there is no shortcut around paying certain dues every successful entrepreneur goes through.

Was there ever a point where you thought about giving up altogether?

There was a point in the summer of 2016 where I heard so many no's, maybes or "Come back to us," I was feeling defeated, because I was the one that was trying to create value to the space for entrepreneurs to connect with VCs. Yet no one wanted to get on board, because it was more of a nuisance than an added benefit. I became demoralized and had to stop for a month. I was very close to saying, "Screw this. Why am I putting all of my time and effort into something that I have a strong belief in, if others aren't buying into it? Why bother?"

During that month break, I remember my father, my greatest mentor, said, "Well, if the problem is monetizing, and the entrepreneurs don't want to pay, and the VCs don't want to pay, surely there's someone that wants to pay. Who is that?" Then all of sudden it hit me. It's not the connectivity that is a problem, but the access to the data and information. And I said, "Well, I guess it's corporations and investors who want data, not connections." That's when we decided to reposition the whole proposition and started focusing on aggregating and packaging data.

So we came up with corporate packages. We managed to sell one or two of them. Then the real turning point was when I got some invaluable feedback from a fellow entrepreneur. Mai Medhat, founder of Eventtus and a close friend, grabbed a coffee me with one day and brilliantly observed, "You've got all of this data, but nobody knows that you do. You've got this huge amount of information from the 1,000 or so registered startups on the platform. Well, nobody else has this information, but nobody knows that you do. Why don't you just kind of share part of it?" I said, "Well, in what format?" She said, "Well, you don't have the money to have a research report, and people don't know who you are to get sponsorship; why don't you just do an infographic and just make it really simple so that people can understand and digest it?" That made sense to me, so I said, "Let's try that."

So as a team, we sat down for the next four weeks and created a list of startups and all this proprietary data from MAGNiTT from what we'd collected. We had so much data, since we asked lots of relevant questions. For example, we asked, "Are you fundraising?" "How much are you fundraising?" "Do you need help with X or Y?" "What industry are you in?" "What country are you based in?" Then we basically released this three-page, very basic infographic that highlighted the data from the MAGNiTT platform. Then all of a sudden, people began saying, "Oh, wow, you have all of this information we didn't know you had."

Our next iteration, we basically gathered all of the funding information that was publicly available on all of the startups listed on MAGNiTT and came out with the 2016 MENA State of Funding. That was a game changer!

Was there an "aha" moment when things started to click finally?

I still remember several VC partners from across the region, many of whom were not quite warm on the idea of MAGNiTT, who after I released the infographics called and emailed me saying, "Wow. Thank you. You have more data on funding than we had, and we can now use the data to pitch to our LPs (limited partners) in a way that we were unable to do before." That's when I realized there is real value here.

This was this lightbulb moment when I thought, "Wow, this data aggregation and more importantly analysis is really key." If corporations are trying to work out what startups in their domain exist in the region, if there are logistics companies looking to find out how much startups are doing in logistics, if there are government entities trying to understand how many startups there are in the UAE and what industry they're in, if there are VCs from outside of the region interested in understanding the fundraising landscape or assessing potential for exits, we now have a very powerful tool we can help them with.

All of a sudden, all these people who previously didn't have this willingness to spend, because they didn't really know what this online community connection platform was, began to get drawn by the fact that there was this underlying very useful information and data.

This became the platform from which MAGNiTT would grow and focus on. I continued to push on this formula, constantly asking, "How do we continue to push on data that is objectively and factually driven? How do we educate stakeholders on what it is they're looking for from the Middle East, while continuing to focus on building out the local community of entrepreneurs?" We looked to be a data-driven platform that would educate stakeholders on the pain points for which they sought answers. Our focus now was to get bite-size data that people could understand relatively quickly, that gave them the kind of high-level information that they needed, and if they needed to get more information and data, they could come back to us.

What were some of the more interesting findings about entrepreneurs and startups when you started looking up the data?

Things got very exciting for me and the team. Each time we would bring out a report, we would look to prove or disprove a hypothesis that would be of interest to the wider public but would each time create a call to action back to the site and create opportunities to monetize the platform.

One example was we took the top 100 startups in the region, broke down who their founders were, who their backgrounds were, and started working out where they were originally to try and come up with data-driven information. The findings indicated that 41 percent had an MBA; 35 percent came from consulting and banking; 35 percent had startup experience; 48 percent had an engineering background. It was fascinating.

Another concept I wanted to dispel was that everywhere you went, everyone was saying, "There are no exits in the region." And I was like, "That can't be true. It's just we haven't heard of the small to medium-size exits." Selling a company for $5 million or $10 million is a great success, because it's damn hard to do it. It's just ten times better when you've done it for $50 million or $500 million, but it doesn't mean that those smaller exits don't exist.

The findings we had unearthed in our exit report confirmed that there is, in fact, a clear path to exit for startups in the region. The first page of the exit report also says that, on average, it takes seven years for a startup to be able to be "exited." How many companies have been around for seven years and are startups? Not many at all. So folks and VCs need to understand that while the potential is there, things take time to build out before anyone can make money. Most importantly, this positioned MAGNiTT as the data analytical hub for the MENA region, as a reference point for institutions. This became the platform for our seed funding.

Fundraising is all about building momentum. With the data analysis MAGNiTT built, on the strength it had achieved in creating awareness for the region, while using the funds to further enhance the platform to focus on data, data analytics and connectivity. We successfully used this to raise a USD $1 million seed round from a collection of regional investors with an aim of further enhancing the platform and expanding into emerging markets.

The fundraising process itself provided vital feedback to me, not only as a founder, but as a user of the platform. The challenges have given us real-time insights on how to solve for issues many founders are facing while highlighting the importance of benchmarking data for the region, a few lessons learned from the fundraising process that I was unaware of.

Thankfully, as MAGNiTT, we knew who the investors in the region were. The MAGNiTT platform actually became a tool for me when I was fundraising to identify who to speak to, what investments they had done, what their focus was and why they should be interested in our platform. The most important was getting a lead investor. Having 500 Startups on board was key. Given their strong track record and investments in similar businesses internationally gave us confidence to go on and build on the MAGNiTT proposition.

I THINK THAT BEING ABLE TO INTERNALIZE AND REALLY TAKE IN FEEDBACK IS A VERY IMPORTANT QUALITY FOR AN ENTREPRENEUR. IF YOU IMMEDIATELY HAVE A KNEE-JERK REACTION TO DEFEND YOUR IDEA OR PLAN, THE PERSON GIVING YOU THE FEEDBACK OR ADVICE WILL JUST SHUT DOWN, NOT TO MENTION YOU MAY ANNOY THEM. OBVIOUSLY, IF THEY'RE A POTENTIAL CUSTOMER, PARTNER, OR INVESTOR, THEN THAT WILL BE MORE DAMAGING.

Fundraising takes time. Longer than expected. Expect the unexpected. Front to end process was about nine months to close the round. Getting the lead investor was critical. If there was one challenge that was unforeseen, it was that we signed our first term sheet officially in mid-July. Unfortunately, in the region, the summer is very quiet as many folks travel abroad then, and this proved to be a big challenge. Fundraising is all about building momentum. This is very hard to do over the summer, when many investors are away and you are unable to get meetings. Plan your fundraising around this so that you can get in front of investors to close deals.

Structuring your investment round is important and costly. This is also something you need to review and think about up front. Many investors at the venture capital stage will ask for you to have an offshore entity. The cost of doing this effectively can be costly and time consuming. Don't leave this to the last minute, as it will only further delay closing the round.

Not every investor may be interested in your startup. That's OK and important to know that, but just as important to thank them for their time and take their feedback on board. Listening to investor feedback is basically getting free advice on your product. Always thank them for their time and learn from what they said when you are building your proposition.

It is important to have good legal support. That was instrumental in advising and helping us with raising funds. They can answer questions on terms, help structure conversations and also allow you to push back when things don't sound right. Having a good legal team can provide you much-needed confidence when speaking to investors.

Remember that you are obsessed with your startup and believe you should be top of investors' minds all the time. The reality is that they are speaking to and closing deals with multiple startups and reviewing hundreds if not thousands of pitch decks. They are busy, and you aren't always their priority. Be sure to keep them up to date and not to be afraid of following up on emails when they don't get back to you, without being pushy.

Prepare yourself. You need to have thick skin. Expect to receive a lot of feedback, questions and criticism. You need to be prepared to have answers. If you don't, don't make something up; it will come back to haunt you. Revert back as soon as you can.

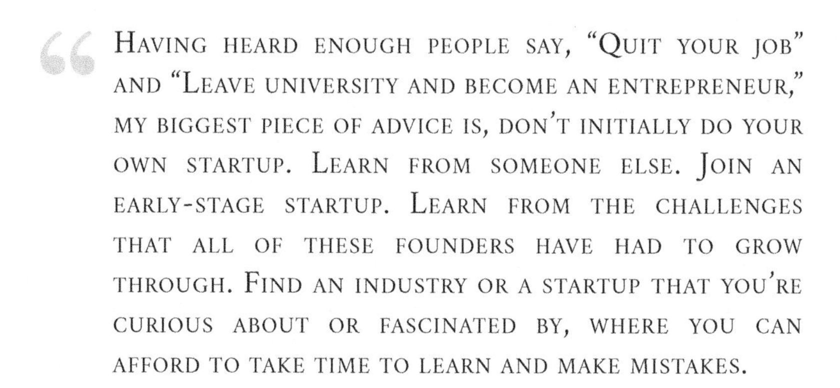

"Having heard enough people say, "Quit your job" and "Leave university and become an entrepreneur," my biggest piece of advice is, don't initially do your own startup. Learn from someone else. Join an early-stage startup. Learn from the challenges that all of these founders have had to grow through. Find an industry or a startup that you're curious about or fascinated by, where you can afford to take time to learn and make mistakes.

What common personality trait have you found to be detrimental to an entrepreneur?

One self-defeating trait that I found to be quite common among entrepreneurs, not just here in the region but everywhere, is defensiveness. I guess it's part of human nature in general. One of the things that I always try to do is to put myself in situations where I'm challenged by different people. If you are stubborn or believe what you're doing is 100 percent correct, and not open to feedback, it will be difficult to grow.

So when everybody was telling me, "You need to pick a geography or you need to pick a market. You can't do both on a global scale," I had to pay attention and really understand the alternatives and make my decision. That's when I decided to focus on the MENA region over picking the niche of the MBA. I had hesitations. I remember wondering after nine months of starting MAGNiTT, I asked a mentor, "Won't the users who have signed up from the MBA be upset if I switch to a Middle East focus?" His response has stuck with me to this day: "If you are successful in ten years, will you worry that your 100 early adopters were upset that you pivoted to a bigger market?"

So I think that being able to internalize and really take in feedback is a very important quality for an entrepreneur. If you immediately have a knee-jerk reaction to defend your idea or plan, the person giving you the feedback or advice will just shut down, not to mention you may annoy them. Obviously, if they're a potential customer, partner, or investor, then that will be more damaging.

Any final advice you'd like to share with aspiring entrepreneurs?

Closing my fundraising provided a lot of learning lessons for entrepreneurs in the region. Having heard enough people say, "Quit your job" and "Leave university and become an entrepreneur," my biggest piece of advice is, don't initially do your own startup. Learn from someone else. Join an early-stage startup. Learn from the challenges that all of these founders have had to grow through. Find an industry or a startup that you're curious about or fascinated by, where you can afford to take time to learn and make mistakes.

If you're fresh out of college, you have plenty of time to get some experience under your belt. The average time it took successful founders to do their startup was nine years; most started their own business. That is because there's no better learning experience than learning from the experience of others and asking them about their journey.

Practice makes perfect. Imagine you are a singer or athlete. Nothing replaces practice and repetition. Know your story and vision and be just as passionate telling it the next time you meet investors as you were when you first pitched your idea. Learn to adapt the story based on feedback from investors; see how they react and develop the rhetoric. Practice, practice, practice.

Accept and expect rejection. It's part of the exercise. It is natural to get upset but important not to get downbeat. Keep yourself going and stay positive but learn from your meetings where investors turned you down by processing what you could have done differently and where you need to improve.

Always keep investors updated on your progress, especially those that might have said no. Fundraising will take months to close. During that period, your product will evolve, your numbers will change, and you will continue to progress. Just because an investor said no at the beginning of the fundraising process, over time if you are making progress and keeping them updated, they may change their mind and close out your round. Finally, hustle. The region is full of people that I look up to in terms of learning how to keep going. Hustle is key to success; there is no way around it.

ACCEPT AND EXPECT REJECTION. IT'S PART OF THE EXERCISE. IT IS NATURAL TO GET UPSET BUT IMPORTANT NOT TO GET DOWNBEAT. KEEP YOURSELF GOING AND STAY POSITIVE BUT LEARN FROM YOUR MEETINGS WHERE INVESTORS TURNED YOU DOWN BY PROCESSING WHAT YOU COULD HAVE DONE DIFFERENTLY AND WHERE YOU NEED TO IMPROVE.

In terms of the startup ecosystem in the region, what's working and what's not working from your perspective?

We have this region with twenty or so countries, with each market having a different infrastructure, different regulations, different levels of development. This is vastly different from what you find in the U.S. or China, where things are more uniform and therefore become easier to target and scale. Granted, the U.S. and China are very competitive environments.

Having said that, what you have here is a fertile ground to create something that many of your global competitors do not have the patience or know-how to build locally. Hence, you have Souq being acquired by Amazon and Careem competing with Uber, etc.

So if you are able to break down the barriers and create a defensible product, in multiple jurisdictions, there will be a buyer out there who may be interested in you. You may also have, as is the case with Careem, potentially created a better solution than their international competitors. That is because you've developed new innovations or new products, out of different problems that use or replicate similar UI and UX of competing companies abroad.

Ultimately, if you already have a potential buyer or an exit, then you're in a much stronger position than if you're someone in the U.S. that's trying to struggle and hustle, because of the strong competition that already exists in that marketplace, to come out with a different proposition.

In short, I think while there are intrinsically issues with regard to the way the Middle East is currently politically, demographically, operationally, regulatory, that is where the opportunity lies with regards to startups.

While I believe that innovation will come from within the region, rather than being borrowed from abroad and adapted to the local market, how fast it will come largely depends on research and development, investment and education, people having coding skills, and the ability to fail and not have a legal risk associated with that.

What are your future plans for MAGNiTT?

MAGNiTT's focus is on data access and data analytics. We want to become the largest platform across all emerging markets, if not the world, that provides a local global platform connecting entrepreneurs to their local stakeholders while supporting global corporations as they discover and connect with entrepreneurs from their specific market.

As such, we will continue to enhance and improve that proposition based on the needs and requirements of our clients. This will include further research and reporting as well as technological enhancements, including APIs, export functionality, and notifications for them to better access what they are looking for, while we look at international expansion of the platform. One step at a time!

CONCLUSION

Are you ready?

It doesn't matter whether you were born in the U.S., in Amman, or in Kom Ombo in upper Egypt. It doesn't matter whether you had a personal chauffeur or had to walk around town in slummy neighborhoods and narrow alleys. It doesn't matter whether you attended English private school and had your own private art tutor or you were squeezed into crowded public-school classrooms. It doesn't matter if your dad owned the factory or if he opened the factory door.

All that matters is whether you care enough to start now, from where you are today.

Do you care enough to live your passions and challenge old-seated traditions and unwarranted bias, to even challenge a culture or a system if you have to? Do you care enough to try to make a difference? Do you care enough about building something so wonderful that it can fulfill your soul and your potential?

Do you care enough to make a change rather than wait for a change?

If there's one recurring theme I encountered writing this book, it's that a can-do attitude and follow-through will triumph over circumstances and challenges. For the first time perhaps in countless generations in the Arab world, our aspirations are no longer pipe dreams but opportunities. Your parents and grandparents had nowhere near the possibilities you have today. No matter what your circumstances, you have access to the world at your fingertips. All you need is a computer, a decent Wi-Fi connection, and your imagination to get started. So, *yalla* startup!

ACKNOWLEDGMENTS

THANKS TO EVERYONE who supported me in this journey and well before, with special acknowledgments to Samih Toukan, Mona Ataya, Mudassir Sheikha, Omar Soudodi, Maaz Sheikh, Delphine Eddé, Idriss Al Rifai, Kunal Kapoor, Bana Shomali, Elie Habib, Omar Gabr, Muhammad Chbib, Sara Alemzadeh, Jon Richards, Fouad Jeryes, Khalil Shadid, Mai Medhat, Amir Barsoum, Zain Alabdin Tawfiq, Niama El Bassunie, Abdulaziz Al Loughani, Philip Bahoshy, Craig Moore, Tarik Amin, Vincent Ghossoub, Ala Alsallal, Mohammed Al-Shaker, Mazen Nahawi, Mohamed Attya, Salman Al-Suhaibaney, Ray Dargham, John Tsioris, Anilesh Kumar, Dhari Abdulhadi, Abdulaziz Aljouf, Sherif Al-Rakabawy, Kaswara Al-Khatib, Rabea Ataya, and Ahmed Moor, for their time helping make this book happen and inshallah (God willing) helping empower the next-gen of MENA entrepreneurs and beyond.

Ahmed Nassef—for help giving life to this project and for all your great wisdom and insights.

Samih Toukan—for being the bedrock of this project and the catalyst for everything I cover in this book.

Omar Soudodi, Raj Gnanamoorthy, Sara Alemzadeh, Fouad Jeryes, Philip Bahoshy, Dina El-Mofty, Ala Alsallal, Vincent Ghossoob, Yasmin Helal—for your encouragement and support.

Amir Farha, Ahmed Alfi, Issa Aghabi, Omar Christidis, Con O'Donnell—for your great feedback.

Fadi Ghandour—for your efforts advocating for and supporting entrepreneurs in the region.

Chris Schroeder and Mo Gawdat—for setting great examples.

Linda Rottenberg—for your encouragement and all the wonderful work you're doing at Endeavor.

Muhammad Yunus—for being a global advocate for social change and entrepreneurship.

Ronaldo Mouchawar, Asif Keshodia, Wisam Daoud, Omar Elsahy, Mohannad Ghashim, Tom Herman, Jordan Banks, Scott Patterson—for your inspiration and support over the years.

Kaleil Tuzman—for your precious influence, mentorship, and friendship.

Chris Kridler—for your generous advice and support, and all your efforts making this book a reality.

Bernadette Valdivia, Shaima Raouf, and Fathurohman—for your invaluable contribution to the making of this book.

Morgan Downey —for your time and valuable advice.

Joanne Wong, Sara Anani, Kristin Muller, Rebekah Berger, Scott Holleran, Camille Culbreath, Moustafa Abou El Ela, Karim Abou El Ela, Maiko King, Tomas Petru, Amal Elsayed, Lubna Farooq, Ruby Luna, Jo Baines, Dalia Ibrahim, Ahmed Moawad, Charlie Scott—for each solving a piece of the puzzle of this project.

Aunt Rawia, Omar Soudodi, Ahmed Soudodi, Reem Soudodi, Rimy

Allam, and Uncle Mostafa—for everything; you're family in every sense of the word.

Nash Salah, Ahmed Nassef, Claudia Bueno, Bernadette Valdivia, Brian Holloway, and Sila Celik, Amr Belal, Dean Adams—for your priceless friendship.

Mariam Allam, Liala El Edwy, and Moustafa El Edwy—I wrote this book with you in mind.

My mother and my father, may they rest in peace—beyond any gratitude or words can express, I owe my best to you.

Special thanks to every member of my extended family, friends, and colleagues, even if you're not mentioned here by name.

ABOUT THE AUTHOR

AMIR HEGAZI is a lifelong entrepreneur, with more than fifteen years of startup, tech, e-commerce, and digital media experience. He is the co-founder and managing partner of intoMENA Group, a consulting firm that helps international companies do business in the Middle East and North Africa region (MENA). Prior, Amir was the director of marketplace at Souq.com, the region's largest e-commerce platform (recently acquired by Amazon.com), where he helped build its marketplace from the ground up to account for a sizable portion of overall sales volume. Amir is also one of the early pioneers of digital media in the region, having launched and managed the largest online TV network in the Arab world at such companies as JumpTV and Talfazat. Amir is passionate about entrepreneurship, technology, and promoting the startup ecosystem in MENA. Amir lives in Los Angeles and Dubai.

GLOSSARY

Acquisition: taking ownership of another business.

Angel investors: individuals who back startups early on; contributions typically range anywhere from $50,000 to $2 million.

API (application programming interface): a set of functions or procedures that act as an intermediary or a connector that allow two applications to talk to each other. For example, each time you use an app like Facebook, Instagram, send a WhatsApp message, or check news on your phone, you're using an API.

B2B (or business-to-business): one business sells products or services to another business.

B2C (or business-to-consumer): a business sells products or services directly to the end-consumer.

Back end: the behind-the-scenes code (while "front end" displays on the screen and in front of users, back end does not).

Beta test: the final stage of product testing before the product is released commercially or goes "live."

Blue ocean strategy: the focus on creating a new, uncontested market space that typically makes competitors irrelevant and that creates new consumer value, often while decreasing costs and maximizing upside.

Business model: a company's plan for generating revenues and profits. It includes the various components and functions of the business, including expenses and money flow.

Business valuation: an estimate of the worth of a business and its assets.

COD (cash on delivery): a type of transaction in which the purchaser makes the payment only when the goods are delivered, typically paying by cash, but possibly by check or other forms of upfront payments.

CRM (customer relationship management): an initiative for managing all of a company's relationships and interactions with customers and potential customers.

CSR (corporate social responsibility): integrating social and/or environmental concerns in companies' business operations and interactions with their stakeholders.

Customer lifetime value (CLV or CLTV): a prediction of the net profit or value attributed to the entire future relationship with a customer.

Due diligence: the inquiry and review process of obtaining sufficient and accurate disclosure of all material documents and information influencing the outcome of the transaction.

Entrepreneur: a person who conceptualizes, plans, organizes, operates, and assumes the risk for a new business venture.

Finance: the management and allocation of money and other assets to support business objectives and growth.

First-mover advantage: an advantage gained by a company that first introduces a viable product or service to the market, allowing it to establish brand recognition or market dominance as a result of attaining consumer loyalty of a new product or service well before other entrants.

Fortune 100 and Fortune 500: an annual ranking by *Fortune* magazine of the 100 and 500 largest U.S. public and privately-held companies, listed according to company valuation or market capitalization.

FMCG (or fast-moving consumer goods) or consumer packaged goods (CPG): products that are typically sold quickly and at relatively low cost. Examples include non-durable goods such as consumer packaged foods, beverages, toiletries, over-the-counter drugs and other consumables.

Gulf Cooperation Council (GCC): political and economic alliance of six Middle Eastern countries—Saudi Arabia, Kuwait, the United Arab Emirates, Qatar, Bahrain, and Oman.

Human resources (HR): the department of a company that has the responsibility for the recruiting, training, and overseeing the welfare of the staff and company culture.

Incubator: provides workspace, coaching, and support services to entrepreneurs and startups.

iOS: an operating system used for mobile devices manufactured by Apple corporation.

Joint venture (JV): a legal entity created by two or more businesses joining together to conduct a specific business enterprise, with both parties sharing profits and losses. It differs from a strategic alliance in that there is a specific legal entity created, whereas a strategic alliance is typically bound by a commercial agreement.

KPIs (key performance indicators): a type of performance measurement or metrics. KPIs evaluate the success of a company or of a particular activity or project in which it engages.

Liabilities: the value of what a business owes.

Logistics: the process of shipping or moving a shipment from the point of origin to the point of destination. Logistics is part of the supply chain, along with ordering, purchasing, forwarding and warehousing.

Market share: percentage of a market (defined in terms of either revenue or units sold) accounted for by a given company product or service adoption in that market.

MENA (Middle East and North Africa): an extensive region stretching from Morocco to Iran, including all Mashriq and Maghreb countries, including the Arabic-speaking territory and Iran.

Monetization: to convert an asset into sources of revenue.

MVP (minimum viable product): a development approach in which a new product or website is developed with sufficient features to satisfy early adopters.

Network effect: the increase in usage as a result of more people using any given product or service, whereas each additional user increases the perceived value of the product or service to the group.

Organic growth: increased output in the form of revenues or user or customer base, without a direct push as in the case of a merger, acquisition or marketing initiative.

Pitch deck: an electronic presentation, typically in PowerPoint or PDF format, which often acts as a proposal to investors by giving an overview of the business and describing the investment opportunity at hand.

Pivot: a structured course correction or shift in strategy designed to test or pursue a new fundamental hypothesis about the product, service or market.

SaaS (Software as a Service): subscriptions are sold, typically via a license fee, to permit use of a given software.

Scalable: a product, service, or company that can grow significantly because the market and demand are big enough or because it tackles an untapped market.

Seed capital: the initial money and funding needed to get a business started.

SEO (search engine optimization): the process of affecting the online visibility or exposure of a website or a web page in a web search engine's unpaid results—often referred to as "natural," "organic" or "earned" results.

Series A round: a startup's first significant round of venture capital financing. The name refers to the class of preferred stock sold to investors in exchange for their investment.

Series B financing: a startup's second round of financing for a business through any type of investment, including private equity investors and venture capitalists.

Silicon Valley: a nickname for the southern portion of the San Francisco Bay Area, which is located in the northern part of California. It is a hub for many of the world's largest high-tech corporations and thousands of tech startups.

Small and medium-size enterprise (SME): an enterprise that employs fewer than 250 people and has an annual turnover not exceeding $50 million and/or an annual balance sheet total not exceeding $50 million.

Social business: a business created and designed to address a social problem. In a social business, the investors and owners can gradually recoup their investment but cannot take any dividend or profit beyond that point.

Startup ecosystem: formed by people, startups in their various stages and different types of organizations in a location (physical or virtual), interacting as a system to start and grow new startup companies. These organizations can be further divided into categories such as universities, funding organizations, support organizations (such as incubators, accelerators, co-working spaces, etc.), research organizations, service provider organizations (such as legal and financial services, etc.) and large corporations.

Sweat equity: shares of your company given in exchange for work done. This is an effective recruiting tool to help a startup attract passionate talent it couldn't afford to pay at standard market rates.

SWOT (Strengths, Weaknesses, Opportunities, Threats) analysis: a rigorous review undertaken by a company to identify its internal strengths and weaknesses, as well as its external opportunities and threats, in an effort to develop a competitive strategy and achieve its business objectives.

Target market: a specific group of customers to which a company tailors its products and services.

Traction: proof that consumers are actually buying and/or using your stuff.

Unicorn: a privately held startup company valued at $1 billion or more.

UI (user interface): how the user interacts with a digital product, typically with a website or mobile app (i.e. touchscreen or graphic interface).

Unit economics: direct revenues and costs associated with a given business model, expressed on a per unit basis.

UX (user experience): the way a user behaves and feels using a particular product or service.

Variable cost: expenses that change in proportion to the activity of a business.

VC (or venture capital): Financing for a company in which the business gives up partial ownership or "equity" and control of the business in exchange for capital over a limited time frame, usually three to five years. Investments range from $500,000 to $5 million.

Viral effect: to spread quickly and widely, typically by word-of-mouth, on the internet and through social media and e-mail.

White-label: refers to a product or service that is offered by one company and re-branded by another company for its own use or distribution.

NOTES

Printed in Great Britain
by Amazon